ASTROLOGY

Using the wisdom of the stars in your everyday life

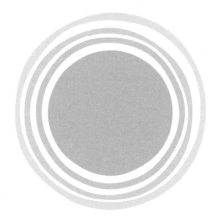

ASTROLOGY

Using the wisdom of the stars in your everyday life

Senior Editors Bob Bridle, Emma Hill
US Editor Kayla Dugger
US Executive Editor Lori Hand
Art Editor Alison Gardner
Editor Alice Kewellhampton
Senior Jacket Creative Nicola Powling
Jackets Coordinator Lucy Philpott
Senior Producer (Pre-production) Luca Frassinetti
Senior Producer Ché Creasey
Creative Technical Support Sonia Charbonnier
Managing Editor Dawn Henderson
Managing Art Editor Marianne Markham
Art Director Maxine Pedliham
Publishing Director Mary-Clare Jerram

Illustrated by **Keith Hagan**

First American Edition, 2018
Published in the United States by DK Publishing
1450 Broadway, Suite 801, New York, NY 10018

Copyright © 2018 Dorling Kindersley Limited
DK, a Division of Penguin Random House LLC
20 21 22 10 9 8 7 6 5
017–310781–Sep/2018

All rights reserved.
Without limiting the rights under the copyright reserved
above, no part of this publication may be reproduced, stored
in or introduced into a retrieval system, or transmitted, in
any form, or by any means (electronic, mechanical,
photocopying, recording, or otherwise), without the prior
written permission of the copyright owner.
Published in Great Britain by Dorling Kindersley Limited

A catalog record for this book is available from
the Library of Congress.
ISBN 978-1-4654-6413-2

DK books are available at special discounts when purchased
in bulk for sales promotions, premiums, fund-raising, or
educational use. For details, contact: DK Publishing Special
Markets, 1450 Broadway, Suite 801, New York, NY 10018
SpecialSales@dk.com

Printed and bound in China

For the curious
www.dk.com

CONTENTS

THE **STORY** OF **ASTROLOGY**   **10**

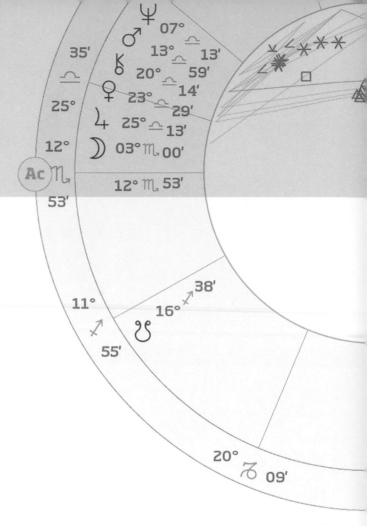

THE **HOUSES** 86

YOUR **BIRTH CHART** 116

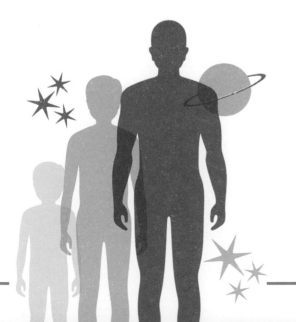

FOREWORD

AN INWARD ART

For many centuries, astrology held an honored position as a source of wisdom, self-knowledge, and connection to a magical world beyond or behind the mundane and material sphere of life.

Astrology was first formed in ancient societies in which humankind viewed itself as intrinsic to the living whole—not detached observers, but participants in the drama of the skies. Over the centuries, it has been part of the great flow of thought that constitutes the Western esoteric or mystery tradition, alongside alchemy, Kabbalah, and magic. It is the product of a philosophy that places us inside an ensouled cosmos in which everything is interconnected and everything has meaning.

As such, it stands in contrast to the contemporary view that we are isolated within the universe and that life is a biological accident, with no inherent meaning or purpose. The birth chart is thus both your individual map, showing personal character and calling, as well as reflecting something bigger—your unique place in the ever-turning wheel.

Esoteric simply means "inner" or "hidden," so astrology is, essentially, an inward art that places the focus on interior experience and the exploration

" The **personal horoscope** encompasses every conceivable area of life, from **birth to death** and all stages in between. It reveals your **motivations and needs**–what drives you to do what you do, go where you go, and seek what you seek. "

of the hidden patterns that underlie each human life, and indeed life itself. From this place of self-knowledge, we can begin to understand better the world around us–our relationships with other people and the experiences we encounter.

The personal horoscope encompasses every conceivable area of life, from birth to death and all stages in between. It reveals your motivations and needs–what drives you to do what you do, go where you go, and seek what you seek. It describes both the literal and the psychological and gathers up past, present, and future into one integrated model.

In short, we might say that your chart is a map of your soul's intent and how you manifest this in the world through being the person that you are.

At the same time, astrology is also a very practical form of knowledge. It opens up psychological awareness, shows you the talents and skills at your disposal, and shows how you might become the best version of yourself. But it also allows you to devise helpful strategies and ways forward in times of crisis, difficulty, and doubt.

In this book, you will find all these layers–a guide to the richness and depth of your own inner world, as well as a practical guide to life.

CAROLE TAYLOR

THE **STORY** OF **ASTROLOGY**

WHAT IS ASTROLOGY?

AN ANCIENT PRACTICE FOR MODERN TIMES

Astrology can be defined as the practice of reading the movements and patterns of the planets and other celestial bodies and correlating them with life on earth. It rests on a view of the cosmos as holistic and interconnected.

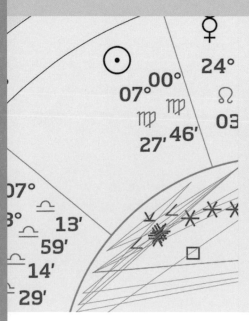

Astrology past and present

Many people today view astrology as archaic and irrelevant, belonging to a bygone era. Yet the practice of astrology has persisted and, indeed, has found new relevance in the 20th and 21st centuries. In the heart of the scientific age, there is perhaps more than ever a need for an alternative view that addresses our human desire for meaning and spiritual connection.

The kind of astrology practiced today, based on the concept of the birth chart or "horoscope," has its roots in the ancient world of Babylon and Greece. To the Babylonians, we can credit the invention of the zodiac and the practice of attributing meaning to the movements of the planets as conveyors of divine will. These ideas were subsequently taken up by the Greeks after the conquests of Alexander in the 4th century BCE and, shaped by Greek cosmology and beliefs, they eventually gave rise to the horoscope we are familiar with today.

What is a horoscope?

A horoscope is a stylized picture of the heavens, drawn for a particular time and place. It is a geocentric or Earth-centered model—a view of the

> The **birth chart** is a **holistic image of you**. Its symbols describe both **inner and outer circumstances** and all levels of your personal history and experience.

sky that puts the observer in the center of the wheel with the heavens arranged around them, above and below the horizon. It is thus a person-centered view of the cosmos that acknowledges a meaningful link between the two.

In this picture will be found the 12 signs of the zodiac as the bounding wheel of the horoscope, plus at least the Sun, Moon, and the planets from Mercury out to Saturn (and often Uranus, Neptune, and Pluto, too), plus any other celestial bodies that the astrologer drawing the chart would like to include, arranged around the wheel according to their position in the sky.

The word "horoscope," meaning "watcher of the hour," originally referred to a very particular point in the birth chart—the rising sign (that is, the zodiac sign that is rising on the eastern horizon at the time of birth). Later, the word came to signify the whole birth chart, and this is the meaning it still has today. A horoscope can also be called a birth chart or natal chart.

What your horoscope tells you

The birth chart is a holistic image of you. Its symbols describe both inner and outer circumstances and all levels of your personal history and experience, from the physical to the psychological. Everything you are and do is somehow contained within its dynamic picture.

Your chart is thus a reflection of your unique character. It acknowledges and validates your deepest feelings, concerns, and desires, showing what is meaningful to you and how you can find ways to shine.

ASTROLOGY
THROUGH THE AGES

A BRIEF HISTORY

Astrology began in Mesopotamia. From the melting pot of the ancient world, it spread to Europe via Islamic scholars, flourishing in Europe during the Middle Ages and Renaissance. Falling from favor during the Enlightenment, it has re-emerged in modern times.

The origins of astrology

Most cultures have practiced some form of sky watching, using knowledge of planetary movements as inspiration for religious rituals and monuments and to chart the passage of time and the changing seasons. There is evidence, for instance, that lunar cycles were being recorded as early as 25,000 years ago. It seems a natural part of human experience to seek meaning in the sky. The Babylonians were skilled astronomers who carefully documented the cycles of the planets. It is from the Babylonians that we have the zodiac, a device based on the constellations through which the Sun travels during the year and created to regulate the calendar and to chart future planetary movements, making prediction possible. Gradually, the zodiac became unhooked from its constellational backdrop and became the collection of 12 equal-sized zodiac signs we recognize today.

The ancient world: Greece & Rome

Astrology spread from Babylon to Greece and Egypt. Alexandria became the intellectual center of the ancient world, and it is here that the concept of the horoscope was born. It brought together the Babylonian zodiac with

> " There is evidence that **lunar cycles** were being recorded as early as **25,000 years ago**. It seems a natural part of human experience to **seek meaning in the sky**. "

Greek notions of the four elements and the celestial sphere, alongside Egyptian symbolism. It also infused astrology with Neoplatonist philosophy, with its belief in a magical correspondence between sky and Earth.

By the 2nd century CE, horoscopic astrology was fully formed and popular in Rome, where it was favored by emperors and commoners alike.

Astrology in the Middle Ages & Renaissance

After the collapse of the Roman Empire and the fall of Alexandria, astrology was kept alive by Islamic scholars who translated astrological works into Arabic. Their work was in turn translated into Latin, eventually finding its way into Europe during the 12th century.

The Medieval and Renaissance periods were a high point in astrology's history. It was taught in several universities as one of the seven liberal arts and formed the basis of many medical practices. Every court had its astrologer-astronomer, and even popes consulted astrologers for advice.

However, the Renaissance also brought a new spirit of humanism and a search for scientific knowledge. Astronomers such as Johannes Kepler practiced astrology but sought a more scientific version of it. Philosophers such as Bacon, Descartes, and Kant emphasized rationality and science as the route to truth.

As Europe moved into the Enlightenment, astrology fell out of favor.

The 19th and 20th centuries

Astrology saw a marked revival toward the end of the 19th century with the increased interest in spiritualism and Eastern religion and philosophy.

The psychiatrist Carl Jung was powerfully drawn to astrology. Drawing on Jung's theories of archetypes and the unconscious, the 20th century saw the development of what is known as "psychological astrology."

Astrology in the 21st century

While astronomers reach literally for the heavens, astrologers understand the cosmos to be as much within as without, the two things inextricably linked. As in ancient times, contemporary astrology emphasizes how we might fruitfully live our lives in rhythm with the heavenly pattern.

ASTROLOGY
TODAY

A REVIVAL OF INTEREST IN CONTEMPORARY TIMES

Most people first encounter astrology via Sun-sign columns and yet this is a relatively recent invention, a commercial application whose simplicity belies the complexities of the full horoscope.

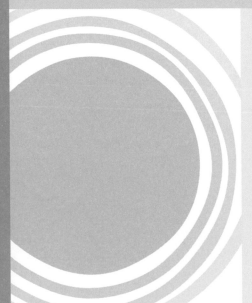

The Sun-sign column

In 1930, an astrologer named R. H. Naylor wrote an article for a Sunday newspaper about the horoscope of the new princess, Margaret. The article proved popular, and he was asked to produce more, this time writing a piece that predicted an aircraft disaster later that year. When a British airship crashed in France, Naylor was applauded for his accuracy and offered a weekly slot. Soon other British newspapers started their own astrological columns.

Naylor invented a system based on the 12 zodiac signs. He placed in order each sign in the position of the first astrological house, noting where the planets fell around the wheel. Thus, for anyone born with the Sun in Aries, the sign of Aries is placed in the position of the 1st house; for anyone with the Sun in Taurus, the sign of Taurus is placed in 1st house position; and so on. This allowed him to create 12 short forecasts based on the one piece of information everyone knows: their own birth date.

Sun-sign columns have waxed and waned in popularity. Many professional

> In recent times, older **traditional forms** of astrology have been revived and renewed for a **contemporary audience**.

astrologers reject them as too simplistic while acknowledging that without them, most people would never know that astrology exists at all.

Traditional and psychological astrology

In recent times, older traditional forms of astrology have been revived and renewed for a contemporary audience. Perhaps the most significant development though has been the incorporation of depth psychology, resulting in "psychological astrology", which has flourished over the past few decades. Psychology has provided what astrology naturally lacks—a theory of human behavior and personality development. For instance, Jung's theory of the unconscious, the concept of archetypes, and the Self as the product of an individuation process have made a very fruitful marriage with astrology.

Astrology now

Astrology is now enjoying a surge in popularity, particularly among the millennial generation—and with unprecedented access to astrological information online, for many, this curiosity now stretches well beyond Sun signs to include awareness of the whole birth chart. Many no longer see it as throwaway entertainment, but as something with substance, meaning, and the ability to provide answers in times of crisis.

Uncertainty about the future certainly pushes many to seek life wisdom from beyond the usual orthodox sources, reaching out to nonmainstream belief systems and spiritual traditions that feel more relevant to the zeitgeist. This renewed interest in magic and mysticism permeates literature, fashion, film, and many other areas, with astrology as a significant strand in this upsurge of alternative spirituality. It addresses deeper questions of meaning and purpose but allows each person to decide for themselves what kind of cosmic force or mechanism might be at work. It is a practical tool that can be learned and applied to every kind of life context, but it also speaks to our need for mystery and spiritual connection, a counterpoint to the rationalism of modern science.

ASTROLOGY AND **PSYCHOLOGY**

UNDERSTANDING YOURSELF THROUGH YOUR CHART

Astrology is an imaginative yet practical art, applicable to all aspects of life. The symbols of the chart connect inner psychology to outer circumstances–thus, the better we know ourselves, the more harmonious and productive our lives can be.

Astrology as a guide for life

We all need a little guidance now and then. Most of the time, life might run smoothly, but in times of crisis or uncertainty, it is useful to have a tool that allows you to glimpse underneath the surface to see what might be going on at a deeper level.

It is this level of life, the inner meaning of events, which psychology seeks to address and which astrology also speaks to with its unique language of symbols.

Astrology encourages self-knowledge and self-reflection, a more thorough understanding of who you are and why you do what you do. It can also help you to understand better the people around you, enhancing your relationships or at least showing you what the purpose of those relationships might be in terms of your own personal story.

It is also eminently practical. For example, if Saturn is active in your chart, it suggests this is not a time to expand and branch out, but a time to focus your energies and knuckle down. If Uranus is active, the best way to respond might be to assert your will,

> **Astrology** encourages **self-knowledge** and **self-reflection**, a more thorough understanding of who you are and why you do what you do.

even if this puts you out of step with others around you.

Following the tides
Astrology allows you to sense and follow the tides; it shows the appropriate time to act and how to make the most of a given set of circumstances.

Nothing we do occurs in a vacuum—our actions are set within the context of our lives and shaped by our particular needs and desires. Whether or not you believe in the idea of the soul's evolution, or even in the idea of soul in the first place, life surely has different phases and cycles and an underlying sense of growth and development.

The one constant in the universe is change, and we are all subject to it.

Astrology frames this in terms of planetary cycles, the planets circuiting the chart and marking out the chapters of our lives, putting each experience and each phase into its proper context.

Astrology and psychology
The birth chart shows both inner and outer circumstances, making the link between the two—thus, it shows how you can change your outer circumstances through a better understanding of your inner psychology and motivations.

With astrology, the emphasis is on personal understanding and personal growth, so that you are not just reacting to life but fully living it by being yourself, becoming who you are meant to be.

How to use astrology
The main practical application for natal astrology is character delineation—identifying skills, potentials, and psychological motivation.

Forecasting then allows you to glimpse into the future—not telling you what will happen, but showing you which way the tide is flowing and suggesting, in symbolic terms, the path you might most fruitfully take.

THE **ASTROLOGICAL MINDSET**

HOW DO ASTROLOGERS THINK?

As a philosophy, astrology belongs to a magical mindset that sees Earth as a reflection of the heavens. You do not have to be a philosopher to use astrology, but it is helpful to understand a little of its underlying view.

As above, so below

The philosophy on which astrology rests is an ancient one, expressed in the Hermetic maxim "As above, so below." This is astrology's basic premise, that life on Earth is a mirror of the heavenly picture.

"As above, so below" is enshrined in the ancient idea of correspondence, where each planet governs everything in the cosmos that reflects or resonates to its particular energy. Thus, the Sun governs solar things (monarchs, heads of state, gold, sunflowers, the heart), while the Moon governs lunar things (mothers and caretakers, food and nourishment, waxing and waning). Each planet has its own domain, reaching through every level of existence and experience from the physical to the conceptual.

Macrocosm and microcosm

This also reflects the ancient view that "man is a microcosm"–in other words, each of us is a cosmos in miniature. Your birth chart, with its bounding circle of the zodiac (the stars), containing all the planets and encoding the connection between Earth and sky, is indeed a miniature cosmos, and you are a reflection of this

> ❝ In order to **fully appreciate** and work with **astrology**, it is necessary to **suspend our conventional way of thinking**. ❞

cosmos at the moment of your birth.

Being a product of the ancient world, of Babylonian star-religion and Greek philosophy, with some Egyptian magic in the mix, astrology only makes sense in an Earth-centered (geocentric) context and in the old pre-Enlightenment frame of mind. It is for this reason that many people today dismiss astrology out of hand, since it cannot hope to fit into our modern scientific view. We are left with astrology as a poetic vision of the world and the birth chart as a kind of magical space in which the usual, "rational" way of thinking gives way to a more symbolic frame of mind.

We might say then, in order to fully appreciate and work with astrology, it is necessary to suspend our conventional way of thinking in order to embrace these ancient ideas of cosmos, based on a holistic view of interconnection where all things of a similar nature resonate in unison.

The nature of symbols

In working with astrology, we must also learn how to interpret symbols. A symbol does not offer a one-size-fits-all description. For example, Venus is our drive to create relationships, but it also describes our aesthetic sense, our artistic potentials, how we dress or style our hair, the fertility of the natural world, and physical or mundane things such as cosmetics and sugar.

Each time we read a chart, we have to think symbolically and use our imagination to interpret it, not just to appreciate that each symbol is being lived at many different levels, but also to acknowledge that symbols, by their nature, only offer symbolic information. This makes it impossible for a natal chart to tell us precisely what a person should do. Indeed, if it did allow for such exact and concrete prediction, it would suggest our lives are fated and mechanical. Instead, it reveals to us the rich and beautiful pattern of our individual life, if we can learn to understand the chart's symbols.

IT'S MORE THAN JUST YOUR SUN SIGN

YOUR PLANETS AND ZODIAC SIGNS

The Sun-sign column is a recent conception, invented to fit the format of newspapers and magazines. Astrology is more complex than this, based on the horoscope or birth chart. Containing all the planets, signs, and much more, the chart is a holistic map of the individual.

YOUR SUN SIGN

We say "she's a Scorpio" or "he's a Gemini" as shorthand to indicate the zodiac sign occupied by the Sun when that person was born. When someone asks you your "star sign," this is what they are referring to. The Sun is the heart center of a birth chart, representing the person's individual creative gift and sense of identity which, like the gold of the alchemists, develops slowly throughout life.

The Sun see pp.62-63

THE BIRTH CHART AS YOUR INDIVIDUAL MAP

Most people know their "Sun sign," the sign occupied by the Sun at the time of birth. But this is only one component of a birth chart, and therefore only one part of a person's character. Astrologically speaking, a person is much more than just their Sun sign.

If you go to see an astrologer or sign up for a course of study (or read this book!), you will be introduced to the concept of the horoscope—the birth chart or natal chart. This is a stylized map of the heavens as seen from Earth, at the exact time and place of your birth. The chart reflects your character and what motivates you, saying something about the circumstances of your life and what you hope to achieve. It is a meeting place of past experiences and family threads, present situations and desires, and future possibilities and potentials.

Your Birth Chart see pp.116-151

YOUR MOON SIGN

The Moon is equal in importance to the Sun and represents our basic needs, instinctive responses, and inner emotional life. Together, the Sun and Moon are termed the "luminaries," since they are the two largest and brightest celestial bodies we see in the sky. In a chart, then, they represent perhaps the two most central forces.

The Moon see pp.64-65

> **The Sun** is the **heart center** of a birth chart, representing the person's individual **creative gift** and **sense of identity**.

YOUR PLANETS

As in the solar system itself, around the Sun circle the other planets and celestial bodies, from Mercury to Pluto, and each plays its unique role in forming the interwoven tapestry of character and life experience.

Each planet represents an archetypal or psychological drive—that is, an impulse that is basic to human life. For instance, Mercury is our impulse to communicate, learn, and make connections. Venus is our impulse to relate, cooperate, and find common ground; by contrast, Mars is our impulse to fight, compete, expend energy, and assert our individual will.

The Planets see pp.58-85

YOUR HOUSES

Each planet resides in a "house." A birth chart is divided into 12 houses, each representing a different area of life. Between them, the 12 houses cover all the important areas of life experience, such as home and family or work and career.

A planet will express itself according to the zodiac sign it occupies and in the area of life denoted by the house in which it resides.

The Houses see pp.86-115

YOUR ZODIAC SIGNS

In a chart, each planet occupies a sign of the zodiac. A person may have the Sun in Scorpio, but their Moon may reside in the opposite sign of Taurus, their Mercury in Sagittarius, Venus in Libra, and so on through the planets. The sign positions of your planets begin to create the unique picture of your birth chart.

The Zodiac Signs see pp.24-57

YOUR ASCENDANT OR RISING SIGN

Your Ascendant is the zodiac sign that was rising on the eastern horizon when you were born. It is one of the four "angles" that quarter the chart and together provide information about identity, relationships, home life, and vocation. More specifically, the Ascendant is the precise degree of that sign, representing your birth at a very particular moment in time.

The Ascendant see pp.120-121

YOUR ANGLES

Each chart has two important axes. The first is the Ascendant-Descendant; it represents the line of the horizon, linking east to west. The Ascendant symbolizes birth and new beginnings. The Descendant lies opposite and is a place where you are drawn into relationships in order to find something of the "other half."

The second axis is called the MC-IC. MC stands for "Medium Coeli" (Latin for "middle of the heavens") and IC stands for "Imum Coeli" ("bottom of the heavens"). In other words, these points represent culmination above the horizon (MC) and a low point below the horizon, dividing the chart vertically south to north. The MC gives important information about your ambitions, career path, worldly status, and achievements. The IC represents home, family, and inner sanctuary.

The Angles see pp.120-123

CHAPTER

2

THE
ZODIAC SIGNS

THE ZODIAC SIGNS
AN OVERVIEW

THE WHEEL OF LIFE

The zodiac is astrology's most ancient and enduring idea. Divided into 12 zodiac signs, it forms the bounding wheel of the birth chart, reflecting the seasonal year through its compendium of mythic images.

The circle of life

We can view the zodiac as a cycle of development—one full circuit of the Sun, from the start of the year at the spring equinox, when the Sun enters the energetic and initiatory sign of Aries, to the completion of the journey in Pisces, whose nature is to dissolve and disperse. Each sign is unique and builds on the story that precedes it to create a complete cycle of experience.

The signs in your chart

A planet represents a particular human drive—for instance, the Moon is our basic need for food and safety, Mercury is our drive to communicate, and so on. By contrast, a sign represents a particular style of expression for something in the chart; it thus determines the way in which your planets and other chart factors express themselves, according to which signs they occupy.

Most of us know our "Sun sign" (the zodiac sign occupied by the Sun on the day you were born) and can instinctively connect to its character and story. As we will see when we look more closely at the Sun (pp.62-63), this sign will form the core of your life experience, a set of qualities and talents that you are in the process of developing. Your Sun sign symbolizes your most essential creative gift, showing where you fit within the zodiac's magical circle.

However, bear in mind that all your other planets occupy a zodiac sign, too. The zodiac is also the bounding rim of your birth chart, and every chart contains all 12 signs. Each sign will therefore have its influence, however small, somewhere in your life.

> Your **Sun sign** symbolizes your most **essential creative gift**, showing where you fit within the zodiac's magical circle.

POLARITY, ELEMENTS, AND MODES

ASSESSING BALANCE IN YOUR CHART

The 12 signs are grouped according to two polarities, four elements, and three modes. Each is a unique combination of these. The overall balance of polarity, element, and mode in your chart gives powerful information about your personality and what motivates you.

The two polarities: positive and negative

+ **The positive signs** have an extroverted and upbeat quality, being outwardly oriented and needing the stimulus of external activity and interaction.

− **The negative signs** are more introverted and low-key, focused on interior experience.

There is no judgment attached to the terms here. We can think of them as similar to the Chinese philosophy of yang and yin, equal and complementary.

The four elements: fire, earth, air, and water

Fire is bold and dramatic, generating heat and energy. When focused, fire can move mountains, sweeping everything along with enthusiasm, vision, and optimistic faith. Planets in fire act with courage, having a strong sense of purpose.

Earth is solid and real, and planets here tend to be grounded, preferring a practical method and a tangible outcome. Theories and "what ifs" do not suit this element, nor are planets in earth given to sentimentality.

Air is the world of ideas and thoughts; planets in air tend to express themselves rationally and verbally, with all the emotional restraint that comes from this element's association with polite interaction and civilized human relations.

Water can appear in the natural world as a cleansing river; a raging torrent; a still, dark lake; or the fathomless ocean. Planets in water act according to feeling, with sensitive intuition.

The three modes: cardinal, fixed, and mutable

▷ **The cardinal signs** begin the four seasons of the year, so planets in these signs take the initiative in whatever way is appropriate to the element. Cardinal makes the first move and needs the stimulus of new projects.

▷ **The fixed signs** reflect the middle of each season, when the weather has settled. Fixed energy is stable and persistent, resistant to change. Planets in fixed signs are steadfast, good at holding and consolidating whatever is signified by the element.

▷ **The mutable signs** mark the end of the seasons, and planets in these signs are given to movement and change. Unlike cardinal, the movement has no focus; thus, the mutable signs allow the unchecked flow of each element.

PISCES

ARIES

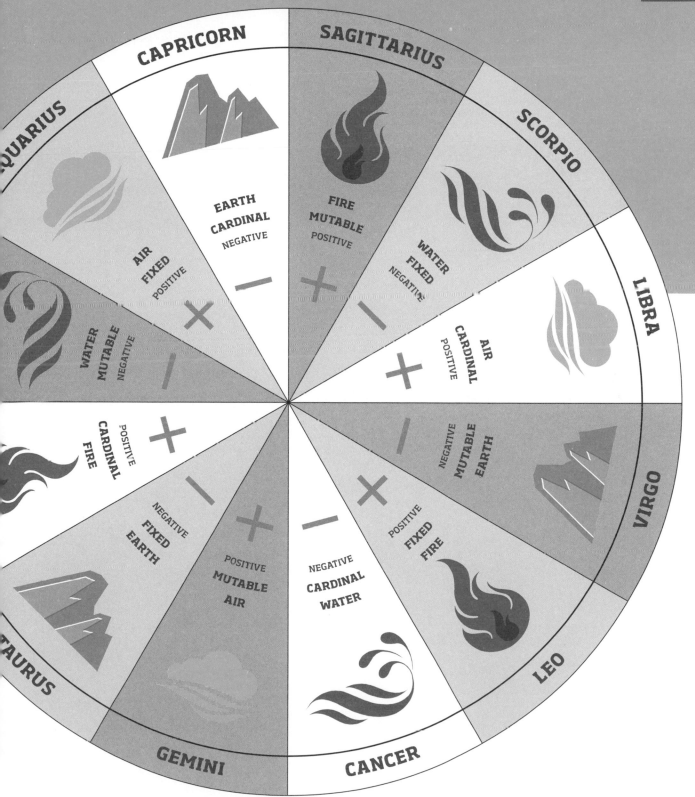

Exploring your chart

Assess the balance in your own chart by noting the signs occupied by your Sun, Moon, Mercury, Venus, Mars, Jupiter, and Saturn. (The sign placements for the outer planets suggest collective rather than personal themes, so we can ignore these.)You can also note the sign in which your Ascendant falls, since this angle describes both physical embodiment and approach to life, thereby adding to the idea of "temperament" in the chart.

When a polarity, element, or mode is strongly represented (for an element or mode, this means having at least two planets there), you are likely to feel ease around it, expressing it without effort. If you have no planets there, you might feel challenged to express its qualities—it forms a kind of "shadow" and a lifelong task to make a more confident relationship to it.

If you have just one planet in a polarity, element, or mode, you will express it just through that planet, often forcefully so.

THE ELEMENTS IN YOUR CHART

ELEMENT	HIGH
FIRE	You tend to be very self-motivated and focused on your own desires and drives. You might have a need to feel pretty special, to be the center of attention or the main player in the drama.
EARTH	Pragmatic and down-to-earth, you are good at managing tasks and getting things done. Life may set you a challenge to move beyond the mundane considerations of material life.
AIR	You tend to live in your head—thoughts and ideas are your reality, and you might be a gifted communicator. The task might be to find ways of bringing your ideas into tangible form.
WATER	You tend to think with your heart and might find it difficult to see things from a dispassionate point of view. Your gift is your ability to connect emotionally and understand others' feelings.

THE POLARITIES IN YOUR CHART

High in positive/low in negative
You like to be involved with the busy flow of things, needing stimulus from the world out there. Spending reflective time alone is much more of a challenge.

High in negative/ low in positive
You tend to be a more introverted type; the inner world of physical sensation and emotional experience is more natural to you than the buzz and noise of the outside world.

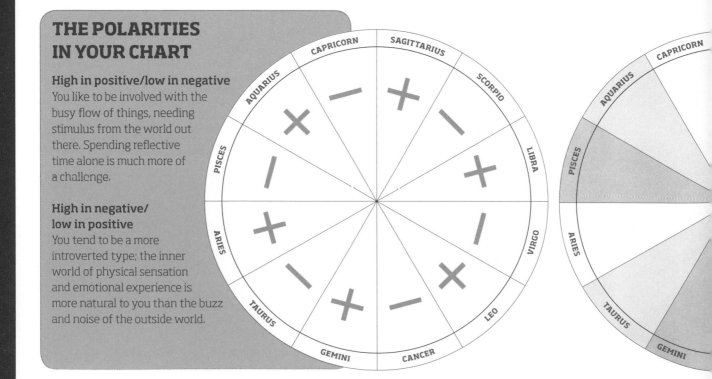

LOW

You can find it a challenge to assert yourself or have confidence, yet you might find yourself in positions where you are challenged to develop leadership, faith, and a vision of your own.

It might be difficult for you to honor your body's needs and adjust to the confines of physical or monetary resources. An unconscious materialism might be at work.

You tend to be wary of too much talking and theorizing, and it might be hard for you to see things with rational objectivity. Your journey might involve slowly developing a body of knowledge.

Overt displays of emotion are not your style, and you might miss subtle cues of body language and emotional expression. Inwardly though, your own emotions take on heightened force.

THE MODES IN YOUR CHART

MODE	HIGH	LOW
Cardinal	You like to seize the initiative and hate to be at the mercy of someone else's plans. It is important for you to set challenging goals and then find ways of achieving them.	You might unconsciously gravitate toward situations that require you to lead from the front or take a role as pioneer or entrepreneur, requiring you to dig deep to develop these skills.
Fixed	Your skill lies in providing continuity and stability, but you might get stuck in situations, afraid to move on. Learning to cope with change might be an important life lesson.	It might be hard for you to stand your ground, particularly if you are high in mutable energy, too. Your challenge may be to stick with something so that you can reap the rewards of commitment.
Mutable	You are highly adaptable—sometimes perhaps too much so, finding it easier to concede than to fight for your territory. Your gift though is your ability to go with the flow and not become too attached.	Your responses tend to be clear and unequivocal—it might be a challenge for you to learn to adapt or feel content in situations that are not completely under your control.

THE **1ST** SIGN OF THE ZODIAC

ARIES

MARCH 21–APRIL 20

As the first sign of the zodiac, Aries is strong and vital, reflecting the vigor of its totem animal, the ram. Positive cardinal fire is extroverted, initiatory, and ardent, focusing its energies to get things going. Aries needs action.

Symbol **♈**
Polarity **Positive**
Mode **Cardinal**
Element **Fire**
Ruling planet **Mars**
Parts of the body **Head and adrenal glands**

The Sun in Aries
Your life purpose is to pioneer and lead the way, breaking new ground for others to follow. As a courageous and conquering hero, you search for challenges through which to prove yourself.

Your planets in Aries
Planets here will act spontaneously, with daring–you like to take the initiative in whatever aspect of your life these planets represent.

Aries on the cusp of a house
This is an area of life where you are competitive and self-motivated, willing to take a risk and step into the unknown.

STARTING OUT

Aries is the herald of spring in the northern hemisphere. Your planets in this sign will express Aries' youthful zest and energy.

THE WARRIOR

The ruler of Aries is the warrior god Mars. For Ariens, it is of the utmost importance to compete ... and to win.

ONLY THE BRAVE

This sign enjoys risk; your planets here will seek out danger as a means of testing and proving their strength.

ENTERPRISE AND INITIATIVE

IF YOU HAVE THE SUN OR MOON IN ARIES, YOU PROBABLY PREFER TO CALL THE SHOTS.

COMPETITION AND FIGHTING

Where Aries falls in your chart, you show competitive spirit and hate to compromise or concede victory.

IMPETUOUS

Planets here thrive on self-generated energy but can act without thinking.

DECISIVE Aries people are clearheaded and can think quickly in an emergency.

GOING SOLO

WITH PLANETS IN ARIES, YOU PREFER TO WORK ALONE.

CHILDLIKE

This sign is candid and sometimes naïve. As an Aries, you can be genuinely perplexed at intrigue and politics or when things do not go according to your plan.

URGENCY

You know what you want, and you want it now— or better still, yesterday.

NEGATIVE TRAITS

The ram is sometimes prone to "locking horns" or acting like a "battering ram"–Aries gets the job done, but can create conflict.

FAST AND FURIOUS

People with planets in this sign take life by the horns.

THE **2ND** SIGN OF THE ZODIAC

TAURUS
APRIL 21–MAY 21

Taurus is calm and measured–the bull is slow to anger and slow to move. Negative fixed earth is reserved, grounded, and resistant to change. Taureans are attuned to physical reality and the rhythms of nature and the body.

Symbol ♉
Polarity **Negative**
Mode **Fixed**
Element **Earth**
Ruling planet **Venus**
Parts of the body **Neck and throat**

The Sun in Taurus
Your life purpose is to build something of lasting value, which will allow you to develop gifts of persistence and resilience. Like a garden, your life's work unfolds slowly, tended with care.

Your planets in Taurus
Planets in this sign are both grounded and sensuous in their expression, channeled through the physical body. This part of you needs time to consider and digest experiences.

Taurus on the cusp of a house
In this area of life, you can show pragmatism, commitment, and persistence. You are willing to let things develop in their own time and have a tendency for patience and endurance.

SLOW AND STEADY AFTER THE SPRING RUSH OF ARIES, TAURUS IS CALM AND CONSIDERED, SLOW AND DELIBERATE.

THE PHYSICAL WORLD

Taureans feel at home in the body and the natural world, appreciating simple sensory pleasures such as delicious food, music, and the arts.

THE GIFT OF PATIENCE

One of your most valuable skills is knowing that good things can come to those who wait. You can sit back patiently with calm acceptance.

ENDURING & PERSISTENT

Once you have committed yourself to a course of action, you stick with it—even at times when making a change might be beneficial.

SLOW TO ANGER Taureans are known for being calm and placid—most of the time! But you can have a formidable temper when goaded or pushed.

SENSUALITY

Taurus is ruled by Venus, the goddess of fertility and sexual love. Your planets here are responsive to the delights of sensual experience and will seek out such pleasures.

NEGATIVE TRAITS

The bull can be immensely stubborn, sometimes to its own detriment. As fixed earth, Taurus can at times be covetous or self-indulgent.

LOVE OF SECURITY

A TAUREAN VALUES STABILITY AND DISLIKES CHANGE AND UPHEAVAL.

MONEY AND MATERIAL SUCCESS

With planets in Taurus, you can have a gift for material accumulation and sound financial sense.

POSSESSIVE

Planets in Taurus can be acquisitive, seeking to own and possess—this sign is often reluctant to let go of objects, situations, or people.

THE **3RD** SIGN OF THE ZODIAC

GEMINI
MAY 22–JUNE 21

Gemini is concerned with duality and movement between opposing sides, providing a bridge between the two. Positive mutable air is sociable and outgoing, light and playful, but easily bored and in need of variety and stimulation for a curious, agile mind.

Symbol Ⅱ
Polarity **Positive**
Mode **Mutable**
Element **Air**
Ruling planet **Mercury**
Parts of the body **Arms, hands, and lungs**

The Sun in Gemini
Your life purpose is to find the "twin." Every Gemini has light and dark sides, and it is your task to recognize both characters within yourself. Communication, learning, and ideas will be central.

Your planets in Gemini
Planets in Gemini tend to adapt themselves easily to new environments and situations. Here, you will need to express yourself with lightness and variety.

Gemini on the cusp of a house
This is an area of life where you apply logic rather than emotion. Here is where you are curious or where you need continual change and mental stimulus.

COMMUNICATION

The image of the twins suggests a need for conversation and social interaction.

NETWORKING

For a Gemini, making connections–while not getting stuck in any one place–is key.

PLAYFUL & CHARMING

As a Gemini, you can be flirtatious, gaining attention through wit and humor.

TWO IN ONE OFTEN ACCUSED OF BEING DUPLICITOUS OR TWO-FACED, GEMINIS CAN FIND THEMSELVES MEDIATING BETWEEN TWO SIDES.

SOCIAL BUTTERFLY

With planets in Gemini, you make friends easily, and your social circle is likely to be wide and diverse.

CURIOSITY & LEARNING

Geminis retain their youthful curiosity and love to learn. New faces and places are a must for a Gemini to thrive.

NOW YOU SEE ME ...

Preferring diversity, sticking with one thing (job, house, opinion ...) for any length of time can be a challenge.

LIGHT & DARK

Geminis are often aware of duality within themselves; the bright celestial twin and the dark earthly twin exist side by side. When not "up," depression can easily take over.

THE NEED FOR CHANGE

Mutable air suggests a restless need for movement, diversity, and stimulation. The worst thing for a Gemini is to feel bored or trapped by routine.

NEGATIVE TRAITS

At worst, Gemini skims the surface, reluctant to engage with deeper feelings and consequences. This sign can play one side against the other.

THE **4TH** SIGN OF THE ZODIAC

CANCER

JUNE 22–JULY 22

Cancer is subtle and sensitive, yet canny and tenacious, too. As its animal symbol suggests, a hard shell protects a vulnerable interior. Negative cardinal water has a receptive nature and the instinct to act on emotions.

Symbol ♋
Polarity **Negative**
Mode **Cardinal**
Element **Water**
Ruling planet **Moon**
Parts of the body **Breasts and stomach**

The Sun in Cancer
Your life purpose is to find your tribe and to develop a central role as the caregiver within it, your life revolving around some form of family (whether personal or professional).

Your planets in Cancer
Planets here will show a self-protective quality, acting according to moods and feelings. Intuition and emotion are the ruling forces.

Cancer on the cusp of a house
This area of your life may form a sanctuary, a place of safety away from the world. You seek to protect and defend the matters of that house.

SIGN OF THE MOTHER CANCERIANS HAVE A DESIRE TO NURTURE BUT MIGHT FIND IT DIFFICULT TO LET GO.

CLOSE BONDS

For Cancerians, the emotions they invest in people, places, and possessions can make separation from them painful.

NEED FOR SECURITY

It is crucial for Cancerians to feel safe. Planets in this sign adopt a low-risk strategy.

HOME AND FAMILY

Cancerians like to feel that they're in familiar territory–anchored by clan, family, and home.

TENACITY When really intent on their goal, a Cancerian won't give up.

WITHDRAWAL UNDER PRESSURE

Cancerians act on instinct, withdrawing into their shell if they sense danger.

POWERFUL INTUITION

People born under this sign easily pick up on atmosphere and feelings.

SIDEWAYS STRATEGY

Being cardinal, Cancerians can be assertive but rarely go straight for the target.

FEELINGS ARE PARAMOUNT

THE CANCERIAN STANCE IS SUBJECTIVE, BASED AROUND PERSONAL EMOTIONS.

EASILY HURT

Cancerians can lash out or become emotionally manipulative, but as a defensive posture, when in a state of stress or anxiety.

NEGATIVE TRAITS

Emotions often take precedence over rational sense. Cancerians can be deeply partisan, closing ranks when challenged by unfamiliar situations.

SEA CREATURE

Reflecting its ruler, the Moon, there is a tidal quality to this sign. Energy levels and emotional states can wax and wane.

CARING

Sensitive and capable of genuine empathy, Cancerians thrive in the healing and caring professions.

THE **5TH** SIGN OF THE ZODIAC

LEO

JULY 23–AUGUST 22

Warm, bright, and charismatic, Leo is a regal sign, but full of fun, too. Positive fixed fire is extroverted, steadfast, and visionary. Leos possess dignity, self-confidence, and a sense of style along with a generous and motivating nature.

Symbol ♌
Polarity **Positive**
Mode **Fixed**
Element **Fire**
Ruling planet **Sun**
Parts of the body **Heart and spine**

The Sun in Leo

Your life purpose is to develop your creative brilliance and take center stage or lead the pack. You attract allegiance in return for your inspiration, support, and strength.

Your planets in Leo

Planets here will act with courage, pride, and a sense of showmanship. These planets radiate star quality, attracting praise from others.

Leo on the cusp of a house

This area of your life will be close to your heart, a place where you can shine and develop your creativity. You invest personal energy here and want to be loved.

SENSE OF FUN Leo is a playful sign; planets here are spontaneous. Leos connect easily to the innocent and uncomplicated world of children.

BOLD & COURAGEOUS

Leos tend to be daring, self-reliant, and self-possessed. Planets here will be brave and spirited.

THE PERFORMER

Leo loves the limelight and puts on a show— this is where we thrive on attention, admiration, and respect.

GLAMOUR & SPARKLE

Planets in Leo can have an air of authority and a sense of grandeur. Leos hate to get their hands dirty and prefer to delegate.

HONOR In a position of trust, Leos are honorable and honest. Integrity is important to this sign.

CREATIVITY

Those with planets in Leo may need to indulge regularly in creative pursuits and hobbies to express their sense of being special.

NEGATIVE TRAITS

You can display arrogance and self-centeredness, or easily suffer hurt pride. Turn this around by developing faith in your creative power.

NEED TO BE SEEN

LEOS TEND TO BE LARGER THAN LIFE AND NEED TO FEEL SPECIAL.

LOOKING TO THE FUTURE

Leos are positive and forward-looking–optimistic, confident, and full of hope.

WARM & GENEROUS

Those with planets in Leo are generous with their time and energy and find it easy to motivate others.

ME, MYSELF, AND I WITH THE SUN AS RULER, LEOS HAVE AN INDEPENDENT WILL AND A FOCUS ON ACCOMPLISHMENT. THE EGO CAN BE STRONG WITH LEO.

THE **6TH** SIGN OF THE ZODIAC

VIRGO

AUGUST 23–SEPTEMBER 22

Virgo extracts what is good and makes something useful out of it. This sign brings order and efficient functioning. Negative mutable earth suggests an ability to do what is necessary without fanfare. Craft and skill are essential to this sign.

Symbol ♍
Polarity **Negative**
Mode **Mutable**
Element **Earth**
Ruling planet **Mercury**
Part of the body **Digestive system**

The Sun in Virgo

Your life purpose is to hone your chosen craft. You feel happiest being useful as part of a team or taking a constructive role in the world. Your Virgo Sun loves practical systems of communication.

Your planets in Virgo

Planets here will act with discrimination. This sign is not given to drama or show, instead focusing on useful efficiency and the development of practical skills.

Virgo on the cusp of a house

This area of your life will probably run like a well-oiled machine–or at least you would like it to! Here, you seek to establish order and method.

THE VIRGIN The symbol for Virgo is the Virgin. In the ancient world, she is the temple virgin, dedicated to the deity. We can translate this as an instinct for self-sufficiency and devotion to practical service.

HEALTH AND WELL-BEING
For Virgos, mind and body are linked; regular exercise and healthy eating help you to maintain effective mind-body balance.

MAKING SOMETHING USEFUL
The Virgin is usually depicted holding a sheaf of wheat. She watches over the harvest, an act of sorting wheat from chaff and using skill to create a useful product.

A SENSE OF ORDER
Virgo's role is to establish and work according to a system. With planets in this sign, you dislike chaos.

PERFECTIONISM
With the emphasis on skill, dexterity, and technique, Virgos tend to demand nothing less than perfection.

HEADSPACE STRESS CAN EASILY BUILD UP WHEN THERE IS NO CHANCE TO PROCESS OR DOWNLOAD.

INFORMATION MANAGEMENT
Virgos have a flair for managing and classifying information and putting it to use.

FOCUS ON DETAIL
Virgos are analytical and discriminating.

Willing to help
This humble sign brings us down to earth after the glitz of Leo. Whereas Leo loves a party, Virgo will organize it—and offer to clean up afterward.

NEGATIVE TRAITS
Virgos can often get lost in the details, unable to see the bigger picture. Sweating the small stuff can turn into an obsessive need for order and control.

HUMBLE AND SELF-EFFACING
A sense of self-value comes from being useful and productive, but Virgos can easily downplay their own talents.

"WE COME **SPINNING** OUT OF NOTHINGNESS, SCATTERING **STARS LIKE DUST**."

Jalal ad-Din Rumi

THE **7TH** SIGN OF THE ZODIAC

LIBRA
SEPTEMBER 23–OCTOBER 22

The scales suggest Libra's task of creating and maintaining symmetry and balance. Positive cardinal air is outgoing and sociable, actively making relationships. Diplomacy, style, and grace are key expressions for this sign.

Symbol ♎
Polarity **Positive**
Mode **Cardinal**
Element **Air**
Ruling planet **Venus**
Part of the body **Kidneys**

The Sun in Libra
Your life purpose is to personify and promote the art of civilized living. You find inner balance through developing poise and grace within yourself.

Your planets in Libra
Planets here will express themselves with polite refinement, seeking to create an atmosphere of harmony and acting with consideration for others.

Libra on the cusp of a house
This is an area of life to which you bring elegance and tact. Here, you are good at sharing or working in tandem with someone else.

THE SCALES

The scales of justice reflect Libra's function of creating peaceful equilibrium and perfect balance.

TACT & DIPLOMACY

You hate to upset anyone or rock the boat, and will win people over with grace and charm.

JUSTICE AND THE LAW

This sign is concerned with fairness and equality; Librans are often drawn to legal work or campaigns against social injustice.

EVENING THE SCORES

Librans, sometimes called "polite Aries," abide by rules of fair play and will go to war against someone who oversteps the bounds.

INDECISIVE

The Libran spirit tries to see all sides, applying the airy gift of objectivity. Indecision can reflect the desire to be scrupulously fair.

NEED FOR RELATIONSHIP LIBRANS NEED THE MOTIVATING PRESENCE OF A PARTNER. PERIODS OF LONELINESS OR ISOLATION CAN SAP THE SPIRIT.

THE PERFECT UMPIRE

Careers in marriage guidance, PR, or mediation might appeal. This is a cardinal sign—fair and polite, but needing to create dynamic movement.

THE ARTS As a
Venus-ruled sign, Libra has a strong association with the arts—many Librans are gifted designers, artists, musicians, and fashionistas.

THE ART OF COMPROMISE

Librans will often be willing to concede personal territory if this results in peace and happiness all around.

BEAUTY AND APPEARANCE

You appreciate life's more elegant offerings—for you, outer beauty reflects inner harmony.

NEGATIVE TRAITS

Perhaps your least attractive trait is insincerity—although your motivation is usually to oil the wheels and make things look good.

THE **8TH** SIGN OF THE ZODIAC

SCORPIO

OCTOBER 23–NOVEMBER 21

Scorpio takes us into the depths. This is a complex and intense sign, concerned with processes of transformation. Negative fixed water is inward-moving and conjures the image of "still waters running deep." Scorpios are masters of controlled passion.

Symbol ♏
Polarity **Negative**
Mode **Fixed**
Element **Water**
Ruling planets **Mars and Pluto**
Parts of the body **Reproductive organs and eliminatory system**

The Sun in Scorpio
Your life purpose is to develop resilience. There is often a story of survival against the odds, and your "solar gold" is the inner fortitude this brings.

Your planets in Scorpio
Planets here will act with passion, intensity, and stoic courage, capable of going into the fire and being reborn in a purer and stronger form.

Scorpio on the cusp of a house
This area of your life is subject to cyclical processes of crisis, elimination, and renewal. Here, you go to the depths and are disinclined to compromise.

WILLPOWER & STRENGTH The symbol for Scorpio is the scorpion, a creature capable of withdrawing into itself to survive the most extreme conditions.

TAKING IT TO THE LIMIT
This sign admires emotional courage and the capacity to survive by one's own wits.

INNER CONTROL
A Scorpio will never admit to feeling powerless. Self-control is paramount.

SECRETIVE & PRIVATE
Scorpio is often the strong, silent type, unwilling to say how they truly feel. Dig at your peril: a Scorpio will use all their resources to avoid emotional exposure.

THE DETECTIVE WITH ITS POWERFUL SIXTH SENSE, THE SCORPION MAKES A GOOD UNDERCOVER SLEUTH.

WORKING AT DEPTH The deep dark is Scorpio's territory. Activities involving research and excavation appeal: archaeology, psychotherapy, or anything that plumbs the depths.

POSSESSIVE
As fixed water, Scorpio suggests emotional possessiveness. This can manifest as unwavering loyalty–but also as intense jealousy.

PASSION UNDER A COOL EXTERIOR
Scorpios possess powerful emotions, usually hidden beneath a seemingly detached exterior.

EMOTIONAL HONESTY
A deep intuition characterizes this sign; you possess a radarlike vision to see into the heart of things.

A STING IN THE TAIL
You would rather die than concede defeat, making you a formidable enemy.

CAPACITY FOR REGENERATION
With Mars and Pluto as co-rulers, inner willpower and determination allow Scorpios to survive the most challenging of circumstances.

NEGATIVE TRAITS
Once hurt, it is difficult for you to forgive or forget. Betrayal cuts deep, and in such instances, your instinct is to take revenge. This sign can seek to dominate and control.

THE **9TH** SIGN OF THE ZODIAC

SAGITTARIUS
NOVEMBER 22–DECEMBER 21

The Sagittarian spirit is optimistic and forward-looking. This is the sign of the traveler and the wanderer, for whom the whole wide world is home. Positive mutable fire is sociable and restless, needing movement and a broad canvas.

Symbol ♐
Polarity **Positive**
Mode **Mutable**
Element **Fire**
Ruling planet **Jupiter**
Parts of the body **Hips and thighs**

The Sun in Sagittarius
Your life purpose is to explore, discover, and set yourself free on adventures. This is a philosophical sign; with the Sun here, you engage in a quest for deeper meaning.

Your planets in Sagittarius
Planets here will radiate fiery confidence, taking a long-range approach and needing breadth and freedom. Any form of confinement would be counterproductive.

Sagittarius on the cusp of a house
In this area of your life, you hear the call to adventure; this is a part of you that invites exploration and where you feel a more exciting world awaits.

THE ARCHER The symbol of the archer suggests an arrow shot into the far distance. For Sagittarians, what excites is a sense of potential and possibility.

THE CENTAUR

Sagittarius is also linked to the Centaur, half-horse and half man, suggesting both a love of wild nature and a world of philosophic contemplation.

BROADENING THE MIND

Long-distance travel, education, religion, and philosophy can all be appealing to Sagittarians.

THE GREAT OUTDOORS THOSE BORN WITH THIS SIGN STRONG IN THEIR CHART OFTEN HAVE A LOVE OF SPORTS AND THE OUTDOORS.

A SEARCH FOR MEANING

At the heart of this sign's wanderings is a search for meaning—an urge to contemplate and answer life's bigger questions.

HONESTY

Sagittarian honesty can appear to others as bluntness. Communication, as with most things, tends to be uninhibited.

BIGGER IS BETTER

Expansiveness is natural for this sign. Sagittarians are good at sensing new opportunities.

AN OPTIMISTIC OUTLOOK

As a fire sign, Sagittarius possesses farsightedness and the confidence to believe that everything will work out well in the end.

DON'T FENCE ME IN

THE NEED FOR FREEDOM AND ADVENTURE CAN RESULT IN AN AVERSION TO COMMITMENT.

A SPLIT NATURE

Ruled by buoyant Jupiter, Sagittarius offers those born under it a sunny optimism. But there can be a darker side, where loss of meaning may bring deep depression.

NEGATIVE TRAITS

Sagittarius is not noted for its carefulness or precision, manifesting in an indiscriminate "scattershot" approach.

THE **10TH** SIGN OF THE ZODIAC

CAPRICORN
DECEMBER 22–JANUARY 19

Capricorn is focused and hard-working, acting strategically and aiming for practical achievements and professional success. Negative cardinal earth is introverted but works patiently and with quiet endurance toward a clear target before moving swiftly on to the next task.

Symbol ♑
Polarity **Negative**
Mode **Cardinal**
Element **Earth**
Ruling planet **Saturn**
Parts of the body **Knees, teeth, bones, and skin**

The Sun in Capricorn
Your life purpose is to develop self-reliance, taking on responsibility for both yourself and others. The path may feel lonely at times, but you always keep your eye on the goal.

Your planets in Capricorn
Planets here will act with mature dignity, aware of tradition and what might be socially acceptable. You develop these gifts slowly over time.

Capricorn on the cusp of a house
Here, you show maturity and seek respect from others. You act pragmatically, with an eye to material gain. You work with purpose in this area and apply a clear sense of structure.

THE GOAT Capricorn's totem animal is the goat, a symbol of this sign's ambitious climb to the top and capacity for quiet endurance.

THE GOAT-FISH This is an ancient symbol of the Mesopotamian god of civilization and fertile abundance.

PLAYING BY THE RULES This is a conservative sign. You understand the rules—indeed, you probably created them.

PRACTICAL ACHIEVEMENTS Capricorns seek to ground their skills in tangible accomplishments.

TAKING ON RESPONSIBILITY
You tend to be organized and reliable. Consultancy or management are good career choices. Status and position are key.

HARD WORKER This sign expects things to be tough and happily knuckles down. You have to feel that you've earned your position.

SELF-SUFFICIENCY You make your own way, preferring not to rely on others. You can be independent and good at maintaining boundaries.

WORLDLY AND PRAGMATIC You know the value of a solid bank balance or an investment in bricks and mortar. As an earth sign, you place faith in the tangible and the real.

PLANNERS THOSE WITH PLANETS IN CAPRICORN WILL ALWAYS HAVE THINGS WORKED OUT IN ADVANCE.

SENSE OF PURPOSE Without a clear aim, structure, or sense of practical achievement, depression can set in. Purposeful work is key for this sign.

NEGATIVE TRAITS This sign can be overly serious at times, hampered by a rigid system or sense of obligation. You can be strategic—but sometimes ruthless and calculating, too.

THE **11TH** SIGN OF THE ZODIAC

AQUARIUS
JANUARY 20–FEBRUARY 18

Highly independent, Aquarius is also paradoxically a very sociable sign. Positive fixed air is outgoing, encouraging involvement in groups and the exchange of ideas. Aquarians often have strong social awareness and a humanitarian vision of a more ideal future along with the determination to bring this about.

Symbol ♒
Polarity **Positive**
Mode **Fixed**
Element **Air**
Ruling planets **Saturn and Uranus**
Parts of the body **Shins and ankles**

The Sun in Aquarius
Your life purpose is to find your place within the group while at the same time asserting your own unique vision. An ideal of social equality may form an important foundation.

Your planets in Aquarius
People with planets in this sign usually march to the beat of their own drum. Planets here tend to show a cool detachment in their expression.

Aquarius on the cusp of a house
You are likely to approach this area of your life from an alternative or highly individual perspective, forming your own ideas and flouting conventions.

SOCIETY

Aquarius represents the ideal of a just and enlightened society. Its symbol, the Water Bearer, pours out the waters of knowledge for the benefit of all humanity.

COMMUNITY YOU TEND TO THRIVE IN GROUPS AND COMMUNITIES HELD TOGETHER BY A COMMON IDEAL.

IDEALISTIC Aquarius is the sign of revolution. You are often in the vanguard of change, with an idealistic vision of how things should be.

UNCONVENTIONAL

Planets in Aquarius like to buck the trend, preferring an avant-garde form of expression.

GROUP DYNAMIC

You are often torn between honoring your own creative power and maintaining the cohesion of the group.

DETACHMENT AND CLARITY

Aquarians tend to feel suffocated if the atmosphere becomes too emotional. You prefer rational conversation with like-minded people.

CREATIVE FREEDOM FREEDOM OF EXPRESSION IS AN ESSENTIAL PLATFORM FOR YOUR CREATIVE ORIGINALITY.

RATIONAL INTELLECT

Your gift for rational detachment often feeds an interest in science or technology.

NEGATIVE TRAITS

A feeling of intellectual superiority can sometimes get in the way of a truly democratic outlook.

RULE BREAKER?

The co-rulership of Saturn and Uranus means you acknowledge the rules but don't always play by them.

FRIENDSHIP

For you, even the closest lover must be a friend, too. Relationships must honor the Aquarian need for space and freedom.

THE **12TH** SIGN OF THE ZODIAC

PISCES
FEBRUARY 19–MARCH 20

As the final sign, the task of Pisces is to find freedom from material limitations and connect with the intangible and the magical, the divine source of life. Negative mutable water suggests focus on an internal world flowing according to feeling.

Symbol ♓
Polarity **Negative**
Mode **Mutable**
Element **Water**
Ruling planet **Jupiter and Neptune**
Parts of the body **Feet**

The Sun in Pisces
Your life purpose is to offer service to a higher principle, a journey that may involve the sacrifice of personal desires. Developing artistic imagination is a key dimension of your life.

Your planets in Pisces
Planets here tend to be unfocused in their expression, moved by subtle feelings rather than practical considerations and lacking in boundaries.

Pisces on the cusp of a house
Pisces brings the lens of imagination to this area of your life. Here, you might be inspired to acts of devotion or find your best strategy is to follow your intuition.

MAGIC & ENCHANTMENT THIS SIGN IS DRAWN TO ENCHANTED WORLDS THROUGH THE PORTAL OF THE IMAGINATION.

THE IMPORTANCE OF DREAMS
For Pisceans, the "virtual reality" of dreams, myths, fantasies, and stories may feel more real than ordinary life.

A NEED TO ESCAPE
This sign's symbol is the two tied fishes, one of which swims along the ecliptic while the other turns its gaze upward, suggesting longing for escape from the ordinary world.

THE NEED FOR RETREAT
Sensitivity and a dislike of pressure mean a need for periodic retreat to recharge physical and psychological batteries.

SAVING THE WORLD PISCES IS THE SAVIOR, COMPASSIONATE AND DEVOTED.

IMAGINATIVE AND ARTISTIC
You can feel like a fish out of water when your creative talents are not being used.

ROMANCE IN RELATIONSHIPS
In relationships, you tend to be romantic and idealistic; you need to retain the magic.

Elusive
It may be a challenge to commit to a long-term partnership or project if this involves binding contracts and obligations.

CHARITABLE & GIVING
You might be drawn to charity or aid work, where you can selflessly assist.

SENSITIVE & RECEPTIVE
Pisces is open to vibration and mood, often feeling overwhelmed by emotions in the world around.

NEGATIVE TRAITS
There can be a tendency to drift or to allow yourself to be taken advantage of. Disillusionment, disenchantment, or a desire to be rescued can sometimes undermine your efforts.

THE
PLANETS

The Sun
Mercury
Venus
The Moon orbiting Earth
Mars
Jupiter
Saturn
Chiron

THE PLANETS
AN OVERVIEW

ASSESSING BALANCE IN YOUR CHART

The planets can be thought of as the actors in a chart. Psychologically, they are archetypal drives, each representing a universal principle that exists within you and also in the world around you. The dynamic relationships between the planets in your chart form the heart of your personality.

SHINE | NURTURE | COMMUNICATE | RELATE | ASSERT

PERSONAL PLANETS

SOCIAL PLANETS

⊙	☽	☿	♀	♂	♃
The Sun	**The Moon**	**Mercury**	**Venus**	**Mars**	**Jupiter**
The central core of our being	Our instinctual responses and nurturing principle	How we think, learn, and communicate	The principle of pleasure and of relating	How we assert ourselves and direct our energy	The principle of expansion, faith, and optimism

The planets in your chart

In your birth chart, each planet represents a basic drive within you, and each can have an array of potential expressions, all flowing from a central idea. Venus, for instance, represents the force of beauty, cohesion, and cooperation in the cosmos; from this, we get the idea of its astrological role as signifier of our capacity to relate and find common ground with others, the notion of romantic love, and our aesthetic and artistic potentials.

Each person's chart contains all the planets, but from chart to chart, the planets will occupy different zodiac signs and different houses, and they will bear different relationships to each other around the wheel of the chart (in other words, different "aspects"). Thus, each chart offers its own completely unique picture, with the planets expressing themselves according to that individual's own particular pattern.

Planetary protocol

Astrology divides the planets into three main groupings, according to their distance from the Sun.

The Sun, Moon, Mercury, Venus, and Mars are the "personal planets," representing the most personal of the planetary drives and the core of our character. (Astrology refers to the Sun and Moon as "planets," too, for brevity.) The Sun and Moon are also called the "luminaries," with the Sun as ruler of the daytime world and the Moon as ruler of the night sky. These two bodies play the most central role in a chart.

Jupiter and Saturn are the "social planets," so called because they represent the processes of socialization and adjustment within our contexts of family and society—Jupiter, as the principle of expansion, connects us to the world at large via education, travel, philosophy, and religious beliefs; Saturn, as the principle of contraction, calls on us to adjust to the rules and regulations that are an inevitable part of human life.

Uranus, Neptune, and Pluto are the "collective," "transpersonal," or "generational" planets. This is because they have very slow orbits and spend a much greater length of time in one zodiac sign. The zodiac sign they occupy tends to describe the collective political and social ideals and preoccupations prevalent during that particular era.

Chiron is a maverick and does not fit neatly into the scheme, orbiting mostly between Saturn and Uranus, so its symbolism unites personal, social, collective, and ancestral themes.

BRIDGING SOCIAL & COLLECTIVE

COLLECTIVE PLANETS

♄	⚷	♅	♆	♇
Saturn	**Chiron**	**Uranus**	**Neptune**	**Pluto**
The principle of contraction, structure, and boundaries	The wounded healer	The force of enlightenment and sudden change	Our ideal vision and what inspires us to devotion	The force that brings about transformation

THE SUN

IDENTITY AND LIFE PURPOSE

Just as the Sun is at the center of the solar system, so the astrological Sun is at the heart of the birth chart, with the other planets in service to the process of self-development and creative fulfillment that it represents.

Rules **Leo**
Day of the week **Sunday**
Metal **Gold**
Colors **Gold, orange, yellow**
Symbol ☉

PURPOSE | VITALITY | CREATIVE POWER | HEART OF OUR BEING
INNER AUTHORITY | SHINING LIGHT | SELF-DEVELOPMENT

The Sun in the sky
In our material world, the sky provides illumination and warmth, regulating the days with its rising and setting and our years with the cycle of the seasons. The Sun is our source of life and energy, around which everything revolves.

The Sun in myth
Solar deities bring light and vitality: the Babylonian Shamash was a symbol of justice, and Helios of the ancient Greeks drove the chariot of the Sun across the sky. In Egyptian Ra, Celtic Lugh, and Hindu Surya as well, we see the life-giving spirit of the Sun.

The Sun in the world around us
Bright yellow and orange flowers are governed by the Sun. St. John's wort, used to treat depression, falls under the Sun. This planet symbolizes monarchs, presidents, and heads of state; it can signify the father, too. Solar places are palaces and theaters.

THE SUN **THROUGH THE SIGNS**

Consider how this planet expresses itself according to the sign that it occupies.

Aries You may be called to be a pioneer, leading the way through courage. Tests of bravery help you to sharpen your warrior's spirit.

Taurus Your creative gift lies in the relationship you make with the physical and natural world. It is important for you to create something enduring.

Gemini The development of language and communication skills informs your identity. Knowledge is your goal.

Cancer Your gift might be to nurture a family or bonded network of people, bringing out your gift as a protective caretaker.

Leo You seek to shine your light boldly and brightly, having the capacity to take on a role of leadership. It is important for you to be admired.

Virgo Your life might revolve around the development of a craft, with the emphasis on skilled working and on practical service.

Libra The expression of harmony and balance may be a key concept for you, either developed through artistic endeavors or relationships.

Scorpio The journey for you may be to dive into the depths, gaining inner strength through weathering tough conditions and emerging transformed.

Sagittarius At the heart of things for you is growth through travel, learning, or breadth of life experience, perhaps via other cultures or belief systems.

Capricorn Life may call you to take on the mantle of responsible leadership. Your life path may encourage the development of self-reliance and reliability.

Aquarius Your life task might be to uphold a principle of equality or to develop a special identity for yourself within an eclectic community.

Pisces You can develop your imaginative gifts in order to bring a sense of pride and achievement—or your life may be selflessly dedicated to serving others.

CENTRAL GOALS | PRIDE | SELF-CONFIDENCE

THE SUN **IN YOUR CHART**

The influence of this planet will be felt according to where it resides and its relationship to other planets.

Central purpose The Sun describes our core sense of identity and the journey we undertake over the course of life to develop the latent creativity within ourselves. The Sun symbolizes our inner guiding light, our essential vitality, and our central purpose.

Our true path The Sun is an orchestrating principle toward which the other planets are somehow leading us. We might liken it to Jung's concept of the Self, where ego can give way to a more holistic version of ourselves once we have gained a measure of self-knowledge and recognized our true path.

Pride Here, we desire to be recognized and admired, since this is a place of pride, where we can develop talents that are of crucial importance to us. It signifies our small portion of the divine light, which we reflect out to the world through our achievements and by which we can be defined and remembered.

Quest As well as who we are, the Sun tells us what we are in the process of becoming. There is a sense of quest with the Sun, at the end of which we eventually come home to ourselves.

Solar potential Where the Sun is in our chart, we can be radiant and magnanimous—an inspiration to others, with the capacity for leadership in our field—or we can lack confidence, or be arrogant and autocratic. What might make the difference here is whether or not our solar potentials have been supported and encouraged by our background, upbringing, and life experiences.

THE MOON

INSTINCT AND PROTECTION

The symbol for the Moon shows the waxing crescent, reminding us that the Moon reflects light from the Sun. In the chart, it takes a less prominent role in our conscious awareness than our solar goals.

Rules **Cancer**
Day of the week **Monday**
Metal **Silver**
Colors **White, silver**
Symbol ☽

PHYSICAL | EMOTIONAL | INSTINCT | FAMILIARITY
MATERNAL | FEED | NURTURE | INTUITION | CYCLICAL

The Moon in the sky
There is something magical about watching the Moon's cycle in the sky. A few days after the new Moon, she appears as a slim crescent and then waxes until at full Moon we see the entire shining disk, before she wanes into darkness again.

The Moon in myth
The Moon's cycle has been charted in triple form as maiden, mother, and crone, and as the three Fates of Greek and Norse myth. It is linked astrologically to the menstrual cycle, conception, and birth, and to mothering, feeding, and nurturing.

The Moon in the world around us
Connected to the ocean and to water (ships, harbors, rivers, and so on), the gravitational pull of the Moon generates the tides, and its phases coincide with natural and biological rhythms. In the human body, for instance, the Moon governs autonomic processes.

THE MOON **THROUGH THE SIGNS**

Consider how this planet expresses itself according to the sign that it occupies.

Aries It does not suit you to be held back or have to wait for others. You might show caring by helping your charges develop their independence.

Taurus It is a prerequisite to take things slowly and calmly, paying proper attention to basic needs. Touch is important for well being.

Gemini What feeds you is verbal contact or learning, reading, and information exchange as part of your daily routines.

Cancer Your primary concern is security. There is a deep instinct to nurture and protect yourself and others. Feelings wax and wane but are powerful.

Leo You seek an active flow of praise and love from others. You may be naturally connected to your own creative talents or seek to nurture these in others.

Virgo Your style of caretaking tends to be practical, quietly attending to humble tasks. Care over diet and exercise can be your key to well-being.

Libra You have an instinct to create relationships and may feel more at home in a partnership than on your own. Calm and peace are needed for well-being.

Scorpio Emotions tend to run deep, and holding on to hurts can at times be destructive. Tough physical exercise can be a way to discharge feelings.

Sagittarius You need room to move and travel around, both physically and emotionally. The best nurturing is a feeling of inner freedom.

Capricorn You may need a structured routine, and you tend to be efficient with your time and resources. Safety comes from feeling you are in control.

Aquarius Naturally gregarious and interested in the alternative option, you might feel most at home living in a community.

Pisces It can be hard for you to identify how you feel, and sensitivity to others' feelings may cloud the issue. Retreat and time alone are needed to recharge.

FEMININE | NATURE | RHYTHMS & RITUALS | SECURITY

THE MOON **IN YOUR CHART**

The influence of this planet will be felt according to where it resides and its relationship to other planets.

Governing influence In early childhood, the Moon is often the governing influence, before awareness of solar individuality and personal will begins to take hold.

Instinct The Moon reflects our instinctive reactions and responses, the ingrained habits and behavioral patterns we develop to ensure our survival.

Intuition Here, you will respond according to your feelings and intuition–the Sun symbolizes the lifelong journey of heroic self-discovery, but the Moon tells us what you are by nature and instinct. The balancing of lunar and solar drives will thus be a major consideration for most of us.

Nurturing The Moon can describe our relationship to our mother–or anyone who plays a mothering role. At heart, it shows what nurturing means to us, and the complex feelings we have around this will inform the relationships we create with anyone who takes care of us. It also describes how we offer nurturing to others.

Self-care Food comes under the Moon, but it shows how we feed ourselves both literally and metaphorically, reaching out for what makes us feel "fed" and satisfied. Eating habits often act as a barometer for deeper feelings.

Relationships Close contact with partners will evoke the lunar side of us sooner or later. The Moon shows what feels "right" to us, and a clash of lunar styles can make or break a relationship. The Moon connects you to your tribe, drawing you to people and places where you feel at home.

MERCURY

COMMUNICATION AND LEARNING

Mercury is our own personal "messenger," describing how we learn and perceive, and then how we communicate to others our knowledge and perceptions of the world around us.

Rules **Gemini and Virgo**
Day of the week **Wednesday**
Metal **Mercury (quicksilver)**
Colors **Gray, multicolors**
Symbol ☿

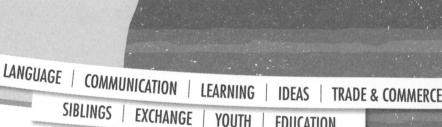

LANGUAGE | COMMUNICATION | LEARNING | IDEAS | TRADE & COMMERCE
SIBLINGS | EXCHANGE | YOUTH | EDUCATION

Mercury in the sky
Never more than 28° from the Sun, Mercury can only occupy the same zodiac sign as the Sun or the adjacent sign. It goes retrograde three times a year, seeming to disappear into the Sun's rays, hence its reputation as trickster and underworld guide.

Mercury in myth
Swift-footed Mercury of Roman myth is a god of language, writing, and invention. His Greek counterpart is Hermes, messenger of Zeus. A clever opportunist who was skilled with his hands, Hermes made the first musical instrument.

Mercury in the world around us
Anything connected to communication falls under Mercury, such as books and telecommunications. Modes of transportation fit here, too–trains, buses, or anything that takes us on a short journey. Schools, stores, and markets are all Mercurial places.

MERCURY **THROUGH THE SIGNS**

Consider how this planet expresses itself according to the sign that it occupies.

Aries You are good at clear thinking and decision-making. Communication is direct and forthright, with the ability to cut to the chase.

Taurus Your thoughts tend to be unhurried and considered. You prefer methodical learning, where you can study at your own pace.

Gemini You are always ready with a witty response. Curiosity inclines you toward diverse interests and a colorful tapestry of knowledge.

Cancer You probably have a retentive memory, absorbing information intuitively. There may be an interest in history.

Leo Leo encourages an extroverted and confident speaking style. You can hold an audience with the power of your voice.

Virgo Systems of classifying and sorting data may appeal to you. You might be good with your hands, possessing practical skills at crafts or DIY.

Libra There are gifts of diplomacy and tact, an ability to charm and persuade others, with this placement. You make sure everyone's opinion is given equal time.

Scorpio This is the probing mind of the detective, researching deeply and sensing motivations. You have the courage to voice things that no one else dares.

Sagittarius Your open-minded outlook and broad knowledge of the world make you fun and interesting to be around.

Capricorn Your practical mind is capable of discharging tasks very efficiently. You may have an inclination toward structured, goal-driven learning.

Aquarius This placement suggests a scientific bent and a capacity to think logically. Rational discussion and truthful, honest communication interest you.

Pisces Yours is an imaginative mind, good at making up stories and giving dry information a magical spin. You learn best in an unstructured environment.

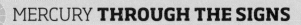

THOUGHTS | OPINIONS | MIND | FACTUAL MEMORY

MERCURY **IN YOUR CHART**

The influence of this planet will be felt according to where it resides and its relationship to other planets.

Communication Mercury suggests the voice itself and how we express to the outside world the ideas that are generated within. Whether our early development of speech and language was easy or difficult, we would expect to find this reflected around Mercury.

Connection Mercury bridges the gap between two sides and represents our need and capacity to make connections, recognize patterns, and create networks. Here, we might often find ourselves acting as an agent or go-between.

Trade and commerce Mercury governs trade and commerce, activities that involve the exchange of money and goods. In the ancient world, this hinged around the traveling trader, whose domain was the crossroads and the marketplace.

Education Early education belongs to this planet—the elementary stages of learning, as well as the learning style that suits us best. It can thus reflect our educational needs and childhood learning experiences.

Youthful This planet possesses a youthful quality and the capacity for dexterity, craftsmanship, and ingenuity. Where Mercury is in our chart, we are likely to show a versatile, inventive, inquisitive, and curious—even childlike or mischievous—response.

Restless Mercury might incline us toward a particular brand of humor and reflect a lightness of touch. And where this planet is, we are often restless, either physically or mentally, and need room to move.

VENUS

LOVE AND PLEASURE

In our chart, Venus is the principle of pleasure and desire, reflecting our aesthetic values and tastes. It is our impulse to relate to others, indicating how we show love and affection and how we create common bonds.

Rules **Taurus and Libra**
Day of the week **Friday**
Metal **Copper**
Color **Green**
Symbol ♀

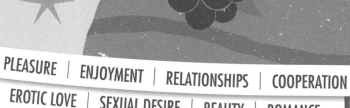

PLEASURE | ENJOYMENT | RELATIONSHIPS | COOPERATION
EROTIC LOVE | SEXUAL DESIRE | BEAUTY | ROMANCE

Venus in the sky

From our vantage point, Venus is never more than 48° from the Sun. It is visible more often than Mercury but follows the same alternating pattern of appearance east and then west of the Sun as evening or morning star.

Venus in myth

This planet has been associated since ancient times with the Great Goddess, mistress of sexual love and fertility. For the Sumerians, she was Inanna; in Babylon, Ishtar; and Aphrodite for the Greeks–all goddesses renowned for their beauty.

Venus in the world around us

She symbolizes art and music, the beauty industry (fashion, jewelry, and cosmetics), and gardens and the beautiful flowers we put in them. Venus signifies the natural world and its fruitful abundance, reflected in her allotted color of green.

VENUS **THROUGH THE SIGNS**

Consider how this planet expresses itself according to the sign that it occupies.

Aries You love the thrill of the chase! Unlikely to hang around waiting to be asked on a date, you'll probably make the first move.

Taurus This Venus revels in the pleasures of the senses–an aromatic perfume or a beautiful garden. Love needs a tactile dimension.

Gemini Communication is a key to love–the art of verbal exchange and the sound of a lover's voice. Relationships need room for you to breathe.

Cancer This is a placement high in sentiment and feeling, creating strong emotional bonds. Your friendship group might feel like family.

Leo This suggests a love of luxury. You no doubt dress to impress and will buy the best you can afford. You show loved ones honest affection.

Virgo For you, the grandness of love is shown through everyday acts of affection and care. Your style is shaped by a love of good tailoring.

Libra You no doubt have a great deal of charm, and a polite deference and gracefulness that wins people over.

Scorpio Relationship is a passionate affair and perhaps a vehicle for powerful transformation. Trust will be important, for when you fall, you fall deeply.

Sagittarius Freedom to roam is important for you– perhaps you need a partner with whom you can share your travels.

Capricorn Your aesthetic sense favors structure and definition–in a face, as well as in clothes or a work of art.

Aquarius Venus here means you value your space and might see love primarily as friendship. Your style may be unconventional.

Pisces Romance flows, inspiring a sense of devotion to loved ones and a need for magic in a relationship. You can be transported by music.

ATTRACTION | LOVE | AESTHETICS | ART & MUSIC

VENUS **IN YOUR CHART**

The influence of this planet will be felt according to where it resides and its relationship to other planets.

Attraction Venus is the desire in us for love and romance–how we make ourselves attractive and what we find attractive in others.

Beauty Beauty is in the eye of the beholder, and the placement of Venus in your chart suggests your definition of this, whether you are moved by the harmonious proportions of classical Greek sculpture or the jagged edges of a Cubist painting. This planet tells us the kind of people we are drawn to and the nature of the erotic charge that drives this; in art, it refers to

what pleases the eye and appeals to our aesthetic sense.

Relationships Here, we desire to form bonds with others, requiring feedback and response; thus we can look to this planet to describe all manner of one-to-one relationships, including friendships.

Worth and value Since Venus offers an image of what we desire and what brings us joy, it is fundamental to feelings of worth and value–the kind of things we might be moved to spend money on.

Peacemaker Venus is known as the peacemaker, bringing the desire for harmony, proportion, and balance (along with the potential for laziness and lack of effort!). Conflict is unwelcome wherever Venus is in your chart.

Vengefulness and vanity True to her mythic role as a goddess of the battle, there is also the potential here for each one of us to react with jealousy and vengefulness when what we have to offer is slighted or rejected. Vanity can also arise around Venus.

MARS

ASSERTION AND ACTION

Without Mars, we would lack the energy that spurs us to action and allows us to further our ambitions. Appreciating your Martial style can be key to feeling energized and fighting fit.

Rules **Aries and Scorpio**
Day of the week **Tuesday**
Metal **Iron**
Color **Red**
Symbol ♂

COMPETITION | SURVIVAL | STRENGTH | CAPACITY FOR ACTION
COURAGE & DARING | ANGER | SEXUAL DRIVE

Mars in the sky
When it is close to the Earth, Mars appears bright red, making it popularly known as the "red planet." This comes, perhaps unsurprisingly, from a concentration of iron oxide, spread over its surface by violent dust storms.

Mars in myth
Greek Ares was the god of warfare, bloodlust, and slaughter. His Roman counterpart, Mars, however, was honored for his warrior spirit, courage, and military skill. His image suggests a more disciplined form of this planet's energy.

Mars in the world around us
Mars is a symbol for civic and military conflict: wars, riots, the armed forces, and police. It also symbolizes more peaceable activities: surgeons, engineers, tool-makers, barbers, and butchers, along with their tools.

MARS **THROUGH THE SIGNS**

Consider how this planet expresses itself according to the sign that it occupies.

Aries This is the most single-minded position for Mars and suggests you channel your energy forcefully and directly.

Taurus Slow to rile, your anger only shows itself after sustained provocation. You are capable of persistent effort.

Gemini Your form of attack and defense is likely to be verbal—you can use words as weapons. You feel liveliest when things are interesting and diverse.

Cancer You see your job as protecting those you love, and you will fight valiantly on their behalf. You tend to take an indirect route to get what you want.

Leo This placement suggests a gallant heroism. You might take great pride in your athletic prowess and lead the team.

Virgo This has the quality of the engineer or practical craftsman—making and fixing things. Anger can be discharged through physical exercise.

Libra You have a way of asserting yourself that acts more like a charm offensive than a battle. You might be roused by issues of unfairness.

Scorpio You can endure and survive the most extreme circumstances. You may act covertly, but the scorpion's sting awaits anyone who crosses the line.

Sagittarius Mars here needs room to gallop; there is a restless need for adventure. The outdoors or long-distance running appeals to you.

Capricorn Your energies tend to be focused on clear targets, maximizing your efficiency and sense of achievement.

Aquarius A cool-headed Mars, you might find you act most effectively when you are defending the group or challenging social injustice.

Pisces Under threat, your strategy might be to disappear until it all blows over, but you can also be a champion for those who cannot defend themselves.

FIGHTING SPIRIT | ENERGY | VITALITY | CONFLICT

 MARS **IN YOUR CHART**

The influence of this planet will be felt according to where it resides and its relationship to other planets.

Competition We might feel inspired to compete in a number of ways—through oratory or sports; as leaders or teachers; or in battles of supremacy with close partners. Mars symbolizes our instinct to survive—not just our physical strength, but the heat and energy that spur us to action.

Warrior Here is the archetype of the warrior and the fighting spirit vital to life. When we are under threat, it is this function in our chart that supplies us with the courage to defend our territory.

Sexual drive Mars also describes sexual drive; it shows our physical needs in this respect and the universal urge to spread our seed.

Energy By extension, Mars will also indicate how we express and release physical energy in more general terms, through sports and exercise. Some prefer the slow burn of yoga, while others prefer the fast-paced action of a tennis match or the long-distance slog of a marathon. Your Mars suggests whether your energy is laserlike or uncontained, sustained or erratic.

Courage Mars inspires us to feats of courage and heroism, each in our own unique style. Bravery can be shown in many ways—physical, mental, emotional, and intellectual—and your Mars suggests where and how you might be prepared to "go the extra mile" to succeed. Under the auspices of Mars come life's pioneers, conquerors, entrepreneurs, adventurers, and athletes, though we should not forget that, in small ways, we each show these qualities daily in our own lives. Courage comes in many different forms, and we are all capable of great strength.

"IF WE CANNOT **EXPRESS MARS**, HOW CAN WE RECOGNIZE AND **RESPECT** OTHER PEOPLE'S RIGHT TO **BE THEMSELVES**?"

Liz Greene and Howard Sasportas,
The Inner Planets: Building Blocks of Personal Reality

JUPITER

GROWTH AND OPPORTUNITY

The largest planet in the solar system, Jupiter's main feature is its Great Red Spot–a vast storm reminiscent of the thunderbolts of Zeus (Jupiter's Greek equivalent). Jupiter is a lawgiver, but a charitable one–its alternative name of Jove gives us our word "jovial."

Rules **Sagittarius; co-rules Pisces**
Day of the week **Thursday**
Metal **Tin**
Color **Purple**
Symbol **♃**

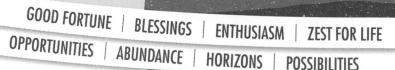

GOOD FORTUNE | BLESSINGS | ENTHUSIASM | ZEST FOR LIFE
OPPORTUNITIES | ABUNDANCE | HORIZONS | POSSIBILITIES

Jupiter in the sky
Jupiter's circuit through the zodiac takes just under 12 years, with the planet spending about 1 year in each sign. Consistent with the image of the well-fed benefactor, Jupiter bulges in the middle.

Jupiter in myth
The equivalent of Roman Jupiter is Greek Zeus and Babylonian Marduk–high gods ruling over their respective pantheons, both beneficent and autocratic. From this, we gain our astrological idea of Jupiter as lawmaker.

Jupiter in the world around us
Under Jupiter's umbrella sit lawyers and legal systems, universities and colleges, religious organizations, publishing houses, and the gambling industry. A Jupiterian object might be a lottery ticket or a hot-air balloon.

JUPITER **THROUGH THE SIGNS**

Consider how this planet expresses itself according to the sign that it occupies.

Aries With Jupiter in Aries, you have the capacity to motivate others through your pioneering vision. When one vision recedes, another soon appears.

Taurus Abundance might be measured in practical terms—a full bank account or an abundant garden. You create your luck by being steadfast and patient.

Gemini Your enthusiasm for learning suggests an attraction to diverse subjects and varied knowledge. You can be inventive with words.

Cancer Joy comes from feeling safe in your group, held together by your generous caretaking. Faith is likely to rest on principles of tradition.

Leo You aim to put on a good show, with a sense for the grand and extravagant. This is a warm and lavish side to you.

Virgo Good luck comes from first paying attention to the details—and joy from hard work and honing your craft. You have a capacity for charitable service.

Libra Growth may come from sharing in a two-way exchange—perhaps a desire to travel with a partner or a career that calls on social skills.

Scorpio For you, learning or travel can never be superficial. You are passionate about what you believe, making it difficult to persuade you otherwise.

Sagittarius Jupiter here brings a powerful sense of abundance and a desire to roam free. You are broad-minded and desire breadth of experience.

Capricorn This practical placement suggests cautious speculation. Your leadership skills are supported by a capacity to take on responsibility.

Aquarius Your vision is eclectic. You may feel most optimistic among your friends or community, promoting your sense of tolerance.

Pisces This suggests the "great escape" to blissful, far-off places—an idyllic getaway perhaps, or daily spiritual practice.

CONFIDENCE | HUBRIS | ADVENTURE | ETHICS | MORALS

JUPITER **IN YOUR CHART**

The influence of this planet will be felt according to where it resides and its relationship to other planets.

Good fortune Jupiter shows where you may feel blessed with good luck. For some, this might be financial; for others, it could mean supportive friends or a happy marriage.

Enthusiasm This deity's mythic zest for life translates in your chart as enthusiasm and a will to find a way. This feeling that anything is possible can also act as a safety net when times are tough.

Opportunities These often present themselves unbidden. As Jupiter is accompanied by abundance,

this can be where you show charity to others, safe in the belief that your own luck will never run out.

Horizons Jupiter expands your horizons, allowing you a glimpse of future possibilities and inspiring you to move beyond current confines.

Confidence Jupiter instills great self-assurance, but it also suggests where you might overreach yourself.

Hubris Jupiter is a dominating presence, and it's possible for you to believe that your way is the only

right way. Jupiter's effect is to desire bigger and better, which can lead to you squandering what you have.

Adventure Jupiter is your spirit of discovery—where you seek knowledge, wisdom, and meaning. It may literally lead you to travel, or the travel may be virtual, intellectual, or philosophical.

Ethics Socially, this planet connects you to moral codes and legal systems. Therefore, Jupiter suggests the area of life where you are most likely to adopt ethical principles.

SATURN

AUTHORITY AND **MATURITY**

The astronomical image of Saturn impresses us with its clean lines and cool dignity. Its rings suggest containment and restraint. In our chart, Saturn is serious and formal, honoring traditions, limits, and rules.

Rules **Capricorn; co-rules Aquarius**
Day of the week **Saturday**
Metal **Lead**
Colors **Black, gray, dark brown**
Symbol **♄**

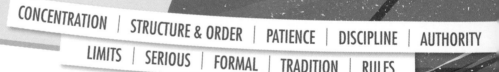

CONCENTRATION | STRUCTURE & ORDER | PATIENCE | DISCIPLINE | AUTHORITY
LIMITS | SERIOUS | FORMAL | TRADITION | RULES

Saturn in the sky
As the outermost planet visible to the naked eye, Saturn was the boundary of the ancient cosmos until Uranus burst through, suggesting its role in the chart as gatekeeper and authority.

Saturn in myth
After the fall of the sky god Uranus, his son Cronus (Greek equivalent of Saturn) established the Golden Age of civic harmony and fruitful husbandry, suggesting Saturn's role as beneficial authority, encouraging abundance through hard work.

Saturn in the world around us
Saturn governs thresholds and doorways, as well as government institutions. As a symbol of age and time, it signifies clocks and watches, rulers and measures. Anywhere cold, dark, lonely, or isolated comes under Saturn.

SATURN **THROUGH THE SIGNS**

Consider how this planet expresses itself according to the sign that it occupies.

Aries Good for athletic or military-style discipline, this Saturn helps you achieve through tests of courage and strength.

Taurus This suggests you possess tremendous patience, carefully guiding your goals to fruition. You create security through conservation of resources.

Gemini You might seek to gain mastery over words, learning several languages or being professionally involved in a field requiring technical knowledge.

Cancer This suggests a strong sense of duty and responsibility in you toward anyone (or anything) placed in your care.

Leo Although performance nerves can sometimes throw you off course, a focus on creative pursuits can in the long run yield concrete results to be proud of.

Virgo Care and precision are the gifts here; your path might be to develop a high level of expertise in your chosen field.

Libra This suggests a capacity in you for fair and impartial judgment. You might uphold a principle of equality as a lawyer or a marriage counselor.

Scorpio Saturn can focus and control Scorpio's passion, and your sense of authority may therefore come from stoically weathering crisis with grit.

Sagittarius Religious faith may not come easily to you, but you can equally become an expert in such areas, keen to learn all you can.

Capricorn Duty and convention are important to you; here, you would play by the rules. You might take on a role as guardian of history and tradition.

Aquarius Your sense of authority comes with a twist—perhaps knowledge of unconventional subjects. You take social responsibility seriously.

Pisces Boundaries may be difficult for you to maintain. But you are good at giving structure to imagination and poetic vision.

HARD WORK | MATURE RESPONSIBILITY | DIGNITY

 SATURN **IN YOUR CHART**

The influence of this planet will be felt according to where it resides and its relationship to other planets.

Structure Saturn brings structure, definition, and clarity—it is where we can be organized, methodical, responsible, and committed.

Authority When we are young, Saturn appears in the guise of authority figures, such as parents, teachers, and community leaders. We see Saturn all around us—the security guard, the policeman, the judge, the referee—setting the rules and making sure they are enforced.

Inner authority Slowly, Saturn emerges in a different guise, as inner authority and guide, a solid bedrock within ourselves. Saturn then becomes a symbol for hard-won proficiency and skill, life experience and wisdom, practical knowledge, and maturity.

Boundaries Saturn adjusts us to necessity—to what is practical, realistic, and achievable in the real world. Here, we all operate within boundaries and limitations of the world at large and of our own human and personal resources. Somehow this is part of the process—the sense of workable limits helping us to shape things appropriately. We must have Jupiter's vision and Neptune's dreams, but Saturn brings our visions and dreams into real life.

Self-contained A final fruitful image might be that of the hermit, who withdraws from the world to concentrate spiritual energy and develop gravitas and self-containment. Where Saturn is in your chart, this can sometimes be a useful strategy—acknowledgment that here you might often find yourself working solo, dependent only on your own resources.

URANUS

CHANGE AND LIBERATION

The discovery of Uranus in 1781 shattered the ancient image of a cosmos safely bounded by Saturn. In our chart, Uranus represents the drive to be different and bring about radical change.

Rules **Co-rules Aquarius**
Day of the week **No allotted day**
Metal **Uranium**
Color **Electric blue**
Symbol ♅

RADICAL | INDEPENDENT | FREE | REBELLIOUS | ORIGINALITY

Uranus in the sky
A feature unique to Uranus is its angle of tilt–its polar axis lies horizontally rather than vertically, consistent with its reputation as a rebel. Slow-moving Uranus spends 7 years in a sign.

Uranus in myth
In Greek myth, Uranus was a sky god, creating many offspring with his wife Gaia–fertile lightning sparks that fell to earth. Another relevant character is Prometheus, who rebelled by stealing fire from the gods to give to mankind.

Uranus in the world around us
The element Uranium is an unstable radioactive metal that eventually stabilizes by decaying to lead, a neat metaphor for the idea that what begins as a brave new world eventually becomes the norm, until a new vision bursts forth.

URANUS **THROUGH THE SIGNS**

As a transpersonal planet, the sign placement for Uranus suggests collective rather than personal themes.

Aries *1927/8-1934/5 and 2010-2018/9* Pioneering technology and the rise of the production line. The car offers individual transportation, bringing freedom.

Taurus *1934/5-1941/2* Deep-seated change. The Great Depression brings financial instability and changes in farming methods. Food rationing begins.

Gemini *1941/2-1948/9* The invention of radar revolutionizes communication. Partitioning in several parts of the world. Innovations in primary education.

Cancer *1948/9-1955/6* Family life evolves to absorb changes brought about by war. Postwar program to rebuild houses and communities.

Leo *1955/6-1961/2* Television revolutionizes personal leisure. Artists and writers of the "Beat" generation shock with new forms of expression.

Virgo *1961/2-1968/9* Innovations in health–the birth control pill brings deep social change. The tiny silicon chip revolutionizes working life.

Libra *1968/9-1974/5* Relationships undergo radical change; equality of the sexes becomes an issue. Thousands gather for the Woodstock music festival.

Scorpio *1974/5-1981* The Punk movement captures the spirit of the age. The "Troubles" in Northern Ireland sees the two sides entrenched.

Sagittarius *1981-1988* Increase in air travel brings new freedom to explore the world. The start of the Internet: technology begins to unite the world.

Capricorn *1988-1995/6* Economic recession brings changes to professional structures and institutions. The fall of the Berlin Wall.

Aquarius *1995/6-2003* Rapid innovation in computing and communications, such as personal computers and cell phones, bring radical social change.

Pisces *2003-2010/11* The arts are revolutionized by technology: digital photography, CGI, and so on. New interest in alternative spiritualities.

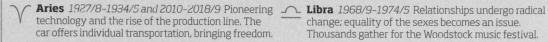

REVOLUTION | INSIGHT | INNOVATION | INTELLECT | RATIONAL | INVENTION | UNCONVENTIONAL

URANUS **IN YOUR CHART**

The influence of this planet will be felt according to where it resides and its relationship to other planets.

Rebel In the birth chart, Uranus is where we can tend to play the rebel, establishing an independent style that sets us apart from everyone else and lifts us above the ordinary.

Intellect is a Uranian gift–here we are clear-thinking, applying cool logic and scientific rationalism. Our Uranian ideas are often ahead of their time, brilliant sparks of intuition.

Rule breaker You are unlikely to play by the rules where this planet is in your chart. Here, we can break down barriers and borders, breathe new life into old traditions, and courageously break convention to bring about social, political, or personal change.

Unconventional We often have the experience of being an outsider in the areas of our lives touched by this planet, feeling called to pursue an unconventional path outside of the mainstream.

Innovation When Uranus is emphasized in a chart, it gives the potential for innovation, originality, a strong will, and freedom of spirit. It can suggest flashes of insight, genius even. Equally, it might give rise to restlessness and the creation of change for its own sake.

Change In your birth chart, you might look to Uranus to describe experiences of separation or radical change, instability, inconsistency, or sudden alteration of circumstances. While Uranus can bring excitement and thrill–life on the edge of your seat–equally it can bring experiences of uncertainty in whichever area of your chart it falls.

NEPTUNE

IMAGINATION AND TRANSCENDENCE

Pictures of Neptune show a wistful and ethereal blue-green planet. In our chart, Neptune represents the desire to move beyond the material world into the limitless imagination.

Rules **Co-rules Pisces**
Day of the week **No allotted day**
Metal **Neptunium**
Color **Sea green**
Symbol Ψ

IDEALISM | ROMANCE | SACRIFICE | CHAOS & DISINTEGRATION
DREAMS & FANTASIES | IMAGINATION | SPIRITUALISM

Neptune in the sky
First sighted in 1795, astronomers were unsure what Neptune was; it was only officially discovered in 1846. Its orbital period is almost 165 years, meaning that it takes about 14 years to go through a sign.

Neptune in myth
God of the sea, Neptune is the Roman equivalent of Greek Poseidon. An invisible god of storms and chaos, Poseidon ruled over the ocean depths, a symbol for the mysterious world of the collective unconscious.

Neptune in the world around us
Neptune can symbolize music, poetry, art, the film industry, photography, and fashion. Mystics, visionaries, and priests come under Neptune, along with hospitals, prisons, monasteries, and other places of retreat or collective confinement.

NEPTUNE **THROUGH THE SIGNS**

As a transpersonal planet, the sign placement for Neptune suggests collective rather than personal themes.

Aries *1861/2-1874/5* New departures in the arts and the birth of modern art. Pioneering efforts lead to changes in spirituality and religious observance.

Taurus *1874/5-1888/9* Financial speculation leads to loss of financial stability. Impressionist painting focuses on natural depictions of light and color.

Gemini *1888/9-1901/2* The beginning of motion pictures as a new form of creative storytelling. Post-Impressionism emerges in art.

Cancer *1901/2-1914/6* Art Nouveau is inspired by curved forms in nature. Dissolution of old European and Asian empires and territories.

Leo *1914/16-1928/9* The glamour of the "Roaring Twenties" and the beginning of cinema. A brief period of indulgence occurs before the Crash of 1929.

Virgo *1928/9-1942/3* A loss of work, routine, and order occurs as stock markets crash and the Great Depression takes hold. More conservative fashion.

Libra *1942/3-1955/7* Longing for peace at the end of World War II. The ideal of a more equal society is seen in the US Fair Deal and the UK National Health Service.

Scorpio *1955/6-1970* The musical revolution of the 1960s. People search for transformative experiences via music, drugs, and sexual liberation.

Sagittarius *1970-1984* Interest grows in the West about spirituality and Eastern religions. The beginnings of Ecstasy and psychedelic dance music.

Capricorn *1984-1998* The fall of the Berlin Wall and the end of Soviet communism. Market deregulation and looser financial controls encourage spending.

Aquarius *1998-2011/2* Globalization and the concept of the "global village" arise—an ideal of a humanitarian society connected by technology.

Pisces *2011/2-2025/6* A subtle shift away from the belief that science offers an answer for everything. People focus on stopping pollution of air and water.

THE DESIRE TO TRANSCEND | A LONGING FOR BLISS | ESCAPE

NEPTUNE **IN YOUR CHART**

The influence of this planet will be felt according to where it resides and its relationship to other planets.

Spiritual escape Neptune is a part of us that desires release from life's limitations to glimpse a world less ordinary. In religious terms, we might think of it as a search for God or a reconnection to the source of life. A spiritually inclined person might find this through holy communion or meditation.

Secular bliss On a secular level, music can offer a similar experience of trance or reverie—or the spirit might be found more prosaically through alcohol and other forms of self-medication.

Chaos and confusion Neptune dissolves boundaries and can bring chaos and confusion. Here, we can fall prey to illusions and surface glitz, believing the hype and forgetting to check for substance. But without Neptune's romantic eye, something would be lost—here, we can be enriched and transported into the parallel reality of imagination, one of our most precious resources.

Sacrifice With Neptune, we willingly offer ourselves in a spirit of charitable service. Devotion can evoke acts of genuine selflessness—

or indeed, occasionally manifest as a form of martyrdom.

Disillusionment True to Neptune, the thing we long for can sometimes feel out of reach, intensifying our longing or bringing sadness, disappointment, and a sense of loss. We can become disillusioned when the reality does not live up to the dream. At such times we can remember that, while a human being might let us down, the deity never will: our dreams remain intact inside us, despite the inconsistencies of the world around us.

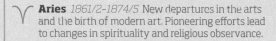

PLUTO

POWER AND TRANSFORMATION

Demoted to "dwarf planet" status in 2006, Pluto remains a "planet" in astrology as a symbol of deep processes that cannot be allotted to any of the other bodies. Pluto brings depth, intensity, and transformation.

Rules **Co-rules Scorpio**
Day of the week **No allotted day**
Metal **Plutonium**
Colors **Maroon, dark red**
Symbol **♀**

CYCLES OF BIRTH & DEATH | TABOOS | CRISIS | SURVIVAL | METAMORPHOSIS
SECRETS | POWER | PROFOUND CHANGE

Pluto in the sky
Pluto takes 248 years to traverse the zodiac and spends an average of 21 years in a sign. Its elliptical path brings it within the orbit of Neptune for part of its journey, so at times it spends 27 years in a sign and only 12 years in another.

Pluto in myth
The word Pluto derives from the Greek *plouton,* meaning "wealth" or "riches." In Greek myth, he is Hades or Dis, the shadowy god of the underworld, the realm of the dead, and of the precious stones and gems buried deep in the earth.

Pluto in the world around us
Pluto suggests the presence of hidden power or wealth: plutocrats, archaeologists, psychotherapists, miners, and underworld crime. Spies, detectives, and secret services are happily embraced by this planet.

PLUTO **THROUGH THE SIGNS**

As a transpersonal planet, the sign placement for Pluto suggests collective rather than personal themes.

Aries *1822/3–1851/3* Pluto was last here at the beginning of the Victorian Age. It reflects new beginnings that sweep away what has gone before.

Taurus *1851/3–1882/4* The upheaval of the American Civil War and Franco-Prussian war impact the economic landscape of the US and Europe.

Gemini *1882/4–1913/4* Communication is transformed by the spread of the telephone and the popularity of newspapers. Invention of the car.

Cancer *1913/4–1937/8* World War I brings threats to home and homeland. Deep changes in family life and in the role of women in society.

Leo *1937/9–1956/8* Rise of dictators and powerful leaders–Hitler, Stalin, and Mussolini. The "cult of personality." The "me" generation: the baby boomers.

Virgo *1956/8–1971/2* The birth control pill brings sexual freedom (Uranus-Pluto conjunction in Virgo). Beginnings of the environmental movement.

Libra *1971/2–1983/4* The political balance of power and Cold War negotiations: SALT and nuclear disarmament. Changes occur in the power balance.

Scorpio *1983/4–1995* Sex and taboo: the issue of AIDS. Power comes to the hidden and dispossessed when apartheid is abolished in South Africa.

Sagittarius *1995–2008* Religious intolerance increases. Exposure of corruption in religious institutions. Financial extravagance.

Capricorn *2008–2023/4* Banking crisis: economic collapse and world recession. This spurs greater fiscal prudence and adjustment to economic necessity.

Aquarius *1777/8–1797/8* Discovery of Uranus in 1781 symbolizes a new age of experiment and invention. Pluto next enters Aquarius in 2024.

Pisces *1797/8–1822/3* The Romantic Period in the arts. Pluto next enters Pisces in 2044, perhaps bringing renewed interest in spirituality and religion.

CONTROL | TRANSFORMATION | PURGING & RENEWING

PLUTO **IN YOUR CHART**

The influence of this planet will be felt according to where it resides and its relationship to other planets.

Life and death Pluto is where we experience a metaphoric death and rebirth, perhaps many times during the course of our lives. Here, we might be drawn to plunge into the depths. This will take different forms, reflecting the house Pluto occupies in your chart and the connections it makes to other planets. Research is one possibility, archaeology another–or you might literally be involved in life-and-death matters where Pluto resides.

Metamorphosis At the core will be the "underworld journey," where all is stripped down to its essence and emerges transformed. We can liken Pluto's process to the metamorphosis of a caterpillar into a butterfly. There is an inevitability and a sense of bowing to necessary development.

Intensity Like the celestial body itself, heavy and dark, Pluto compresses into concentrated form. In this area of your life, you will feel this at work. Poetically, we might think of intense passions and the urge to surrender ourselves completely. Prosaically, we might think of involvement in recycling or waste management. At the end, there is resurrection in a new form.

Secrets Pluto signifies things we want to hide or that lie in shadow, perhaps out of shame or because they are surrounded by a taboo. Secrets often abound where Pluto is, made potent by suppression.

Power Pluto is where we can become powerful, although it can also be a place where at times we feel disempowered, invisible, or persecuted. At the end of the tunnel, though, is the light of regeneration.

CHIRON

HEALING AND COMPASSION

Chiron has been defined variously as asteroid, comet, and minor planet–it seems to defy categorization. In our chart, Chiron represents our desire to heal and make whole, and can indicate aspects of our life where we have been wounded.

Rules **None**
Day of the week **No allotted day**
Metal **None**
Color **None**
Symbol ⚷

WOUNDED HEALER | MAVERICK | OUTSIDER | SCAPEGOAT | COMPASSION
ALIENATION | DISPLACEMENT | ALTERNATIVE

Chiron in the sky
Discovered in 1977, Chiron is infinitesimally smaller than any of the other astrological planets, yet it has taken on importance as a symbol relevant to the times. It was described as a "maverick" by the astronomer who first plotted its path.

Chiron in myth
The centaur Chiron's parents, the nymph Philyra and Cronus, rejected him, and he was fostered by Apollo, god of music, prophecy, poetry, and healing. Chiron in turn became a wise prophet, healer, teacher, musician, and mentor to many.

Chiron in the world around us
Being a relatively recent discovery, Chiron has few associations with the material world. But we can certainly see Chiron's image reflected in the world of complementary health, alternative spirituality, and ecology.

CHIRON **THROUGH THE SIGNS**

Consider how this planet expresses itself according to the sign that it occupies.

Aries Self-assertion can be a challenge—perhaps early on you were discouraged from going your own way. Healing arises from finding your independence.

Taurus You might have experienced an early lack of material security, leading to a need to develop your own grounding.

Gemini You might have encountered challenges in speech development or a disrupted education, but you can have a gift for language and communication.

Cancer There may be a feeling for you of not belonging; perhaps you were adopted or separated from family.

Leo Perhaps you were not allowed to shine, be playful, or perform. Uncovering your creativity can inspire others to find their creative courage, too.

Virgo You may seek to achieve perfection but feel you fall short of this. Psychosomatic illnesses can reflect a mind-body tension.

Libra Early experiences of being treated unfairly might have led you to develop a role as an advocate for those who have suffered injustice.

Scorpio Disempowerment might be a theme from your childhood years. You can find creative ways to work with deep feelings.

Sagittarius You might have sacrificed opportunities for further education or travel. Or loss of faith may have led to restless searching for your own beliefs.

Capricorn You may have shouldered responsibility at an early age. A feeling of not fitting into the system can lead you to carve your own image of authority.

Aquarius A commitment to social equality and acceptance of diversity might emerge from an early situation where you did not fit in.

Pisces This may suggest an early experience of loss, illness, or sacrifice. You can develop your own holistic spiritual vision and assist others to do the same.

MENTOR | TEACHER | VULNERABILITY | HEALING

 CHIRON **IN YOUR CHART**

The influence of this planet will be felt according to where it resides and its relationship to other planets.

Wounded Chiron indicates an aspect of your life where, through no fault of your own, you have been wounded in some way. Sometimes it will reflect an ancestral theme in the family passed down through generations. We may take personal responsibility, absorbing guilt for things that are not our fault and that we could never have changed, and it may take many years for us to acknowledge this.

Alternative Here, we may find ourselves taking an alternative path. We may end up feeling we have not

achieved very much or that we do not fit in. We can feel vulnerable here, painfully aware of our perceived shortcomings.

Outsider Here, we can feel like outsiders, outcasts, and scapegoats: the migrant, the foreigner, the one who feels different.

Healing Through a philosophical and self-accepting response, we can eventually forgive ourselves and others, healing painful feelings of alienation or displacement. Eventually, Chiron is where we

grow to become a "healer" in our own right, mentoring and helping others and the world at large. We become instruments of healing according to the nature of our own wound, because here we have developed experience and wisdom.

Individuality Where Chiron is in your chart, you find your own individual way forward and carve a distinctive path for yourself. Here, you can capitalize on your differences and alternative point of view to offer a valuable and unique personal perspective.

THE
HOUSES

THE HOUSES
AN OVERVIEW

THE 12 HOUSES

The 12 houses reveal which areas of life are most important to you. Each house describes a focus of experience, such as your relationships or career. Each planet will occupy one of the houses and any given house can contain more than one planet. Here's how to locate and interpret the houses in your chart.

> The **houses** are like **territories**. They are **dimensions of the psyche**, but also places and areas of **everyday experience**.

11TH *Friendships*
• Communities
• Social life

12TH *Service*
• Self-sacrifice • Seclusion

Ac

Ascendant
The place where the zodiac cuts the horizon in the east. It is symbolic of dawn and the moment of birth.

1ST *New beginnings*
• Birth • Self-identity

2ND *Resources*
• Possessions
• Money

Houses in a birth chart
The Ascendant, which is also the cusp of the 1st house, is placed at "9 o'clock," with the other houses radiating around the chart in a counterclockwise direction.

Cusp of the 3rd house

HOW THEY WORK

The Ascendant, Descendant, MC, and IC form the four "angles" of the birth chart. These move against the backdrop of the heavens, one turn of the wheel as the Earth rotates each day. The planets move very little over that time, but the angles and house cusps move like the hands of a clock, creating a unique picture for your chart. Apart from the Moon, the planets for two people born on the same day will broadly share the same zodiacal positions. However, unless they were born at precisely the same time (and in the same place), the house positions can differ considerably.

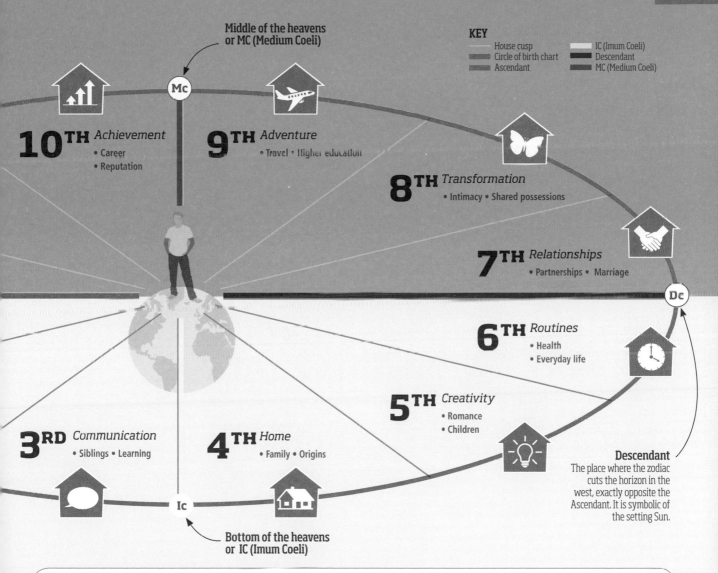

Middle of the heavens
or MC (Medium Coeli)

KEY

House cusp	IC (Imum Coeli)
Circle of birth chart	Descendant
Ascendant	MC (Medium Coeli)

10TH *Achievement*
• Career
• Reputation

9TH *Adventure*
• Travel • Higher education

8TH *Transformation*
• Intimacy • Shared possessions

7TH *Relationships*
• Partnerships • Marriage

6TH *Routines*
• Health
• Everyday life

5TH *Creativity*
• Romance
• Children

3RD *Communication*
• Siblings • Learning

4TH *Home*
• Family • Origins

Bottom of the heavens
or IC (Imum Coeli)

Descendant
The place where the zodiac
cuts the horizon in the
west, exactly opposite the
Ascendant. It is symbolic of
the setting Sun.

▶▶ INTERPRETING THE HOUSES

We can approach the interpretation of a planet in a house in two ways: from the perspective of the house and from the perspective of the planet.

From the perspective of the house, you will experience this area of life through the lens of the planets that occupy it. For example, with Mercury in the 1st house, to feel confident about making your way in the world (1st), it will be crucial to develop your communication skills (Mercury).

From the perspective of the planet, on the other hand, the house it occupies shows which areas of life to focus on in order to develop that planet's characteristics. For

example, with Mars in the 2nd house, an important testing ground for developing your competitive edge (Mars) might be to engage with your finances (2nd house).

Untenanted houses

Although the houses that contain the most planets are areas of key importance, most charts will have a few empty houses. This doesn't mean that these areas of life are meaningless or unavailable–for example, an empty 2nd house doesn't mean an empty bank account! It simply suggests that your attention is more naturally focused elsewhere.

1ST **HOUSE**

SELF AND **PERSONALITY**

The 1st house opens the show. It describes our earliest circumstances and how we were received into life. Your planets here, the signs they occupy, and the sign on the cusp of the 1st house set the tone for your approach to all new beginnings and to the world in general.

First impressions

The 1st house symbolizes birth and new beginnings. It reflects how things seem to us and the impact of our earliest encounters. From a young age, we adapt ourselves according to this view, and it becomes the lens through which we see the world.

Appearance

The 1st house can be likened to the window display of a store. Here, we create an image for ourselves, either consciously or unconsciously, through the way we dress, the car we drive, or the way we like to present things.

Sense of identity

Planets in the 1st house often loom large, and we identify strongly with them. If you have planets in this house, you are likely to be consciously aware of their influence on your character. Indeed, you may be quite *self-conscious* about them.

The physical body

Traditional astrology equates the 1st house with your physical body and with vitality. Planets here, and the sign on its cusp, have a lot to say about your relationship to the body and what might support its vital energy.

PLANETS IN THIS HOUSE

Take a look at which planets fall in your 1st house to reveal how they influence your energies and focus. A full house will point to this being a highly significant area of your life.

☉ **The Sun** You might have a strong sense of identity, with self-development at the center of your life. Your father may have been a very powerful influence.

☽ **The Moon** Inner feelings lie close to the surface and inform how you see the world. Your mother may have been a very powerful influence.

☿ **Mercury** Your first instinct might be to start a conversation or create a connection. You are curious and eager to learn. A sibling might have been an early role model.

♀ **Venus** Physical beauty might be important to you, and you always try to look good. You might see your role in the world as a peacemaker or mediator.

♂ **Mars** You probably came out fighting from the start and continue to do so. Your instinct is to take the initiative and demonstrate your strength and will.

♃ **Jupiter** You are optimistic and philosophical and see the chance for self-development everywhere. People react positively to your confidence.

♄ **Saturn** When it comes to a new project, you like to be prepared. Perhaps you took on responsibility early in life and continue to counsel those around you.

♅ **Uranus** You might present yourself differently to others or feel somehow out of step. You can play the role of outsider, bringing valuable insight to outmoded situations.

♆ **Neptune** The presence of Neptune brings an element of glamour to your outer persona. It gives you a sixth sense with which to navigate the world.

♇ **Pluto** Naturally private, it is hard for you to open up. New projects illicit a need to be in control. You may go through several distinct "chapters" in your life.

⚷ **Chiron** The wounded healer is your guiding daemon. Any loneliness might blossom into a life along the "road less traveled" and a role as mentor, healer, or teacher.

ZODIAC SIGNS AND THIS HOUSE

Refine the picture by considering the signs in which your 1st-house planets reside and the sign on the cusp of the 1st house in your chart.

♈ **Aries** You are probably self-motivated and eager to get going—your own birth might be reflected in a lifelong pattern of seizing the initiative.

♉ **Taurus** You are slow to start but steady on the road. You might need to pace yourself and not allow yourself to be rushed into taking action.

♊ **Gemini** You have a need for dialogue and exchange. You may feel like you're two people in one, or perhaps a sibling had a strong influence on you growing up.

♋ **Cancer** Your first instinct might be to protect yourself and others or to establish your territory. A good approach might be to trust your instincts and act accordingly.

♌ **Leo** You have a capacity for bold action and standing your ground. Perhaps you were encouraged to be playful and creative in early life.

♍ **Virgo** You have a gift for creating order, a hallmark of the way you approach each new task or chapter. Physical health and nutrition might be particular interests.

♎ **Libra** You move gracefully and dress with a sense of style. Your primary instinct might be to mediate and find balance, creating symmetry and a peaceful atmosphere.

♏ **Scorpio** There may be an element of self-defense here—an awareness of danger and the need to protect. So you might take a warrior stance in life.

♐ **Sagittarius** You might find each new phase or project begins with a grand vision or a longing for travel. A change of scene can bring a sense of renewal.

♑ **Capricorn** You might seem mature and reliable to others. Before you begin a task, your instinct may be to plan ahead and follow a tried-and-true method.

♒ **Aquarius** Whatever might be going on inside, you usually maintain a cool exterior. You can analyze rationally and bring mental clarity to a situation.

♓ **Pisces** Practical navigation might not be a strong point, but you can use your imagination. You feel your way into new beginnings to avoid confining yourself to a set path.

2ND HOUSE

POSSESSIONS, MONEY, AND FINANCE

The 2nd is the house of personal income and financial resources, reflecting our sense of material security. What we seek to possess can be shown here, our "movable property." Notions of value, cost, and worth belong to this house.

Money and income

The 2nd house denotes money and income—financial resources that are under our control. Thus it can reflect our attitude toward money and the feelings it generates in us. It indicates how we earn a living and spend money.

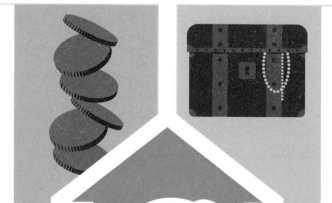

Intangible wealth

The "wealth" of the 2nd house is both tangible and intangible. We build our resources here, both literally and metaphorically. If all our worldly goods were to disappear, whatever remains is perhaps our most fundamental resource.

Worth and value

We often use money as a shorthand to describe worth or value. Thus the deeper meaning of this house lies in revealing our sense of value—what we place value on and ultimately how we value ourselves.

Material possessions

The 2nd gives us a sense of "what is mine"—what you own and what you would like to own. Traditionally, it is the house of "movable property"—in other words, objects, possessions, and all the material goods we accrue.

PLANETS IN THIS HOUSE

Take a look at which planets fall in your 2nd house to reveal how they influence your energies and focus. A full house will point to this being a highly significant area of your life.

The Sun Connecting to the material world or earning your own income might feel like a marker of success or a reflection of your creative power.

The Moon Emotional and material security are powerfully connected, and possessions are invested with emotional significance. You like to have a nest egg.

Mercury Communication skills can be an important resource, perhaps the basis for an income. Treasured possessions might be books and other objects that value language.

Venus There is a sensual quality at play here, a desire for physical contact or to be surrounded by beautiful things that bring material pleasure.

Mars You might possess an ambitious drive to improve your material conditions. It can be important to you to survive on your own resources.

Jupiter Feelings of abundance and a confident attitude toward money mean it naturally flows in. You can feel financially buoyant no matter what your bank balance.

Saturn Careful and canny with money, your approach might be to work hard for it and expect nothing for free. You value practical goods and self-sufficiency.

Uranus Financial fortunes might be subject to sudden changes, perhaps a result of not playing it safe. Income might come from independent freelance sources.

Neptune Your value system might be guided more by a charitable principle than practical considerations. Imagination or artistic gifts can be a source of income and self-worth.

Pluto Material resources can be subject to change, which might feel like a metaphorical death and resurrection. Such times test your survival skills and create inner strength.

Chiron Through your own experience, you might be sensitive to the notion of poverty or lack of resources. Your work might involve providing assistance to others.

 ZODIAC SIGNS AND THIS HOUSE

Refine the picture by considering the signs in which your 2nd-house planets reside and the sign on the cusp of the 2nd house in your chart.

Aries Planets in Aries here will take action to establish and maintain security. Aries on the cusp gives an independent and self-motivated approach to personal finance.

Taurus Taurus sits happily here, being associated with slow accumulation and the delights of the tangible. You might feel in rhythm with the natural world.

Gemini Gemini brings a sense of light playfulness—so perhaps you don't take this area of your life too seriously. Income might come from two sources.

Cancer You may feel a need to guard possessions, as well as sensitivity toward the ebb and flow of income. But you can also be resourceful around personal finances.

Leo Your material assets can perhaps bring you a sense of pride and self-value. Things you like to own or collect might have a gilt edge to them—you enjoy good quality.

Virgo Thrift might be the hallmark here, and a skill at taking care of the pennies so that the dollars take care of themselves—with a spreadsheet to keep it all in check.

Libra Libra desires harmony, artistry, and good taste, an approach you apply to your possessions and material assets. "Going Dutch" might suit you.

Scorpio Scorpio here can bring cycles of boom and bust, with each crisis building resilience and greater acumen. You prefer to keep your financial life private.

Sagittarius You might prefer to make a splash than count the pennies—monetary restriction does not suit you. You need to be free to spend or donate as you please.

Capricorn Common sense and financial planning prevail, with income generated from your own hard work. A good inventory keeps the material world in order.

Aquarius You believe in share and share alike, economic equality, and making sure everyone gets a slice of the cake. You might value gifts of the intellect above possessions.

Pisces You can take an unworldly approach to finances, never quite knowing how much is in the bank. Generosity can sometimes spill over into sacrificing what you own.

3RD HOUSE

COMMUNICATION

In the 3rd house, we develop language and communication skills. Experiences of early education belong here, as well as relationships to siblings, cousins, and school friends. Your planets here suggest how you develop your ideas and your style of communicating them.

Communication and language

The 3rd house is the territory of the mind, indicating how we develop language and our style of communication. Planets here show mental perception and how you express your ideas.

Siblings

Through sibling relationships, we explore our world and flex our communication skills. Where we fit in the sibling tree and how these early peer hierarchies influence us can be shown here, setting a pattern for the way we act in later life.

Short journeys and the local environment

Here, we interact with the area around us, networking or traveling around via our preferred forms of transportation. In contrast to the 9th house, this is the local world on our doorstep.

Early education

This house describes early education and our approach to gaining knowledge. The school environment moves us into a more complex peer environment, and your planets in the 3rd house will show what feelings this evoked.

PLANETS IN THIS HOUSE

Take a look at which planets fall in your 3rd house to reveal how they influence your energies and focus. A full house will point to this being a highly significant area of your life.

☉ **The Sun** With your Sun here, language and communication, or the development of ideas, lie at the very heart of life. A sibling may have been an early role model.

☽ **The Moon** Learning might feel natural to you, with an ability to absorb information easily or perceive intuitively. Perhaps you had a strong emotional bond with a sibling.

☿ **Mercury** Your mind works quickly, making connections between disparate pieces of information. You might play the joker in your peer group or develop a role as a storyteller.

♀ **Venus** With Venus here, you might enjoy romantic literature or exploring ideas around love and beauty. Harmonious relationships with siblings rest on mutual appreciation.

♂ **Mars** Mars here suggests a competitive edge to your communication. At home, you might have had to fight to be heard. For you, words have force and power.

♃ **Jupiter** You probably never run out of things to say, your mind a fertile generator of ideas. Foreign languages might appeal. You have an optimistic perspective.

♄ **Saturn** You approach learning seriously. Perhaps you took a role of responsibility toward siblings or have gained authority through mastering a subject.

♅ **Uranus** Your mind works at lightning speed. You can be single-minded in the way you think, with a talent for presenting the opposite view.

♆ **Neptune** Intuitive perception is at the fore here, the facts less important than the feeling they convey or the story that might be woven around them.

♇ **Pluto** You may have a detective's mind, penetrating deeply to find the information. Learning and language can be transformative, the words carrying power.

⚷ **Chiron** This might suggest an unorthodox schooling experience, perhaps initially denting your confidence but giving rise to a unique perspective.

 ZODIAC SIGNS AND THIS HOUSE

Refine the picture by considering the signs in which your 3rd-house planets reside and the sign on the cusp of the 3rd house in your chart.

♈ **Aries** Your mind moves fast, and you speak your thoughts directly. Perhaps there is rivalry with a sibling and you sense a need to assert yourself in their presence.

♉ **Taurus** Learning needs to be paced and methodical, and the end result practical and usable. You might seek knowledge of tangible things—gardening, sculpture, or how to build a wall.

♊ **Gemini** You might be good at noticing patterns, as well as networking and making connections within your local area. There is an urge to verbalize each thought as it arises.

♋ **Cancer** You probably choose nonverbal forms of communication, which can better convey sentiment. You may feel protective toward siblings.

♌ **Leo** You can be bold and confident in the way you express your thoughts, since your communication skills and knowledge base can be sources of pride.

♍ **Virgo** Local places get the clean treatment—keeping the garden neat and the path swept. Information needs to be organized, and you might have a gift for precise observation.

♎ **Libra** Fair and equal communication might be a feature here, a diplomatic approach and ability to liaise and mediate between different perspectives.

♏ **Scorpio** You might enjoy research and learning about any subject you study, if it engages your passion … and you probably know exactly what the neighbors are up to.

♐ **Sagittarius** The local environment might feel like a wide territory with endless possibilities. Education needs to feel like a quest, full of anticipation and a spirit of adventure.

♑ **Capricorn** You might be a practical thinker, able to marshal information easily and ensure that time spent learning or planning is fully productive.

♒ **Aquarius** Perhaps you had an eclectic peer group at school and felt like "one of the gang." Your approach to learning is democratic and with a rational bent.

♓ **Pisces** You absorb information by osmosis and do not respond well to rote learning. You might speak poetically, and books provide an escape route into the imagination.

4TH HOUSE

HOME AND FAMILY

The 4th house describes our home and place of safety and retreat, both literally and metaphorically. It is the crucible of the family and the container of lineage and ancestry, contributing to our sense of our heritage.

Home

The 4th describes both our concept of "home" as a place of retreat and belonging, as well as the bricks and mortar of the house we live in. It will reflect the role your home fulfills for you—a place to lay your hat, or sanctity and security.

Ancestry and history

Our sense of the past as both personal ancestry and the concept of history are features of the 4th house, as is the notion of cultural inheritance and connections to homeland and the ancient idea of guardianship of the land.

Family

Our blood family and the family we make for ourselves are shown here. The 4th reflects a desire to belong, and for those with personal planets in this house, a sense of being "from somewhere" might be particularly important.

Foundations and private world

Here, we find an inner center of gravity in terms of developing a place of safety within ourselves. The 4th is our place of sanctuary, what we are like when the front door is closed and we are no longer on display to the world.

PLANETS IN THIS HOUSE

Take a look at which planets fall in your 4th house to reveal how they influence your energies and focus. A full house will point to this being a highly significant area of your life.

The Sun Home is your center of gravity, a place where your light can shine most brightly. You might strongly identify with your ancestry, country, or culture.

The Moon You might feel emotionally very close to your family. Being in your private space allows you to recharge your emotional batteries.

Mercury Home might be a place of lively conversation and exchange, or perhaps your early life was marked by frequent changes and moving around.

Venus You might create a peaceful living space for yourself. Artistry may be a family trait, or a sense of culture was cultivated in the family home.

Mars Perhaps there was a sense of competition at the root in early life, the atmosphere tinged with conflict. Retreat for you might mean energetically tackling the housework.

Jupiter You might travel far from home before settling down–or indeed feel like a traveler discovering new worlds just on your own patch.

Saturn You tend to need bricks and mortar, a solid foundation beneath your feet. In the family, you might be the one who shoulders responsibility.

Uranus Early independence may have been high on the agenda. You might opt to rent rather than buy so you can change the scenery from time to time.

Neptune Neptune here suggests a search for the perfect sanctuary, a place of soulful retreat. A spiritual principle can be your inner and outer foundation stone.

Pluto Home can be your power base. Pluto here suggests home renovation–perhaps describing a literal activity or a desire to renew your life by moving to a new home.

Chiron This can suggest an early sense of displacement or not belonging. It might take you a while to find your own territory and put down roots.

 ZODIAC SIGNS AND THIS HOUSE

Refine the picture by considering the signs in which your 4th-house planets reside and the sign on the cusp of the 4th house in your chart.

Aries Aries can signify an atmosphere of rivalry in your early home situation, and you might have learned to stand your ground in the family group.

Taurus Your home base needs to be solid and secure. This part of your life is where you can slow down and take things at a more leisurely pace.

Gemini Perhaps you have two homes or two distinct strands in your ancestry, maybe an awareness of having split loyalties or moving between two cultures.

Cancer Cancer makes the 4th house into a cosy nest, a place of security and protection. You can create this for your family and probably need it for yourself, too.

Leo Home can be a place of pride, where you feel moved to show creative flair or introduce a bit of bling. Owning your own property might be important.

Virgo Perhaps you need to complete tasks around the house before you feel able to rest. A sense of duty toward family members might see you taking a role as caretaker.

Libra Your upbringing might have emphasized a principle of sharing, and fairness may still be important to you. Your role in the family might be as bridge-builder or diplomat.

Scorpio The bond with your parents can be powerful, with perhaps much left unsaid. Your ideal retreat is a place of complete privacy, where you can shut out the world.

Sagittarius A multicultural element might characterize your family, with an "open door" atmosphere. Coming from or making a large family would be consistent with this sign here.

Capricorn You may have a down-to-earth approach to matters of the home. Feeling that things are well-organized there can give you a firm platform from which to operate.

Aquarius Community living might suit you–a collective or a commune, or just a place where you can have an eclectic group of interesting friends around you.

Pisces A house by the water, or one that is filled with music, can bring a sense of inner peace. Perhaps music or art runs in the family and is part of your inheritance.

5TH **HOUSE**

CREATIVITY AND **CHILDREN**

The 5th house encompasses creativity, play, and leisure. Our activities here bring joy and delight, serving to reinforce a sense of being a special and unique individual. Children come under this house, as do romance and gambling.

Creativity and self-expression

Traditional astrology places children in this house, surely the ultimate joyful expression of our creative capacities. The 5th speaks to the idea of "legacy," of creating something that will be a lasting testament to our inner spirit.

Romance

Planets here might indicate how we show love to others, how we make others feel special as well as ourselves. Lovers and romance are encompassed by this house—the aspect of a relationship that arouses passion within us.

Recreation

The 5th is the "inner child." As adults, this part of ourselves is often tucked out of sight—we feel guilty for putting ourselves first or taking time out to smell the roses. Yet acts of pure pleasure and recreation reinforce the life spirit.

Taking a gamble

Gambling belongs here—all forms of risk-taking and speculation, literal and metaphorical. With 5th-house activities, we often put our heart on the line, and it requires courage and self-belief to see the project through.

PLANETS IN THIS HOUSE

Take a look at which planets fall in your 5th house to reveal how they influence your energies and focus. A full house will point to this being a highly significant area of your life.

The Sun You can be a natural performer or creative artist, happy to take a place in the spotlight or put your heart into your creative work. You seek attention and praise.

The Moon Attuned to the playful world of children, you have an easy creativity and fun-loving side. You might also want your personal needs to be placed center stage.

Mercury Your creative impulse might involve words and communication—inventive writing or storytelling. You seek praise for this, since this is a side of you that can shine.

Venus Romance needs to be at the heart of a relationship for you, a sense that your worth and attractiveness are admired. Creative skills might involve design or fashion.

Mars For you, sexual potency might be a form of self-expression. Games are competitive, and having children could bring your fighting spirit to life.

Jupiter You might opt to have a large family or just enjoy indulging in vacations and recreation. Taking time out to play can be rejuvenating.

Saturn Your chosen pastime might be chess or something equally strategic. Creative work can become a honed skill, from event planning to sculpture or pottery.

Uranus You have potential for genuine creative originality, although your challenge might be to allow it to land and take form, because each idea is rapidly superseded by the next.

Neptune Music or poetry might appeal to you, and you may find it easy to lose yourself in artistic activities. These can bring a sense of emotional and spiritual fulfillment.

Pluto Having children, or being creative in other ways, can be an all-consuming and transformative experience, giving rise to a deep and unassailable power within yourself.

Chiron Perhaps adoption or surrogate children are part of your experience. Any form of play can help to nurture the wounded child within, both in yourself and in others.

 ZODIAC SIGNS AND THIS HOUSE

Refine the picture by considering the signs in which your 5th-house planets reside and the sign on the cusp of the 5th house in your chart.

Aries Sports might need to be action-packed, a way for you to use up spare energy, or perhaps with an edge of danger. Taking a risk might come naturally to you.

Taurus Earthy media might appeal when it comes to your choice of creative activity—making tangible objects. A sensuous quality pervades romantic encounters.

Gemini For you, a love affair might be a meeting of minds, and attraction to lovers relies on intellectual connection. Your form of creativity is likely to be verbal.

Cancer It might be your caretaking skills that give you a sense of pride—or the family you have created. A vacation by the ocean or in a place of retreat might suit you.

Leo Leo here reinforces the power of creativity as a means by which to feed a sense of life being joyful and meaningful. You bring warm-heartedness to love and romance.

Virgo You apply precision to your creative projects but might also have a tendency to hide your creative light. A working vacation might suit you more than complete relaxation.

Libra For you, a creative work must be beautiful and well-designed, and you aim for perfection in this respect. With lovers, too, you find classical beauty attractive.

Scorpio Romance can be supported by loyalty and passion—although it might sometimes be broken by intrigues and jealousies. Your sense of humor may have a risqué edge to it.

Sagittarius Long-distance running or archery might be the kind of sport you would enjoy. Your first choice of vacation would probably be somewhere far away.

Capricorn You probably aren't much of a gambler—or if you are, you like to lower the odds and take only a calculated risk. Creativity and children get your serious attention to duty.

Aquarius Being acknowledged for what makes you different can increase a sense of being special and valuable. Romance might grow out of friendship and favor an open honesty.

Pisces You can lose yourself in a romantic affair, transported to paradise—or at times, taken for a ride, seeing your beloved through rose-tinted spectacles.

6TH **HOUSE**

HEALTH AND **WELL-BEING**

The 6th is the house of work and service. Here, we humble ourselves to the tasks at hand—the daily routines, duties, and maintenance that put bread on the table and keep the body and mind in good working order.

Daily work

In the 6th house, we engage with the day-to-day reality of working life. It shows what the daily grind feels like to you and the adjustments you can make to improve it. Your attitude toward work is also revealed here.

Health

The 6th house describes health as daily maintenance. Physical routines keep everything running well, and this house will show what kind of daily workout or health regime might suit you best.

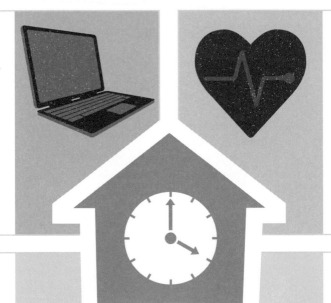

Routines and rituals

Activities here can be an important anchor, encompassing all the mundane rituals that form the backdrop to life. Most of us would rather go on vacation than mop the floor, but things grind to a halt if we neglect chores.

Service

In the 6th, we find our relationship to those who serve or work for us. It also describes how we serve others and what feelings this evokes in us. Those who work in service industries might have planets in their 6th house.

PLANETS IN THIS HOUSE

Take a look at which planets fall in your 6th house to reveal how they influence your energies and focus. A full house will point to this being a highly significant area of your life.

The Sun Working life can be an important focus for you, perhaps in a field of health or service. You gain a sense of purpose from being productive.

The Moon Some kind of hospitality work might appeal to you, being good at looking after daily needs. Being in touch with your inner feelings might be a key to good health.

Mercury Your particular craft might involve using your hands for practical communication or a manual skill. Daily work might involve networking in a mobile environment.

Venus Popular among work colleagues, you might be the one who unites the workforce or solves industrial disputes. You need a peaceful environment in which to work.

Mars Everyday life is no doubt full of dynamic movement, and you feel liveliest when you can work at your own fast pace. An active daily workout keeps you in good health.

Jupiter You like to get heavily involved in chores, gaining satisfaction from a job well done. You might take on too much, overestimating how much you can achieve in 1 day.

Saturn You can take your duties very seriously. You might be good at DIY or construction, with an eye to ensuring things work efficiently.

Uranus You probably need some excitement in your daily routine. Being a freelancer might suit you, so you can set your own routine and timetable.

Neptune Your skill might be to play a musical instrument, with daily practice to perfect your artistry. A pressured work environment may not suit you.

Pluto Chores might be left until they feel overwhelming, followed by a great purge. An intense daily workout and attention to nutrition keeps the system in good order.

Chiron You might have a particular interest or profession in complementary health. You can be a compassionate mentor to your colleagues.

 ZODIAC SIGNS AND THIS HOUSE

Refine the picture by considering the signs in which your 6th-house planets reside and the sign on the cusp of the 6th house in your chart.

Aries Your routine is likely to be active, pushing yourself to achieve a lot in just 1 working day. You probably get through the housework in no time at all.

Taurus A slow working pace might suit you best, allowing you to carry out each task without undue pressure. Good health is supported by honoring your body's physical needs.

Gemini You no doubt have a busy daily life, and your well-being benefits from this variety. You can be dexterous with gadgets and curious to know how things work.

Cancer Workmates might feel like family, and it is important for you to feel emotionally in tune with them. Perhaps you take on a motherly role, or your work involves caretaking.

Leo Because your sense of identity is linked to it, daily work needs to be stamped with your authority and be a dimension to which you apply your own unique and creative approach.

Virgo You pay attention to the humble chores and are happy to spend time doing the background work properly. Care and discrimination over your diet can support your health.

Libra Diplomacy can be a useful tool in the workplace, helping you to create the harmonious environment you need. Well-being comes from physical balance and poise.

Scorpio Health can be supported by an intense workout or by throwing yourself into your daily tasks. Periods of intense activity need to be followed by rest to prevent burnout.

Sagittarius Your daily routine might take you far afield, and you need freedom in your working life, as well as an atmosphere of good humor among colleagues.

Capricorn You like to know that things have been done properly and that attention has been paid to the details. You like useful and productive systems.

Aquarius You might work in a community of people or in a technological or scientific field. A belief in equality for the workers can underpin your choice of job.

Pisces Daily life has its own flow, and timekeeping may not be your forte. You might resist the ordinary nature of daily chores, but these can bring some much-needed structure.

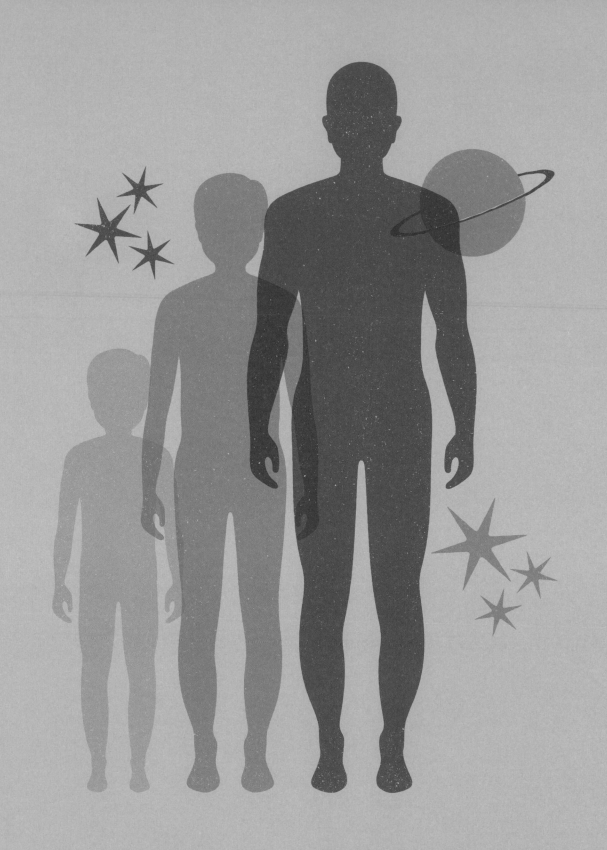

"**CONCEIVED IN THEIR TOTALITY**, [THE HOUSES] UNFOLD A PROCESS OF SUPREME SIGNIFICANCE– THE STORY OF THE **EMERGENCE AND DEVELOPMENT OF A HUMAN BEING**."

Howard Sasportas, The Twelve Houses

7TH **HOUSE**

RELATIONSHIPS

The 7th house traditionally denotes marriage and partnership, but also the idea of "open enemies," quarrels, and disputes. It is the house of contractual partnership, but also of litigation. A deeper look reveals the interesting links between these things.

The other half

The 7th is our sense of "other." We might say that it constitutes our "shadow," being a set of characteristics we do not consciously identify with. We are attracted to whatever is in our 7th, sensing it to be a missing part of the picture.

Projection

The psychologist Carl Jung talked about projection as a mechanism by which a person identifies a trait or behavior as belonging to someone else, unaware that it actually belongs to themselves. In the 7th, we are prone to this.

Relationships

This is the house of marriage and other contractual partnerships. Whether your desire is to put a ring on it or you prefer to be footloose, the sign on the Descendant and planets in the 7th will have a large part to play.

Open enemies

The 7th house is the "house of open enemies." It is the place of litigation and the lower courts, where disputes between two warring parties are settled. We might indeed see partnership as a form of combat.

PLANETS IN THIS HOUSE

Take a look at which planets fall in your 7th house to reveal how they influence your energies and focus. A full house will point to this being a highly significant area of your life.

The Sun For you, relationships are at the heart of life–but you need to find your own individuality through the relating process, an important arena for your self-development.

The Moon You reach out to others in a spirit of caring, being attuned to their needs and sensitive to their feelings. You may seek and offer nurturing and protection in your relationships.

Mercury You might be attracted to intellect or a need for relationships based on communication and mental connection. You stimulate the thought process in others.

Venus Relationships are a mirror for your own sense of value, making it important for you to receive positive feedback. You seek a partner who is gracious and cultured.

Mars Relationships are a medium for developing self-assertion–but they can also become a place where you either fight for supremacy or let others take charge.

Jupiter You are able to motivate and teach, but you may see others as more knowledgeable and confident than you. You might be attracted to a partner from a different culture.

Saturn A serious approach to partnership is suggested, committed through good times and bad. You might choose an older partner, slowly developing your own inner authority.

Uranus You may prefer to break up with someone who curtails your freedom. Partners may seem unpredictable, but perhaps an assertion of your independence is at the root of it.

Neptune A longing for a perfect union is suggested here, and it might be hard for you to see people as they really are, rather than as you would like them to be.

Pluto Partnerships are crucibles for transformation, though not without times of crisis and power struggle. But you can become strong through it and able to empower others.

Chiron You can offer compassion and acceptance to others and be motivated by a desire to heal. A relationship that defies convention might suit you.

 # **ZODIAC SIGNS** AND THIS HOUSE

Refine the picture by considering the signs in which your 7th-house planets reside and the sign on the cusp of the 7th house in your chart.

Aries With Libra rising, you aim for fairness and impartiality–yet in the relating process, you develop a more warriorlike side that complements and balances this.

Taurus You seek stability and long-term loyalty in your dealings with others. This can counterbalance your Scorpio Ascendant's intense approach to life.

Gemini You are drawn to dialogue with others and may need variety and humor in a relationship. You learn to articulate to others the visions of Sagittarius rising.

Cancer Relationships bring out a more sentimental side than your Capricorn persona initially suggests. Wanting to create a family and a safe nest might determine your choice of partner.

Leo A secret desire for praise and attention might lie behind your friendly Aquarian Ascendant. Through relationships, you learn to shine your light and assert your specialness.

Virgo You might look to others to provide some real-world grounding, finding in a relationship a practical foundation to counterbalance the poetry and daydreams of Pisces rising.

Libra The assertive front of Aries rising is challenged by situations where you must learn to compromise. Although frustrating, relationships encourage a fair-minded approach.

Scorpio Intensity and passion are hallmarks of your relationships, a dimension belied by placid Taurus rising. Relating brings empowering transformation on both sides.

Sagittarius Being with other people allows you to synthesize and find meaning in the interesting information collected by your Gemini Ascendant.

Capricorn You look to partners, friends, and associates to help provide containment and stability for the daily inflow of feelings and impressions via your Cancer Ascendant.

Aquarius Relationships challenge you to develop a more democratic outlook than comes naturally to Leo rising. Relationships must be supportive of freedom on both sides.

Pisces You might use your practical skills (Virgo rising) to selflessly assist others. With a partner, you can be transported beyond the ordinary to a place of blissful union.

8TH HOUSE

INTIMACY AND SHARED POSSESSIONS

The 8th is a house where we encounter many of the darker aspects of life. Here, we can experience loss and emotional crisis, but also deep transformation. The 8th covers the intimacies of relationships and the complexities of shared finance.

Deep, dark, and mysterious

Death, loss, and compromise of power are all dimensions of the 8th house, challenging our sense of personal control. Much of what belongs here is deeply private and arouses primitive and powerful emotions.

Shared resources

The 8th house describes shared money and assets, making this a potentially deadly battle ground if we are not careful. The 8th is a territory of trust and mistrust, and a house of debt and financial obligation.

Intimate relationships

After the contractual relationships of the 7th, the 8th house takes us into the murkier territory of emotional bonds and under the surface of our relationships: the power plays, the unspoken contracts, and deeper intimacies.

Death and transformation

Crisis and loss followed by regeneration tend to be experienced here. Often what we encounter in the 8th are the suppressed emotions of the past, but experiences of disempowerment can become a place of enormous inner strength.

PLANETS IN THIS HOUSE

Take a look at which planets fall in your 8th house to reveal how they influence your energies and focus. A full house will point to this being a highly significant area of your life.

The Sun Your life purpose might be to explore deep territories. You might do this through your work or maybe through intimate relationships that test your mettle.

The Moon You can be very sensitive to emotional undercurrents, intuitively picking up what is not being said. Looking after people in crisis might be a particular skill.

Mercury A penetrating mind might see you interested in research or in secret codes and clandestine communication. Superficial information is never satisfactory to you.

Venus You might find power seductive or find you gain financially through partnerships. In intimate dealings, you show diplomacy, affection, and an ability to negotiate.

Mars You can be decisive in a crisis, pitting your strength against the toughest of situations. Joint finances can be a proving ground for developing your independent will.

Jupiter A buoyant attitude toward extreme situations can allow you to survive and also support others. Faith may undergo a crisis and transformation, renewed in a strengthened form.

Saturn Intimacy may not come easily, as you might prefer to keep your boundaries and stay in control. People trust you with their money and with their deepest secrets.

Uranus You can shine intellectual light on to life's mysteries, bringing clarity and rational discourse. It might be important to you to maintain your distance in intimate encounters.

Neptune Giving your all in a close relationship can bring the spiritual or emotional connection you seek with a partner. But it can also mean making sacrifices or feeling vulnerable.

Pluto You have a nose for power battles and can play opponents at their own game. Your survival skills might be tested in difficult situations or through financial losses.

Chiron You might benefit from or practice deep forms of therapy. You can understand others' pain and reach out in a spirit of compassionate healing.

ZODIAC SIGNS AND THIS HOUSE

Refine the picture by considering the signs in which your 8th-house planets reside and the sign on the cusp of the 8th house in your chart.

Aries You tend to charge headlong into deep waters, acting first and reflecting later. You might fall in love on an impulse or take a risk on an investment without thinking it through.

Taurus Your attitude toward shared finance is safe and steady—and you have an eye for a profitable investment. You can contain a crisis through being sensible and grounded.

Gemini Articulating deeper meanings might be a skill fueled by curiosity about hidden motivations. Intimacy for you might be created in the linking of minds.

Cancer You might protect your private world extremely closely and be very in touch with emotional undercurrents—which can make a profound impression on you.

Leo You might have the Midas touch when it comes to getting a good return on your investments. Having autonomy over joint finances is important to you.

Virgo It might take you a while to process experiences of crisis and catastrophe, but equally you can bring your critical faculties to bear in such situations.

Libra You like joint finances to be fair; you need to know everything you share with your partner is split down the middle, and that the partnership itself is even-keeled.

Scorpio When you fall for someone, you might fall strongly, giving intensely of yourself the more involved you become. There may be power plays with a partner over money.

Sagittarius Investing in riskier ventures might be appealing to you. You view an intimate relationship as an adventure and a route to expansion and greater knowledge.

Capricorn You prefer not to entwine your resources with those of a partner. You might keep a similar boundary around your heart and resist deeper commitment in relationships.

Aquarius A rational approach to the unexplained allows you to sort what is real from what is shadow. Even in a committed relationship, you need the clear air of distance.

Pisces For you, deeper intimacies can be a route to transcending the ordinary, lifting you into a more magical world in the arms of a partner.

9TH HOUSE

QUEST AND ADVENTURE

The 9th house is our sense of what lies beyond the horizon. It invites us to travel, both physically through long-distance journeys and mentally through higher education, philosophy, and religious contemplation. It covers ethics and ideals, and the spirit of the law.

Quest for meaning

The 9th house is concerned with the exploration of unfamiliar territory, the purpose of which is to reach for experience, wisdom, and greater understanding–of ourselves and the world around us.

Teaching and higher education

In the 3rd, we learn the basics via early education, but in the 9th, we go beyond facts and analysis into meaning and synthesis. Our planets here suggest how we deal with this more complex level of learning.

Philosophy, religion, and belief

Here, we seek answers to life's bigger questions– philosophy, politics, and law all belong in the 9th, along with religion, faith, and belief. This is a house of moral principles and political ideals, the ethics and codes by which we live.

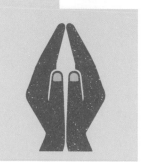

Adventure, travel, and long journeys

The 9th suggests long journeys. What you consider to be a "long journey" will depend on your perspective–it is not the mileage that counts, but your sense of something over the hills and far away.

PLANETS IN THIS HOUSE

Take a look at which planets fall in your 9th house to reveal how they influence your energies and focus. A full house will point to this being a highly significant area of your life.

The Sun Through travel or education, you can grow in stature and confidence. To truly find yourself, you might need to move beyond the familiar territory of home.

The Moon The whole world can be your home. Perhaps you have lived abroad (or would like to) or simply feel nurtured by travel and arrival at exotic destinations.

Mercury This suggests a gift for languages, as well as curiosity for further study. Full of questions, you are no doubt interested in a wide range of subjects—a perennial student.

Venus Perhaps your purpose for study or travel is to evoke your sense of beauty or develop artistic skills. Friends and lovers from other cultures might bring this alive in you, too.

Mars You can be an intrepid pioneer into the unknown, carving a path for others to follow. Tough journeys test your strength and resolve, making you fearless.

Jupiter Faith may come easily, and you approach the unknown with trust. Higher learning is expansive and joyful, and your capacity to teach or broadcast is equally bountiful.

Saturn "Fear of flying" might describe not just your approach to air travel but also to unfamiliar situations. Faith may be hard-won, and you like to be well-prepared for the journey.

Uranus Going to college or grappling with religious principles can bring enlightenment, but you might also be inclined to question, rejecting orthodoxy and tradition.

Neptune The 9th is a house of prophecy—Neptune here suggests a gift for spiritual vision or for intuiting future trends. Travel might invoke a longing for an island paradise.

Pluto A few with Pluto here might be reaching for global domination. Most might simply seek to be transformed by learning—or perhaps by faith.

Chiron You take your own path through the moral maze, seeking a deeper wisdom. You can be a true teacher leading others to their own form of understanding.

 # ZODIAC SIGNS AND THIS HOUSE

Refine the picture by considering the signs in which your 9th-house planets reside and the sign on the cusp of the 9th house in your chart.

Aries You do not like to be held back in exploration and adventure, whatever the nature of these. You might prefer to travel solo and go to places that few have visited.

Taurus Luxury travel might suit you, or at least a journey where creature comforts are taken care of. A patient approach to learning brings rich rewards.

Gemini Curiosity might be your main reason for study or travel. You tend to analyze complex concepts so they can be articulated in clear and simple terms.

Cancer The rhythms and rituals of foreign cultures might be of interest. You take an intuitive approach to higher education, studying what you feel emotionally connected to.

Leo You prefer to travel in style, and your motivation might be to stimulate personal growth. Taking a risk beyond familiar territory strengthens your sense of identity.

Virgo You deal with the unknown by checking the details and taking a map, a compass, and a contingency plan. You can be excellent at analyzing complex ideas.

Libra Equality and civil relationships might be the basis of a moral code for you, a principle held high. Subjects of further study might be social sciences, art, fashion, or design.

Scorpio You might engage deeply with philosophical questions or with further training or study, not content until you have uncovered the last word on the matter at hand.

Sagittarius The world might seem an open place to you, with no borders or restrictions to limit your scope. Called to adventure, you want to experience it all.

Capricorn You might take a practical and businesslike approach to learning and teaching, perhaps excelling as a professional trainer, with an interest in gaining qualifications.

Aquarius Moral principles for you might revolve around supporting what is best for the community rather than the individual. Faith is approached rationally and intellectually.

Pisces You long for escape into the wild blue yonder, perhaps not knowing what your destination is going to be but lured by the siren call of faraway lands that inspire your imagination.

10TH HOUSE

CAREER AND VOCATION

The 10th house is a place of culmination and fruition. It describes our public image, shaping what we do for a living and our role in the wider world. Here, we reach for achievement and success, and toward a true calling.

Career and vocation

The 10th house represents the idea of culmination—a high point to be reached. It describes career and is where we reach for success and achievement. It is also a place of inner vocation.

Parents and authority

The 10th represents authority figures, particularly our parents. How you yourself govern—how you take charge and find leadership skills within—will also be shown, perhaps based on how your parents did this.

Ambition and status

In the 10th, we seek credit for our achievements and want to flourish—to flower and come into our own. So it plays to the notion of growing up, achieving through work, and taking our place in the world.

Public image

The 10th is our public face, what we are famous for. The profession we choose invites us to profess what matters to us. Thus in the 10th, we seek work that is a happy marriage of worldly ambition and inner calling.

PLANETS IN THIS HOUSE

Take a look at which planets fall in your 10th house to reveal how they influence your energies and focus. A full house will point to this being a highly significant area of your life.

The Sun You identify strongly with the work you do, making it important to choose a vocation that allows you to take a central or dominant role.

The Moon You lead through a caring touch. Perhaps being a parent is your vocation–or your work involves fostering, catering, or a domestic element.

Mercury Your career might revolve around communication and networking; developing these skills gives you a sense of achievement. You admire articulate and clever people.

Venus People might recognize you for your diplomatic skills and ability to lead by bringing the team together. You always pay attention to how you look.

Mars You might choose a competitive profession where drive and ambition are required. You prefer to assert yourself as the boss, rather than take orders from someone else.

Jupiter For you to feel content, your career needs to offer possibilities of betterment and promotion. Your parents might have encouraged you to aim high.

Saturn Your style of leadership might be to shoulder a lot of responsibility by yourself. Although it might be lonely at the top, this can bring you a sense of solid achievement.

Uranus Bowing to authority is not your style, and you may choose work that encourages your independent vision and allows you to change track when it suits you.

Neptune A career in the arts might appeal, or something that allows you to use and develop your imagination and put your imaginative gifts on display to the world.

Pluto Others might see you as carrying great influence, although inside it may take you a while to feel comfortable taking on that mantle of power.

Chiron A career in healing or mentoring might be your goal. Although you may only find your true niche after time spent in the "wilderness," it can unfold as a true vocation.

 # ZODIAC SIGNS AND THIS HOUSE

Refine the picture by considering the signs in which your 10th-house planets reside and the sign on the cusp of the 10th house in your chart.

Aries You might be a self-starter when it comes to your career path, eager to show what you can do and get ahead of the pack. In your work, you prefer to lead the way.

Taurus A long, slow climb might characterize your choice of employment, with a practical, down-to-earth element. You might tenaciously stay in one job or field for a long time.

Gemini Your career path might have two distinct strands, and it is the variety and cross-fertilization that feeds your ambition. You strive to be seen as articulate and intelligent.

Cancer A job involving nurturing and caretaking might suit you, where you can be part of a professional family. You rise to the top by using intuition and instinct.

Leo Public image is important, and you show a regal face to the world. Perhaps you believe in principles of self-promotion and self-reliance in making your way.

Virgo A type of work revolving around the development of craft and precision might appeal: making things, creating order, or sorting wheat from chaff.

Libra A certain amount of PR or bridge-building might be involved in your choice of profession–and you aspire to be seen as someone who deals fairly and takes no sides.

Scorpio Grit and determination characterize your professional path, perhaps following your parents' example. You might choose work requiring passion and commitment.

Sagittarius The world is a place where you can achieve exponentially, limited only by your own vision. There might be an international or educational dimension to your work.

Capricorn Administration, organization, and good planning are all skills that can be coaxed out by your world of work. You prefer a traditional career with professional training.

Aquarius You would choose not to work alone, but in a team of like-minded people who share a common goal. Your style of management is friendly, democratic, and inclusive.

Pisces You might want to be known for being compassionate or for your artistic skills. It may take you a while to find your vocation if you have no clear sense of what you want.

11TH HOUSE

FRIENDSHIP AND COMMUNITY

The 11th house is where we find our place within the wider group, through friendships and social networks of all kinds. Your planets here suggest the unique role you play as a member of the team.

Friends and allies

If the 5th is the house of play, the 11th is the playground, where we share space and time with others and create a social circle of friends and acquaintances. Here, we find our allies and supporters, those whose actions benefit us.

Teamwork

Aside from our social circle, the 11th suggests all kinds of group endeavors—councils, committees, and clubs—and therefore our mode of participating in and contributing to something larger than our individual concerns.

Hopes and wishes

The 11th reflects our hopes for the future and the extent to which we believe life will buoy and support us. It shapes our attitude toward making plans and the strategies we can usefully employ to bring them to fruition.

Common goals

The 11th says a good deal about our political views and social ideals—our view of utopia and how society should be. The extent to which we are prepared to lay aside personal glory for the good of the group is revealed here.

PLANETS IN THIS HOUSE

Take a look at which planets fall in your 11th house to reveal how they influence your energies and focus. A full house will point to this being a highly significant area of your life.

The Sun You may have a life at the heart of the community. You define yourself through your friendships and shine brightest when your actions have collective significance.

The Moon You might be naturally gregarious, thriving on mutual support. Your role in the group may revolve around nurturing and protection.

Mercury In a social environment, you may have excellent networking skills and a need to be mobile. Knowing who's who can assist you in making the most of opportunities.

Venus You perhaps find a way to fit in with the crowd through diplomacy and polite exchange. You can get allies on board by using charm, tact, and grace.

Mars Your competitive spirit is likely to be stimulated in group and social situations. Mars here is also a warrior for the community, perhaps fighting for social or political causes.

Jupiter Where Jupiter is, things often feel effortless. Getting along in the group will be facilitated by this planet's capacity for broad-minded tolerance and love of jovial company.

Saturn The image of fruit ripening over time is evoked by Saturn. In this house, it can suggest a serious commitment to friendship—less in number, but standing the tests of time.

Uranus This placement offers a paradox: how to maintain your freedom and autonomy within a democratic context. You could play the role of agitator, bringing radical change.

Neptune You might believe in the motto that we are "all members, one of another" and be prepared to sacrifice personal desires to serve the community.

Pluto You might form intense friendships or commit yourself unequivocally to a political ideal. Both have the capacity to transform and empower.

Chiron Chiron often inhibits us to reach high and yet, in the 11th, you might develop a role as a mentor and wise teacher, carrying out the work of healing that binds the community.

 # ZODIAC SIGNS AND THIS HOUSE

Refine the picture by considering the signs in which your 11th-house planets reside and the sign on the cusp of the 11th house in your chart.

Aries You might lean toward independent action when it comes to groups and friends. You can be a social pioneer, lead the group, or feel energized by a hectic social life.

Taurus You tend to look for loyalty from friends and return it in good measure. Your approach to friendship will emphasize constancy and longevity.

Gemini Friendships ideally involve verbal exchange and diversity. Gemini here suggests a need for networking and a varied social schedule.

Cancer For you, friends might feel like family—you gravitate toward the safety of the tribe. Your ideals might reflect this as a belief that society should provide support and nurturing.

Leo This house provides an arena for you to shine your light. You might take charge of the group in regal fashion or be socially generous with your time and attention.

Virgo Your instinct might be to focus on the general welfare of the group; for you, it would be less important to stand out from the crowd than to play a useful role in the group.

Libra This sign brings a sense of fairness and harmony to joint ventures, so you might find yourself playing the role of mediator between friends.

Scorpio Friendship is unlikely to be a frivolous endeavor for you, with Scorpio lending depth and intensity to any planets here. Force and passion may characterize your friendships.

Sagittarius You could have the capacity to lead the group on a shared adventure. You may find joy in participating and meeting people from different cultural backgrounds.

Capricorn You perhaps strike a serious note and have a tendency to take control. You might play the role of elder, bringing a mature perspective to the party.

Aquarius You might take an egalitarian stance, believing it important that each person in the team is treated equally and any benefits distributed are for the good of all.

Pisces You may deal sensitively and sympathetically with friends. Being in a community can evoke a capacity in you for altruistic service.

12TH HOUSE

SERVICE AND SACRIFICE

The 12th house suggests dissolution and release, a place outside of time where life returns to the primal waters before the cycle of the houses begins again at the Ascendant. Here, we can experience sacrifice, but also selflessness and devotion.

Behind the scenes

This is the house of "self-undoing," suggesting we might not give ourselves full credit for our capacities, needing reflection back from others in order for those skills or traits to seem real. This is also a house of escape and withdrawal.

Higher service

The notion of sacrifice sits well in this house. Meaning simply "to make sacred," it perfectly describes the idea that whatever is given in a spirit of universal love, compassion, and charity is a true gift to the world.

Universal and collective

Traditional astrology places many institutions here–hospitals, prisons, religious retreats. In such places, it is easy for the sense of "I" to be replaced by a merging with everyone else. Planets here take on an otherworldly quality.

Transcendence

Perhaps the ultimate meaning of the 12th house is the idea of transcendence: leaving the wheel of life, if only for a short time, in order to be in a timeless state of bliss, tranquility, and reconnection with everything-that-is.

PLANETS IN THIS HOUSE

Take a look at which planets fall in your 12th house to reveal how they influence your energies and focus. A full house will point to this being a highly significant area of your life.

☉ **The Sun** Your identity and purpose can emerge from a life dedicated to service. You may shine as a performer or actor, easily shifting into character.

☽ **The Moon** Care work might appeal. Focusing your compassionate efforts in this way can be more fruitful than trying to care for the whole world.

☿ **Mercury** You might be curious about the spiritual or intangible dimensions of life, including myths and symbols. Imaginative storytelling allows your voice to be heard.

♀ **Venus** The perfect lover probably does not exist—but hold the image in your head, and you might then recognize it as a projection of your own beauty or gifts.

♂ **Mars** On your own, you might feel as though your efforts do not hit home—yet you can fight effectively and courageously on behalf of those who are weaker or less fortunate.

♃ **Jupiter** Bliss might be the perfect trip abroad or time spent celebrating in jovial company. For as much as you give generously, you might also feel blessings magically arrive.

♄ **Saturn** Remembering you are not responsible for the world's suffering can help you to focus your dedication on truly worthy causes. You have a gift for bringing order to chaos.

♅ **Uranus** Perhaps you hide your unconventionality so you can fit in—reclaiming this can help set you free. Your radar for collective trends can put you ahead of your time.

♆ **Neptune** Perhaps you give everything to the cause, leaving nothing for yourself—but you can be a beacon of compassion in a troubled world.

♇ **Pluto** If you do not accept your own power (or feelings of powerlessness), you can undermine your efforts. You have the capacity to probe the psychology of the collective mind.

⚷ **Chiron** This suggests a desire to heal the collective and show compassion to all. Perhaps you have had to conceal your own suffering, making you sensitive to others' hidden pain.

 ZODIAC SIGNS AND THIS HOUSE

Refine the picture by considering the signs in which your 12th-house planets reside and the sign on the cusp of the 12th house in your chart.

♈ **Aries** Involvement in charitable works can evoke the fighting spirit in you, and you might lead the crusade, bringing initiative and focused energy to it.

♉ **Taurus** Getting away from it all might involve relaxing in comfort—time spent in the garden or walking in the country. The natural world brings a sense of relief and release.

♊ **Gemini** You can provide a bridge across to the world of the imagination using the gifts of the concrete mind to enquire into and articulate its complexities.

♋ **Cancer** Your role behind the scenes might be as a nurse or caretaker, looking after those who are unable to look after themselves. The perfect sanctuary might be your own home.

♌ **Leo** You might feel your brilliance has been overlooked but you can impress with your creative or performance skills, gaining confidence from the adulation of the crowd.

♍ **Virgo** You might serve through small, practical acts—metaphorically arranging the church flowers or sweeping the path. Such acts are made in a spirit of universal love.

♎ **Libra** Getting away from it all can revive a sense of balance in you—perhaps a yoga retreat or time spent restoring the harmony and peacefulness of your chosen sanctuary.

♏ **Scorpio** Although suspicious of what might be hidden from view, equally you can have a strong intuition for it. Research into mysteries or the mystical might be of interest.

♐ **Sagittarius** You are a traveler into the unknown, a spiritual seeker perhaps. Blissful escape for you means getting as far away as possible.

♑ **Capricorn** You can bring structure and purpose to the imaginal world, perhaps through work in an artistic field. Equally, you might distrust whatever you cannot see or prove.

♒ **Aquarius** You might seek a scientific explanation for life's more mysterious dimensions. Being with friends can be your escape—or walking to blow cobwebs away.

♓ **Pisces** You can be sensitive to feelings and atmospheres; it might be important to lay down a boundary so you are not overwhelmed by the grief or sadness you pick up in others.

YOUR
BIRTH CHART

YOUR BIRTH CHART
AN OVERVIEW

SEEING THE WHOLE PICTURE

Your birth chart is a never-to-be-repeated arrangement of planets, signs, angles, houses, and aspects. Most importantly, your own free will and the many possible interpretations of the symbols means your life path is an expression of you as an individual spirit.

You are unique!

A birth chart is a view of the heavens for a precise time, date, and location. At any given moment, each planet occupies a particular place in the zodiac, and these placements, by degree and minute of the sign, are exactly the same for anyone (or anything) born at that moment, anywhere on Earth. But if we take the charts of two people born at the same time and date but in different locations, the angles and the house cusps would be different in each chart. Each would offer a different version of that same arrangement of planets in the sky.

Move forward in time and the picture changes again—the planets move on, and so do the angles and house cusps.

In other words, your chart is singular and shared by no one else. In the charts of twins, even a difference of a few minutes in the birth time can mean a planet changes house or the angles move into the next zodiac sign.

What your birth chart says about you

A birth chart offers a great deal of information. It reveals character and temperament, motivations and desires, potential skills and talents. It looks back into the past in suggesting the ancestral themes that have made their impact on you and forward into the future in suggesting what you might strive to create and achieve for yourself.

Interpreting symbols

Each symbol in the chart has many different meanings, operating at all different levels of life experience. Whenever you identify something in your chart that seems to pose an issue or that you feel negative about, it can be instructive to switch your perspective and play with the symbolism: for instance, Saturn can evoke fear but is also an invitation to focus and professionalize; Neptune can indicate loss of structure but equally a release of imagination; the Moon can carry difficult emotional memories but also shows how we might offer ourselves supportive self-care.

Keep an open mind

Try to be flexible and imaginative in your thinking around any chart, including your own. While being honest about the challenges, take time to honor the talents and skills that are present or that could be developed. Aim to articulate what you see in a way that is open and exploratory. Each chart offers a sense of a life unfolding, so there is never a final word on anything, only more potentials to explore.

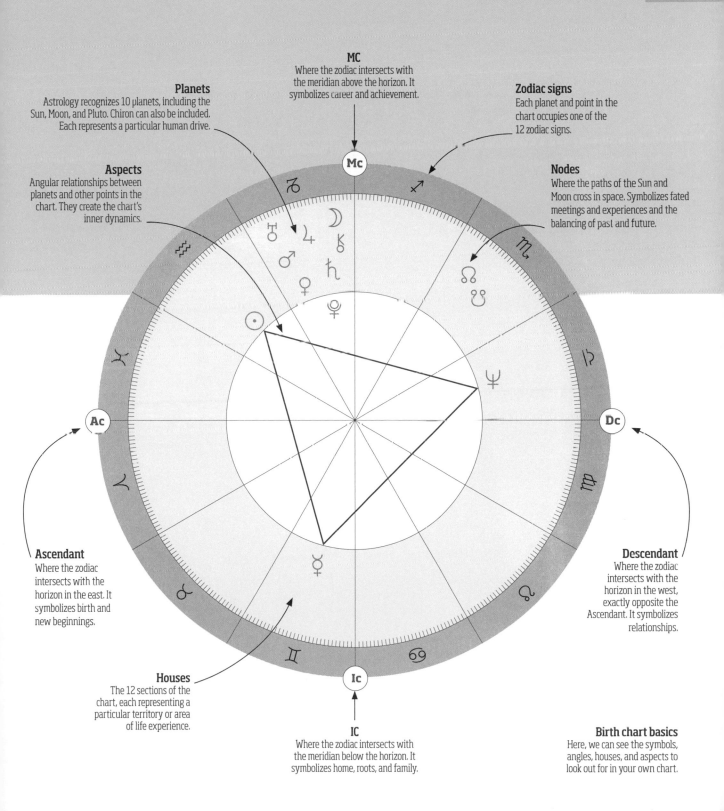

MC
Where the zodiac intersects with the meridian above the horizon. It symbolizes career and achievement.

Planets
Astrology recognizes 10 planets, including the Sun, Moon, and Pluto. Chiron can also be included. Each represents a particular human drive.

Zodiac signs
Each planet and point in the chart occupies one of the 12 zodiac signs.

Aspects
Angular relationships between planets and other points in the chart. They create the chart's inner dynamics.

Nodes
Where the paths of the Sun and Moon cross in space. Symbolizes fated meetings and experiences and the balancing of past and future.

Ascendant
Where the zodiac intersects with the horizon in the east. It symbolizes birth and new beginnings.

Descendant
Where the zodiac intersects with the horizon in the west, exactly opposite the Ascendant. It symbolizes relationships.

Houses
The 12 sections of the chart, each representing a particular territory or area of life experience.

IC
Where the zodiac intersects with the meridian below the horizon. It symbolizes home, roots, and family.

Birth chart basics
Here, we can see the symbols, angles, houses, and aspects to look out for in your own chart.

THE **ASCENDANT-DESCENDANT**

YOUR EAST-WEST AXIS

The Ascendant and Descendant represent the horizon. They form an axis across the chart, linking our conscious sense of ourselves (the Ascendant) with its opposite and complementary energy (the Descendant), which we seek and encounter through our relationships.

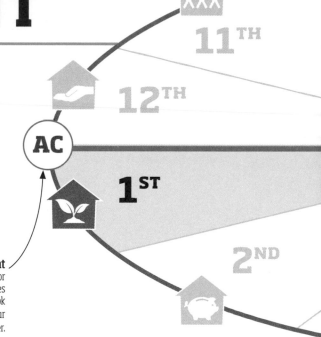

The Ascendant

The Ascendant or rising sign (more specifically, the rising degree) is symbolic of the birth moment, your entry into the world. It shows the conditions and circumstances around you at that time, or at least how you sensed them to be.

New beginnings

This imprints itself and sets the pattern for all new beginnings—starting a new day, a new project, or a new phase of life; how you meet and greet and come across to others; how you answer when someone engages you; how you want others to see you and how they do see you; and your sense of how things are out there in the world and how you adjust to it.

Persona

We can think of the Ascendant sign and any planets close to the Ascendant as

Ascendant
The Ascendant sets the pattern for all new beginnings and provides important clues about our outlook on life. The planet that rules your Ascendant sign is your chart ruler.

our aura, the atmosphere we create. We might think in terms of "persona," too—a mask we wear or the way we dress and present ourselves. As the cusp or beginning of the 1st house, it is part of our store window, or what is most on display.

Everything we experience is filtered through the Ascendant, so it gives us important clues about our basic outlook on life.

The chart ruler

This is the planetary ruler of the Ascendant sign and plays a key role. Your chart ruler is like the helmsman, and its position by sign, house, and

The Ascendant-Descendant axis

Here, we see how the Ascendant-Descendant axis cuts through the chart from east to west, from the cusp of the 1st house to the cusp of the 7th.

aspects shows a range of experiences and skills, the development of which directly serves the unfolding story of your chart (in particular, the central story of your Sun). Being the planetary ruler of the 1st house, your chart ruler gives you further information about everything the Ascendant describes.

The Descendant

This is the point exactly opposite the Ascendant, immediately implying an

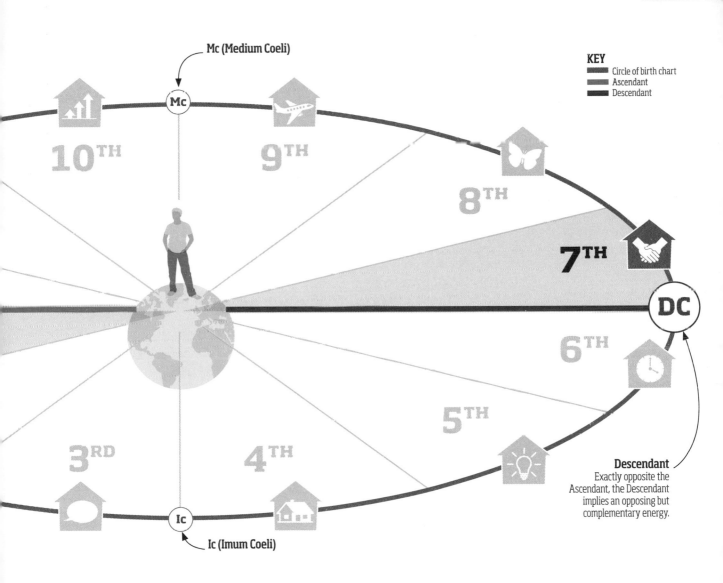

KEY
- Circle of birth chart
- Ascendant
- Descendant

Mc (Medium Coeli)

10TH

9TH

8TH

7TH

DC

6TH

5TH

4TH

3RD

Ic (Imum Coeli)

Descendant
Exactly opposite the Ascendant, the Descendant implies an opposing but complementary energy.

opposing but complementary energy via an opposing pair of signs. The two ends of the axis are linked as one horizon stretching from east to west across the chart.

"Not me"

If the Ascendant is "me," then the Descendant is "not me," a set of traits and behavior patterns we do not associate with ourselves, figuring they must belong to someone else. You will

often be attracted to other people because they reflect the qualities of your Descendant sign and planets close to this point (and planets in the 7th house).

Relationships

The Descendant is the part of you that interfaces with others directly in one-to-one encounters of personal and professional partnership. The Descendant and the 7th describe

relationships as a learning curve, pivoting on opposition, difference, and the courage to recognize that the traits we thought belonged to "those people out there" really belong to us or are ones we need to develop. It can therefore describe characteristics that we both dislike and admire in others. In the thrust and parry of relationship, we slowly develop the skills and qualities of our Descendant sign and planets.

THE **MC-IC**

YOUR NORTH-SOUTH AXIS

This axis connects the IC, representing home, ancestry, and private space, to the MC or Midheaven, representing our vocation, ambitions, and highest aspirations. It is like a tree, whose roots form our foundations at the IC and whose crown flourishes at the MC.

Ascendant

Ac

11TH

12TH

1ST

2ND

The observer's meridian

At the time and place of your birth, if you could have drawn a line linking the north and south points of the horizon with the points directly above and below you on the celestial sphere, you would arrive at the concept of the observer's meridian. Where this meridian intersects with the ecliptic (and therefore the zodiac) are the points in your chart known as the Midheaven or MC (Medium Coeli) and the IC (Imum Coeli).

The MC

Being above the horizon and the place the Sun reaches around noon each day, the MC represents a point of fruition and culmination. It is our occupation and also our calling or vocation, what we aspire to achieve out in the world (which may be different to the actual job we do for a living).

In the sign on the MC and any planets

close to it, we find qualities for which we want to be known, admired, and respected, along with activities that can bring us honor and recognition. We may of course become notorious for these things, too; either way, it is a place that indicates our public profile.

As the cusp of the 10th house, the MC traditionally represents mother. We might extend this to say it represents both of our parents in their role as authority figures who have had a hand in socializing us and shaping our future. If you have children of your own, then the MC (and the 10th) can suggest what it feels like for you to carry the responsibility of being a parent.

The MC-IC axis

Here, we see how the MC-IC axis cuts through the chart from south to north, from the cusp of the 10th house to the cusp of the 4th.

The IC

The tree image is a useful one for this axis. The IC (which begins the 4th house in the Placidus house system) forms the roots, so we can think of this point as representing a very deep part of ourselves, connected to the family, to previous generations, and to the past. It forms our foundation stone in terms of our early family life, the home and family we create for ourselves, our

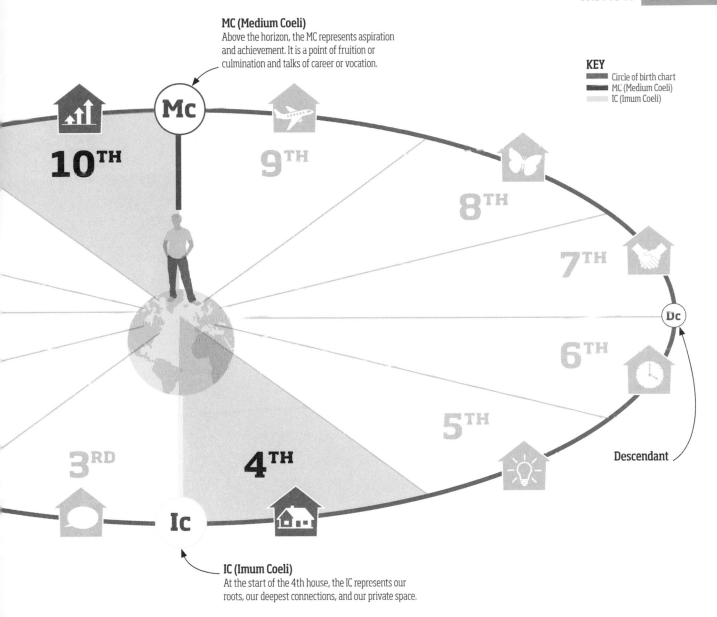

MC (Medium Coeli)
Above the horizon, the MC represents aspiration
and achievement. It is a point of fruition or
culmination and talks of career or vocation.

KEY
Circle of birth chart
MC (Medium Coeli)
IC (Imum Coeli)

10ᵀᴴ

9ᵀᴴ

8ᵀᴴ

7ᵀᴴ

Dc

6ᵀᴴ

5ᵀᴴ

Descendant

3ᴿᴰ

4ᵀᴴ

Ic

IC (Imum Coeli)
At the start of the 4th house, the IC represents our
roots, our deepest connections, and our private space.

deepest principle of what matters
to us, and our sense of being on firm
ground (or not, depending on the sign
of the IC and any planets close to it).

As the cusp of the 4th house,
the IC traditionally represents father.
Like the MC, we might extend that
to say that it represents both of our
parents in their role as conduits of
the family lineage and tradition.

> In the **sign on the MC** and any planets close
> to it, we find qualities for which we **want to
> be known, admired, and respected**.

THE MOON'S NODES

BALANCING PAST AND FUTURE

The Nodes are the two crossing points of the paths of Sun and Moon. These points form an opposition across the sky, North Node on one side and South Node on the other. Myth associates them with the head and tail of a cosmic dragon.

The Nodes in your birth chart
The Nodes form an axis; there is therefore an inherent tension between the two ends but also complementarity and a sense of it working as one integrated dynamic.

South Node A set of habitual patterns that we readily fall into, often because they were laid down in early life and have been reinforced through endless repetition. This can be the basis of a useful set of skills that we may take for granted in ourselves but that we can always rely on. Equally though, it can describe negative, even destructive, patterns that embed themselves and to which we return because they are familiar. At the South Node, we are invited to engage in self-reflection

and to move beyond patterns that no longer serve us. Here, we can reclaim an inheritance of unassailable skills and talents, make our peace with the ancestors, and lay old ghosts to rest.

North Node Represents a path to tread and a future to be made. Unlike the South Node, this is unfamiliar territory. This end of the axis challenges the ingrained assumptions and patterns of the South Node. The Nodes work as an axis and are of equal value– we oscillate back and forth between the ends. The Nodes represent cycles of crisis, re-evaluation, release, and then forward motion, a pattern that continues throughout life in rhythm with the 18.6-year cycle of the Nodes around the chart.

Moon at its
lowest point

An astronomical view of The Moon's Nodes
Here, we see the path of the Sun, the Moon's orbit, and the line of the Nodes. When the Sun and Moon simultaneously occupy the Nodes, solar and lunar eclipses occur.

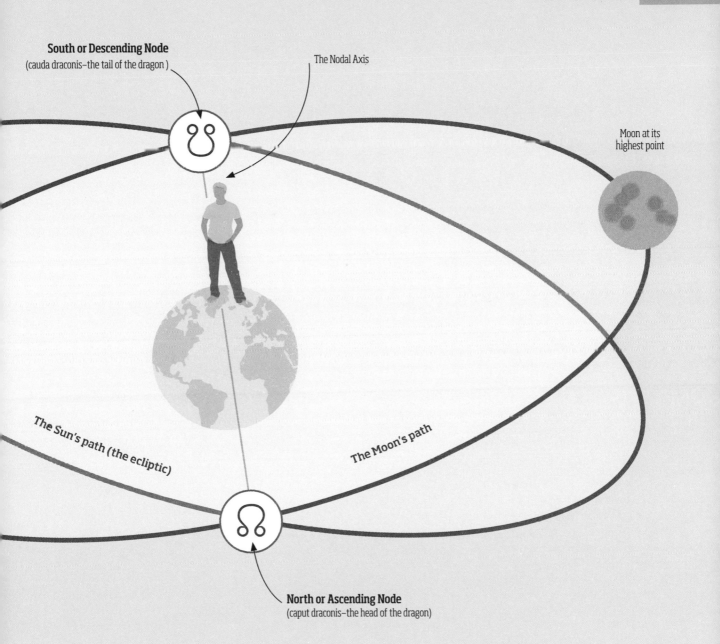

South or Descending Node
(cauda draconis–the tail of the dragon)

The Nodal Axis

Moon at its
highest point

The Sun's path (the ecliptic)

The Moon's path

North or Ascending Node
(caput draconis–the head of the dragon)

> The Nodes represent cycles of **crisis**, **re-evaluation**, **release**, and then **forward motion**, a pattern that continues throughout life.

THE WHEEL
OF **RULERSHIP**

PLANETARY RULERSHIP
OF THE ZODIAC SIGNS

Each sign is ruled by the planet (or planets) with which it has the most affinity. Traditional astrology uses only the seven "traditional" planets, from the Sun through Saturn; contemporary astrology adds Uranus, Neptune, and Pluto into the rulership scheme.

Using rulership in your birth chart
Everything in a chart occupies a zodiac sign. Each of your planets occupies a particular sign, and so will the four angles (the Ascendant, the Descendant, the MC, and the IC) and the other house cusps, along with the Nodal Axis and any other chart factors that an astrologer might use.

The zodiac sign occupied by a planet or angle will give us information about the style in which that planet or angle expresses itself. The sign occupied by a house cusp (in other words, the beginning point of a house) indicates how you approach the issues and activities of that house. So the sign modifies anything that is placed in it.

The planetary ruler of that sign will then give us further information about how that planet, angle, or house cusp expresses itself. For instance, for a person with the Sun in Capricorn, Saturn (the ruler of Capricorn) gives further information about what shapes that person's sense of identity and their goals in life. We can then look to Saturn's position in their chart—if it is in the 7th house, for example, then committed (Saturn) relationships (7th) will be at the heart of this person's life journey (Sun). Or if you have Virgo on your 11th-house cusp, your friendships will be shaped both by Virgo and by its planetary ruler Mercury, including Mercury's position in your chart.

PISCES

ARIES

Planetary rulership
Here, we can see which sign(s) each of the planets rules. The Sun rules Leo and the Moon rules Cancer; then each traditional planet rules the next two signs, working outward toward Saturn. There is no established rulership for Chiron.

 Everything in a chart occupies a **zodiac sign**.
Each of your **planets** occupies a particular sign.

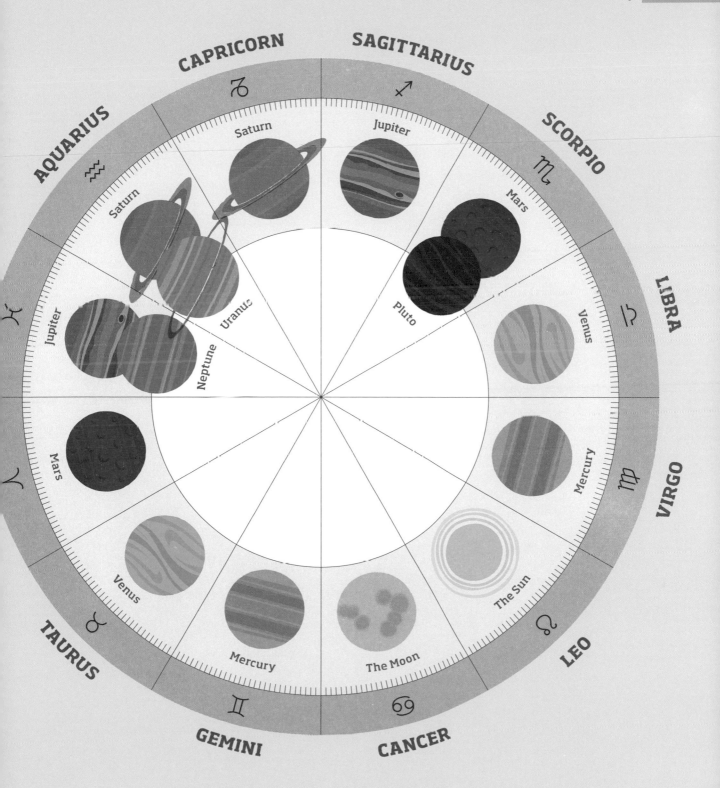

" ... **THE CHART** IS A KIND OF **TREASURE MAP**, AND THE REAL SEARCH IS AN **INTERNAL ONE**."

Kim Farley, Journey Through Astrology:
Charting the Astrological Voyage of Discovery

THE **ASPECTS**

DYNAMIC CONNECTIONS IN THE CHART

Aspects are connections between the planets in a birth chart or between planets and the angles or the Nodal Axis. They create dynamic movement that reflects inner psychological patterns.

Aspects and number symbolism

Aspects are based on number symbolism. Each is formed from a root number by which the circle of the chart is divided to create an angular relationship.

Most astrologers use the basic set of aspects listed here. Those based on 1, 2, 3, 4, and 6 are called "major aspects"; they form the main dynamics of a chart. Those based on 8 and 12 are classed as "minor aspects," although they still have influence.

The opposition and square are "hard aspects." The semisquare, sesquiquadrate, semisextile, and quincunx are also hard in nature. These are based on numbers that reflect tension and friction. The trine and the sextile are "soft aspects," being based around the number 3, representing harmonious flow.

Each aspect has an "orb," meaning that it holds true for a certain number of degrees on either side of exactitude. The tighter the orb, the more intensely we feel it, a bit like a photograph: at one point, the image will be pin-sharp (exactitude), with its effect lessening as the image goes out of focus.

Astrologers disagree on orbs, but the ones in the tables to the right are a good place to start. Major aspects have a larger orb than minor aspects.

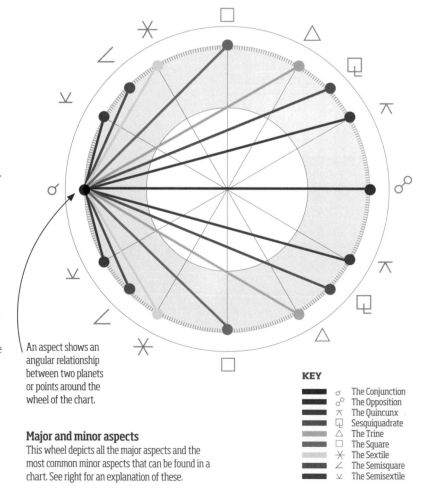

An aspect shows an angular relationship between two planets or points around the wheel of the chart.

Major and minor aspects

This wheel depicts all the major aspects and the most common minor aspects that can be found in a chart. See right for an explanation of these.

KEY

☌	The Conjunction
☍	The Opposition
⊼	The Quincunx
⏚	Sesquiquadrate
△	The Trine
□	The Square
✶	The Sextile
∠	The Semisquare
⊻	The Semisextile

MAJOR ASPECTS

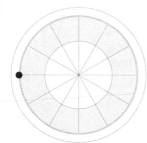

The Conjunction
Root **1** Symbol ☌ Angle **0°** Orb **8°**

Planets in conjunction form a unity. They are inseparable from each other, blending their energies into a kind of "third force."

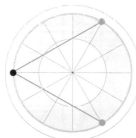

The Opposition
Root **2** Symbol ☍ Angle **180°** Orb **8°**

Planets in opposition reflect an internal dilemma arising from conflicting needs. We might identify with one side and project the other, unconsciously playing out the conflict in our relationships.

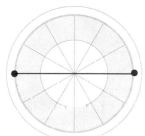

The Trine
Root **3** Symbol △ Angle **120°** Orb **8°**

The trine creates an easy flow between planets. They represent reservoirs of talent and things we find easy and enjoyable. However, we may take these talents for granted and not develop their deeper capacities.

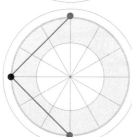

The Square
Root **4** Symbol □ Angle **90°** Orb **8°**

Planets in square tend to be very productive. The expression "squaring up to a challenge" is appropriate. Here, we can be inhibited to express our drives fully, but equally we strive to hone and perfect our skills.

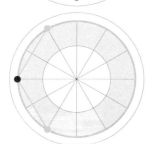

The Sextile
Root **6** Symbol ✳ Angle **60°** Orb **4°**

With sextiles, we are motivated to put in a little work, but also feel relaxed about expressing whatever is indicated by them. We tend to enjoy the busy creativity of the planetary combination.

MINOR ASPECTS

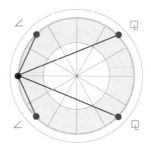

The Semisquare
Root **8** Symbol ∠ Angle **45°** Orb **2°**

The Sesquiquadrate
Root **8** Symbol ⟥ Angle **135°** Orb **2°**

These carry a similar quality to the square, although without the same intensity. Like the square, we want our efforts to produce concrete results, and we set ourselves goals and targets.

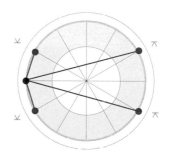

The Semisextile
Root **12** Symbol ⊻ Angle **30°** Orb **2°**

The Quincunx
Root **12** Symbol ⚻ Angle **150°** Orb **2°**

These aspects can generate frustration, making us feel thwarted in our efforts. They can be a blind spot, a desire or set of skills that needs our conscious focus in order to achieve or fulfill.

ASPECT PATTERNS

DYNAMIC FORMS IN THE CHART

Astrology recognizes a number of patterns formed from particular combinations of aspects. Each pattern represents a complex psychological dynamic, a source of tremendous talent and potential but also its own inherent challenges.

Planetary connections

Aspect patterns are combinations of three or more planets which together create an inherent pattern of behaviour within you.

KEY

- The T-square (or T-cross)
- The Grand Cross
- The Kite
- The Grand Trine
- The Minor Grand Trine
- The Hard Rectangle
- The Mystic Rectangle
- The Finger of the World
- The Yod

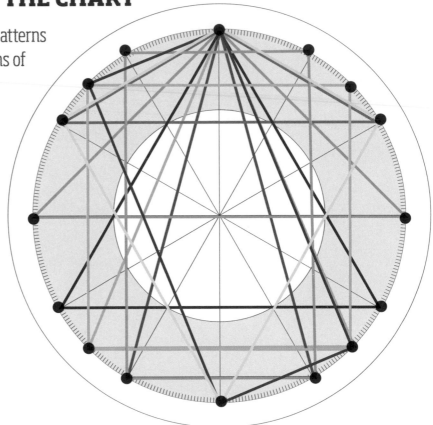

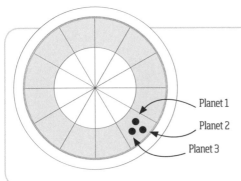

Planet 1
Planet 2
Planet 3

THE STELLIUM

Not strictly an aspect pattern, this is a conjunction of at least three planets occupying the same sign or house. It creates a concentrated, even obsessive, focus on one area of life. Conjunctions have a subjective quality, so with a multiple conjunction the person may resist challenge from outside opinions and influences. Equally, it can represent an area of expertise.

SQUARE PATTERNS

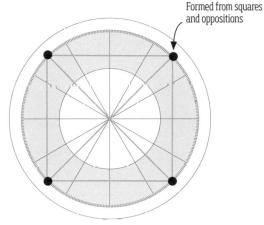

Formed from squares and oppositions

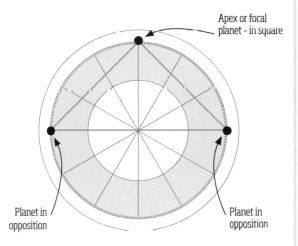

Apex or focal planet – in square

Planet in opposition

Planet in opposition

The Grand Cross

Formed from two oppositions at right angles to one another, meaning that each "leg" of the pattern is also receiving two squares. It suggests a high-energy dynamic, generating immense work and effort but without the "escape route" of an apex planet.

So it may seem to the owner of a Grand Cross that challenge is ever-present and life is never still, and this can lead either to a sense of being superhuman or a victim of one's circumstances. With two oppositions, there will be two sets of internal paradox to resolve; with four squares, there is continual task-setting, challenge, and expenditure of energy in the process of trying to achieve that.

The Grand Cross can be either cardinal, fixed, or mutable. Cardinal energy is centrifugal, making the cardinal Grand Cross like a dynamo; fixed energy is centripetal, meaning a fixed Grand Cross holds a great deal of internal tension which tends to explode with great force under extreme pressure; and mutable energy makes the mutable Grand Cross rather like a dancer in constant motion.

The T-square (or T-cross)

Formed from two planets in opposition, with a third in square to both. The planet forming the squares is known as the apex or focal planet.

The opposition will reflect an inner tension, conflict, or paradox and the desire to unite the two planets into a common activity, talent, experience, or mode of behaviour.

The apex planet receives two squares, meaning that much of the dynamic movement takes place here. It drives the reconciliation and synthesis of the opposition, but it can also serve to exacerbate the tension between them; it can be experienced both as a point of release and as an obstacle.

T-squares (unless "dissociate") can be either cardinal, fixed, or mutable. A cardinal T-square is driven, dynamic, and forceful; a fixed T-square is resistant and capable of sustained effort; and a mutable T-square may generate a tremendous restlessness and need for movement and change.

 It may seem to the owner of a **Grand Cross** that **challenge is ever-present** and life is never still. 🙶

TRINE PATTERNS

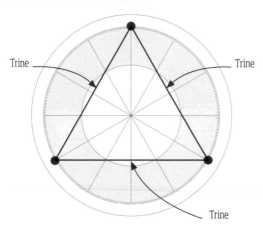

Trine

Trine

Trine

The Grand Trine

A triangular figure formed from three trines and characterized by the trine's easy flow. A Grand Trine reflects a well of natural talent which seems to produce its fruits with little effort. Consistent with the contented enjoyment of the trine, it describes behaviours and activities which come easily and can often be taken for granted.

Unless one of the "legs" is dissociate, the planets in a Grand Trine will occupy signs of the same element – fire, earth, air, or water.

A Grand Trine in **fire** can bring easy confidence and a sense that life will be supportive - an enjoyment of risk or an inner sense of being special.

A Grand Trine in **earth** suggests being "lucky" in the material world and perhaps pleasure gained from making and doing things in this medium.

A Grand Trine in **air** brings natural skills of communication and social interaction. There might be wide interests, a love of reading and learning, and a facility for language.

A Grand Trine in **water** suggests a deep reservoir of sensitivity and feeling, a skill at picking up emotional undercurrents and ability to tune in on a deeper psychic level.

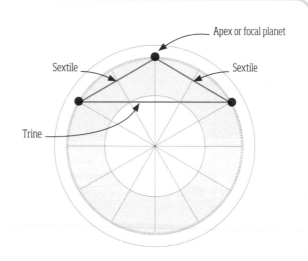

Apex or focal planet

Sextile

Sextile

Trine

The Minor Grand Trine

Formed from two planets in trine, with a third apex planet forming sextiles to both. Because it receives two sextiles, the focal apex brings creative movement and effort as an outlet for the talent of the trine.

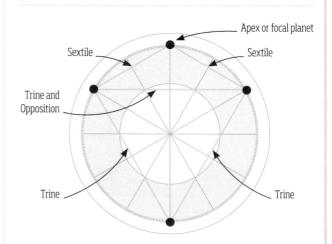

Apex or focal planet

Sextile

Sextile

Trine and Opposition

Trine

Trine

The Kite

Formed from a Grand Trine and a Minor Grand Trine together, creating a kite shape. It combines the easy potentials of the Grand Trine with the busy creativity of the two sextiles and some added tension from the opposition. There is a clear apex or focal planet which galvanizes the action and provides motivation for developing the Grand Trine's latent skills.

RECTANGLE PATTERNS

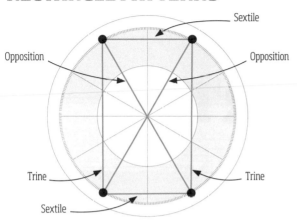

The Mystic Rectangle

Formed from two oppositions, the ends of which are linked by two sextiles and two trines. Here, the two oppositions find resolution through the confidence and opportunities provided by the trines and sextiles. We might think of this pattern as a gift for finding creative solutions to difficult dilemmas.

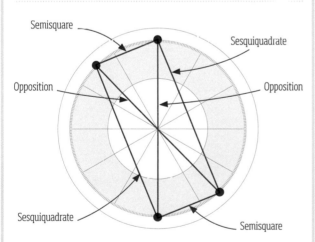

The Hard Rectangle

Formed from two oppositions, the ends of which are linked by two semisquares and two sesquiquadrates. The four minor hard aspects create a sense of perpetual tension. There is no apex planet and therefore no outlet that leads the action, generating a feeling that the work is never fully accomplished.

FINGER PATTERNS

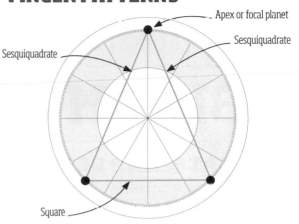

The Finger of the World

Formed from two planets in square to each other, and both making sesquiquadrates to a third planet that acts as apex point. There is likely to be a great deal of conscious work and effort generated, a development of the apex planet's gifts and expressions as a funnel for the dynamic tension of the planets in square.

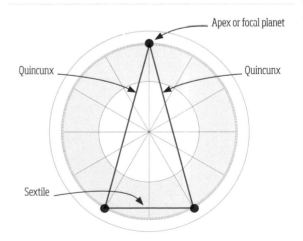

The Yod (Finger of Fate or Finger of God)

Formed from two planets in sextile to each other, and both making quincunxes to a third apex planet. The person may struggle to bring the gifts of the sextile to life, since the apex planet can feel unattainable. So it can generate feelings of waiting for something to happen before we can move forward.

CASTING
A BIRTH CHART

TIME, DATE, AND PLACE

To calculate a chart, all you need is your time, date, and place of birth. It is possible to cast a chart by hand using an ephemeris and a table of houses, but most astrologers take the short cut and use astrological software.

Your time of birth

Most of us know our date of birth, but the more accurate you can be about your time of birth, the better. The MC and IC move through each zodiac sign in exactly two hours and the Ascendant and Descendant take an average of two hours through each sign, so they are moving relatively quickly and a discrepancy of even just an hour can change the picture of a chart quite significantly.

If you do not know your time of birth at all, it is not possible to set up the full horoscope. You will only be able to cast a "flat" chart in which the four angles will be absent and also the house cusps, missing out a great deal of basic information. The Moon's position will also be in question, since the Moon moves an average of 13° 11′ through the zodiac each day.

So it is worth making every effort to find out. The time of birth is recorded on the birth certificate in some countries but not in others, and some countries offer a "long form" of birth certificate, which includes the time of

birth. It is also possible that the hospital may record birth times. Family records and baby books are also helpful. In the absence of written evidence, family members can often be a godsend, perhaps remembering that you were born "around teatime" or "in the evening", which gives you a starting point. If you have no record at all, some professional astrologers will "rectify" a chart – this is a skilled process of matching significant dates and events in your life to astrological significators in order to arrive at a suggested time of birth.

Your place of birth

Regarding location, it is helpful to be as accurate as possible, although if you were born in a rural area then the nearest town should be sufficient to use as your birth place. If you were born in a city, astrological software usually lists different city districts and suburbs, to create the most accurate chart.

If there is no town nearby, it is possible to use just the co-ordinates for the place you were born.

Casting your chart

For many years until the arrival of astrological software, astrologers calculated their charts by hand. It is still perfectly possible to do this and any good astrological training course will teach you how to do it, because in the process you learn a great deal about the nuts and bolts of a chart and how its various components are arrived at. Calculating and drawing up a chart by hand can be a magical undertaking, connecting us to astrology as a traditional craft. Most astrologers, however, use software to calculate and print their charts and some software producers offer a free trial version.

It is possible to get a copy of your birth chart from the internet without having to visit an astrologer or obtain a software programme. There are several online sites that will calculate a copy of your chart for free. Some produce charts that can be a little difficult to read if you are new to astrology, so astro.com and alabe.com are good places to start (see pp.244-45).

THE IMPORTANCE OF TIME

An accurate time of birth gives the most accurate chart. With no birth time, we cannot calculate the angles and house cusps.

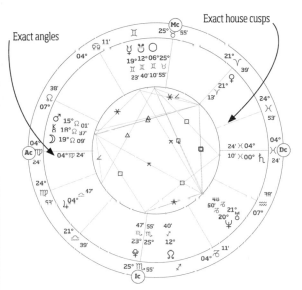

Exact angles

Exact house cusps

Birth chart with known time of birth
This reveals the four angles and the house positions of the planets.

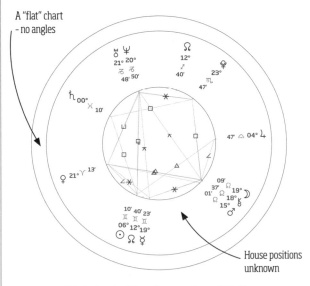

A "flat" chart – no angles

House positions unknown

Birth chart with unknown time of birth
The four angles and the houses are missing from the chart.

A DIFFERENCE OF 15 MINUTES

Twins will have very similar charts but often with a few quite significant differences. These are charts for twins born 15 minutes apart.

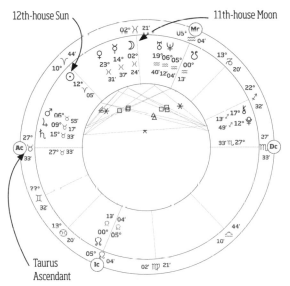

12th-house Sun

11th-house Moon

Taurus Ascendant

Twin one
Both twins have Aquarius MC, but twin one has a Taurus Ascendant, a 12th-house Sun, and an 11th-house Moon.

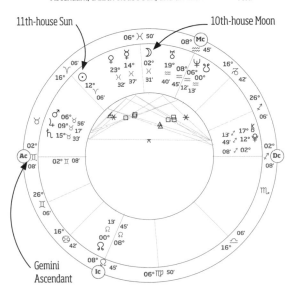

11th-house Sun

10th-house Moon

Gemini Ascendant

Twin two
Twin two has Gemini Ascendant, an 11th-house Sun and a 10th house Moon. Neptune has also changed houses.

READING THE WHOLE **BIRTH CHART**

FIRST STEPS

Before you apply your knowledge to interpreting your birth chart, it is helpful to methodically review the role each chart factor plays in building the whole picture of your character and life story. Here is an overview of what you need to consider. Take notes along the way.

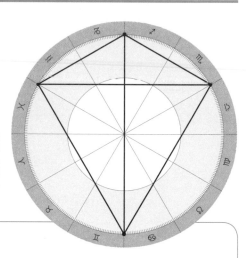

Example aspect pattern
Look for any aspect patterns (see step 6) such as this kite. These will carry significant influence in your chart.

STEP 1: **FIRST IMPRESSIONS**

A missing polarity, mode, or element will powerfully shape a person's character and motivations. We can also consider the distribution of planets around the chart.

PERSONAL PLANETS

SOCIAL PLANETS

❯ **Polarity/element/mode balance**
Use just the seven personal and social planets (Sun through Saturn) and the Ascendant.

☉	☽	☿	♀	♂	♃	♄
The Sun	The Moon	Mercury	Venus	Mars	Jupiter	Saturn

❯ **Distribution of planets**
This reveals basic orientation toward spheres of public/private and self/other. For this, use all 10 planets plus Chiron.

Upper half
The upper half is above the horizon. Having the majority of planets here suggests orientation toward the outside world and public life.

East
Having the majority of planets in the eastern half suggests a focus on the self.

Lower half
The lower half is below the horizon. Having the majority of planets here suggests a life away from the limelight in a more private space.

West
Having the majority of planets in the western half suggests focus on relationships and collaboration.

STEP 2: **THE ANGLES** AND **CHART RULER**

The Ascendant shows your style of meeting the world, and its ruler (the "chart ruler") describes a territory that is crucial to unfolding your life story.

The Descendant complements the Ascendant as the axis of self and other, and the MC-IC shows the interplay between private and public life. Interpret each angle separately, and then contemplate each pair as an axis.

Take note of:

❯ **The Ascendant** (or rising) **sign**.

❯ **The Descendant sign** Contrast this with the Ascendant.

❯ **The chart ruler** Note which sign and house it occupies and its aspects to other planets. If Mercury, Venus, Mars, Jupiter, or Saturn are your chart ruler, check to see if it also rules another house in your chart.

❯ **The ruler of the Descendant** by sign, house, and aspect.

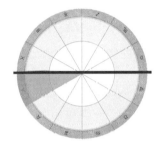

The Ascendant
Which sign sits on the eastern horizon of your chart?

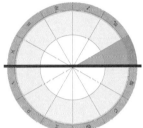

The Descendant
Which sign sits on the western horizon of your chart?

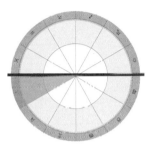

The chart ruler
Which sign and house does it occupy?

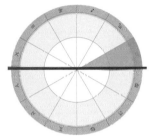

Descendant ruler
Which sign and house does it occupy?

Repeat this for **the MC-IC axis**

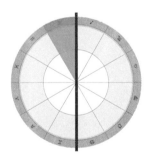

The MC
Which sign does the cusp of the 10th house occupy?

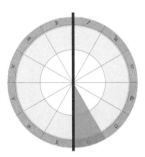

The IC
Which sign does the cusp of the 4th house occupy?

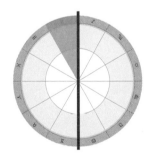

The MC ruler
Which sign and house does it occupy?

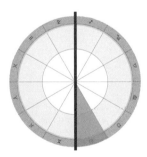

The IC ruler
Which sign and house does it occupy?

❯ **Planets conjunct the angles**
Any planets that fall within an 8° orb of the angles ("angular planets") will strongly color your experience of that angle.

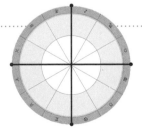

Angular planets
Conjunct within 8° of an angle.

CONTINUED

STEP 3: **THE SUN** AND **MOON**

Along with the chart ruler, the Sun and Moon are your central drives. Explore them by sign, house, and aspect, and note the house that each of them rules.

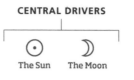

CENTRAL DRIVERS

The Sun   The Moon

STEP 4: **THE PERSONAL** AND **SOCIAL PLANETS**

Explore the remaining personal planets (Mercury, Venus, and Mars) to complete the inner core of the personality, and then the social planets (Jupiter and Saturn) to suggest experiences of the wider social world.

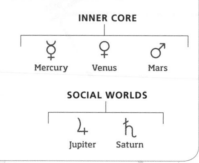

INNER CORE

Mercury   Venus   Mars

SOCIAL WORLDS

Jupiter   Saturn

STEP 5: **CHIRON** AND **THE OUTER PLANETS**

Chiron and the outer planets are a powerful presence if they make major aspects to personal planets or angles. Note their sign and house position and the aspects they make, plus the house each outer planet rules.

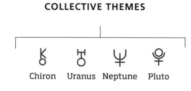

COLLECTIVE THEMES

Chiron   Uranus   Neptune   Pluto

STEP 6: **ASPECT PATTERNS**

With an overview of each planet, the aspect patterns become easier to spot. Not all charts have one, but for a chart that does, this will form an important dynamic.

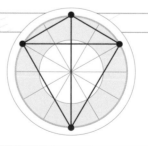

STEP 7: **THE MOON'S NODES**

The Nodal axis often makes more sense once we understand the rest of the chart and its themes.

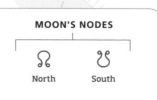

MOON'S NODES

North   South

IDENTIFYING THEMES IN YOUR CHART

The main work of chart interpretation is to pick out your chart's most important features. Here, we are looking for threads that weave together to create distinct themes, as well as the tensions and contradictions that all charts contain.

STEP 1: **IDENTIFYING THE KEY ASTROLOGICAL FACTORS**

The Ascendant, chart ruler, Sun, and Moon These are the four most important factors in any chart, because they define your self-image and worldview (Ascendant and chart ruler), your heroic purpose (Sun), and your inner "soul life" (Moon). The houses they rule will also reflect key areas of personal expression.

Angular planets Any planet conjunct one of the four angles ("angular planets") will play a leading role, and we can extend its influence to the house (or houses) that planet rules in your chart. The angles are the most basic life areas—identity (Ascendant),

choice of relationship (Descendant), home/family (IC), and vocation (MC)—and a planet conjunct one of them brings both the planet and the angle into sharp focus.

Unaspected planets An unaspected planet plays a key role, too. It represents an inner drive that the person may find difficult to connect to or feel in control of.

Aspect patterns Aspect patterns reflect a complex inner pattern.

What is emphasized and what is missing Three or more planets in one element or mode will make that your dominant style; alternatively, the lack

of an element or mode means it can dominate by its absence. Heavily tenanted houses or an empty hemisphere are worth noting, too.

Aspects with the tightest orbs These are usually felt the most keenly. "Tight" is a relative term. For instance, an orb of 1° is tight for a square if our maximum orb is 8°; on the other hand, 1° is not tight for a sesquiquadrate if our maximum orb for these is only 2°. Tight major hard aspects provide the core material of a chart—the grit in the oyster.

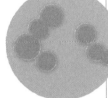

STEP 2: **IDENTIFYING THE MAIN THEMES**

A theme emerges when two or three chart factors all point in a similar direction—and a theme will be strongest when it involves key chart factors from the list above.

At the same time, we want to think about a chart's strengths—the main skills and talents—as well as the challenges, tensions, and paradoxes it contains. There is no such thing as

a "good" or "bad" chart; each has its difficult areas and its positive potential, and indeed these can be one and the same.

69

" ... **ASTROLOGICAL EVENTS** MAY WORK OUT QUITE **DIFFERENTLY** FROM HOW WE MIGHT IMAGINE, **FEAR,** **OR PREDICT THEM**, BUT THEY ALWAYS EXPRESS THE ASTROLOGICAL SYMBOLISM IF WE ARE **OPEN TO SEEING IT.**"

Richard Idemon, Through the Looking Glass:
A Search for the Self in the Mirror of Relationships

CASE STUDY 1

AMANDA

Here we will see the process of chart interpretation in action, using the chart of Amanda, a body therapist and writer. Her interests encompass theatre, psychology, spirituality, and the mind-body link. She is politically aware and is an active environmental campaigner.

STEP 1: IDENTIFYING THE KEY ASTROLOGICAL FACTORS

The Ascendant
& chart ruler

Ascendant and chart ruler Her **Scorpio rising** suggests a guarded approach and a strong intuitive radar, sensitive to undercurrents and desiring to penetrate beyond the surface – and with **co-chart ruler Mars**, this depth allows Amanda to make an impact on the community (Mars in 11th) via actions that bring balance and equilibrium (Mars in Libra).

The **Mars-Chiron** conjunction adds the healing element which informs Amanda's bodywork and **Mars-Neptune** adds artistry and sensitivity. **Mars** rules both the 5th and 6th houses, so a total of three houses in the chart, further increasing its importance and making a strong link to creativity/children (5th) and to the world of everyday work and physical health (6th).

The other **co-chart ruler Pluto** is in

Leo in the 9th. The sign is shared by everyone of Amanda's generation, but **the 9th house** is personal to her chart: she will probe deeply to find ultimate (Pluto) answers to life's bigger questions (9th).

The Sun and Moon Her **Virgo Sun** is on the MC, suggesting a prominent public role and work as a vehicle for self-expression. **Virgo** suggests craft and precision; she is ideally suited to bodywork and can feel pride in professional expertise and a connection to the physical realm.

The Sun does not rule a house, but it rules the three planets in Amanda's **9th house**, so the determined urge towards higher knowledge which they represent will be gathered up and elevated by the **Sun via its conjunction to her MC.**

The Moon is in **Scorpio** in the **12th**, a very private placement. Emotions will be deeply felt but kept in reserve, heightening the powerful emotional radar. Personal needs may not be openly articulated. The **square to Saturn** is almost exact, making this perhaps the chart's most influential aspect and continuing the theme of self-containment. The **conjunction to Jupiter** adds natural positivity alongside this.

The Moon rules the 9th, again highlighting travel and learning; being ruled by the Moon takes that world and links it to Amanda's inner soul life (Moon). Much of the "travel" may therefore be inward and of a metaphysical nature.

Angular planets As well as the Sun, **Mercury** is also **conjunct the MC**. In addition, these two planets occupy each others' signs, so they are linked,

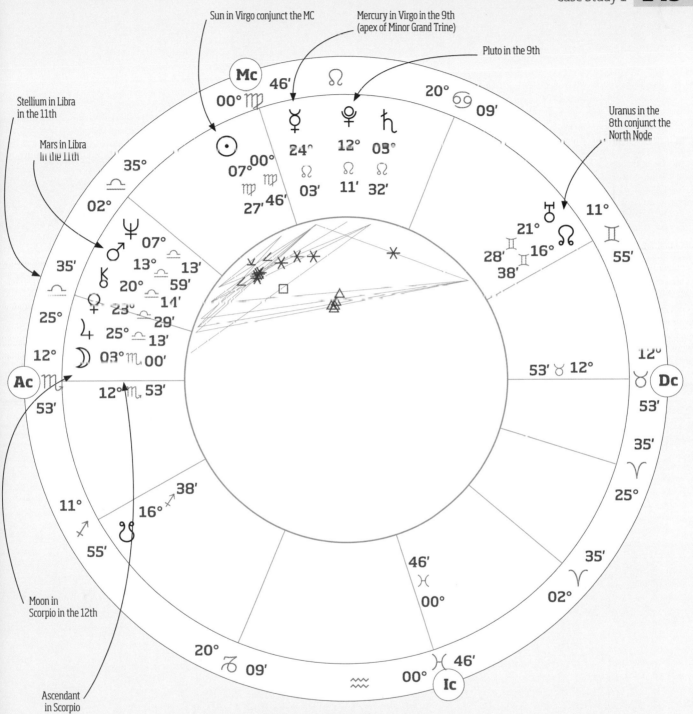

Sun in Virgo conjunct the MC

Mercury in Virgo in the 9th
(apex of Minor Grand Trine)

Pluto in the 9th

Stellium in Libra
in the 11th

Mars in Libra
in the 11th

Uranus in the
8th conjunct the
North Node

Moon in
Scorpio in the 12th

Ascendant
in Scorpio

Amanda's birth chart
The 9th, 10th, and 11th are key houses, connecting
Amanda to areas of travel and philosophy, as well as
community and the need for a public role or profile.

CONTINUED »

reinforcing manual dexterity and craft and the development of ideas and communication skills as key elements in the career.

Unaspected planets None

Aspect patterns The **Libra Stellium in the 11th** emphasizes this sign and house. Fairness and balance become key motivations, as do relationships and social interaction, all centered around community. The enthusiasm and motivation of **Mars** and **Jupiter**, the artistry of **Venus** and **Neptune**, and the "wounded healer" dimension of **Chiron** combine to create a sense of life as a beautiful and energetic healing dance.

The **Minor Grand Trine** (involving Uranus, Chiron, Venus, Jupiter, and Mercury) adds an image of the "alternative healer" motivated by dramatic performance (Mercury in Leo in the 9th as apex planet).

What is emphasized and what is missing The Sun carries the earth function, so there might be an emphasis for Amanda on developing a relationship to the physical realm (earth) as a medium for self-expression (Sun), and this could be one reason for her love of the natural world. The Sun is also the only planet in a mutable sign, so she may have been challenged to develop flexibility, perhaps through her work or her role as a parent (MC).

The southern hemisphere contains all the planets; she is oriented outward toward collective and interpersonal areas. The eastern hemisphere is more dominant than the western–so although the Libra planets suggest a need for relationships, she will have a sense of herself as being the driver.

Aspects with the tightest orbs Apart from the Moon-Saturn square, Pluto tightly squares the Ascendant-Descendant axis. Perhaps there have been distinct chapters in Amanda's life, punctuated by dramatic transformation via travel, education, or ethical questioning (Pluto in 9th). Such changes may transform both her sense of identity (Ascendant) and her relationships (Descendant).

STEP 2: **IDENTIFYING THE MAIN THEMES**

Transformation and regeneration
Amanda may undergo cycles of transformation and regeneration, and her life may have distinct chapters separated by times of instability and change.

❯ **Scorpio Ascendant**, co-ruler **Pluto** high in the chart and **tightly square the Ascendant-Descendant**
❯ **Moon** in **Scorpio**
❯ **Uranus conjunct** the **North Node** in the **8th**
❯ Angular **Mercury** on the MC (and linked to the Sun) rules the **8th house**

Philosophical
Amanda is likely to have a philosophical way of thinking and be interested in probing deeply to find answers to complex questions. There may be an interest in spiritual and esoteric matters.

❯ **Scorpio rising**, co-ruler **Pluto** in **9th**
❯ **Saturn** and **Mercury** also in the **9th**
❯ **Saturn** in the **9th** rules the **3rd**
❯ **Moon** in **Scorpio** rules the **9th** and is **conjunct Jupiter** in the **11th**
❯ **Uranus-North Node conjunct** in the **8th**
❯ Angular **Mercury** on the **MC** rules the **8th**

Career as a healer
Amanda has made a career as a healer and healing gifts are well-starred in her chart. The idea of physical "therapy" is shown, manipulating the body to release tension and bring healing:

❱ Co-chart ruler **Mars** is conjunct **Chiron**
❱ Co-chart ruler **Mars** also rules the **6th**
❱ **Venus** (ruler of the **12th**) is **conjunct Chiron**
❱ **Scorpio Ascendant** and **Moon**
❱ Angular **Mercury** rules the **8th**
❱ **Sun** in **Virgo** and on the **MC** (Sun is the only planet in earth)

Social and political
Amanda may have a strong social and political awareness, being interested in moral and ethical issues generally and the idea of social fair play. Indeed, this may underpin much of her life:

❱ A packed **11th house** with a **Stellium in Libra**, including **Jupiter**
❱ **Venus** in **Libra** in the 11th rules the **11th**
❱ Three planets in the **9th**
❱ Ruler of the **9th**, the **Moon**, is **conjunct Jupiter**

Sensitivity
Amanda's chart suggests a high degree of sensitivity and a "sixth sense", an ability to pick up "vibrations" and unspoken communication. She is skilled at seeing below surface appearances:

❱ **Ascendant** in **Scorpio**
❱ **Moon** in Scorpio in the **12th**
❱ **Uranus** in the **8th**
❱ **Mercury** rules the **8th**

Writing
Writing features as a potential talent. The prominent Sun and Mercury suggest it is important for Amanda to use communication in her work and as a means of conveying her creativity:

❱ **Mercury** and **Sun** on the **MC** – they rule each other, and Mercury rules the MC
❱ **North Node** in **Gemini**, ruled by **Mercury**
❱ **Saturn** in the 9th rules the **3rd** and **tightly squares the Moon**

Relationships
Relationships of all kinds are likely to be a consistent theme, but with some tensions to deal with. Venus in Libra (Descendant ruler) might reach for a peaceful, loving, and affectionate relationship, but it is also trine independent Uranus on the North Node ("fated encounters"). The Scorpio Moon square Saturn is self-contained and the weight of planets is to the eastern side. So a need for relationship sits alongside a need for personal space and autonomy:

❱ **Stellium in Libra**, including co-chart ruler **Mars** and **Venus** (ruler of the Descendant)
❱ **Moon in Scorpio** square **Saturn**
❱ **Venus trine Uranus** and **North Node** in the **8th**
❱ **Eastern hemisphere** is dominant

CASE STUDY 2

JACK

Here, we will see the process of chart interpretation in action, using the chart of Jack, who works as an estate agent. He is hard-working and career-minded, and would eventually like to run his own business. He enjoys traveling and has a dream to live in the US.

STEP 1: IDENTIFYING THE KEY ASTROLOGICAL FACTORS

The Ascendant
& chart ruler

Ascendant and chart ruler Jack's Ascendant is in Virgo, so his initial approach to anything will favor efficiency, expediency, and a critical eye. With Pisces on the Descendant, he might at times in life be challenged to develop a more fluid and less analytical style, a theme that might arise in partnerships and relationships in particular.

Mercury is his chart ruler, in Aquarius in the 5th house. There is a sense here of enjoying information

networks and social exchange, and indeed that Jack sees his ability to communicate as a key "calling card" (Mercury as chart ruler) that enables him to express his mental creativity (Mercury in the 5th). Mercury in Aquarius inclines toward open and honest communication and suggests a facility for technology and innovation. Mercury also rules his Gemini MC.

The Sun and Moon The Sun is in the 6th house in Pisces and conjunct the North Node. This might reflect a strong sense of his own destiny, yet also a lifetime's journey to find identity, creative

expression, and a true sense of purpose (Sun conjunct North Node). This might be found through practical service of some kind (Pisces, 6th house). The Sun rules his 12th house, reinforcing the idea of shining in a role that is essentially behind the scenes.

Angular planets None

Unaspected planets None

Aspect patterns There are two T-squares. Both involve the Mars-Pluto opposition, with the Moon at apex of one and Venus at apex of the other. The Mars-Pluto opposition brings

> ❝ **Polarity** is tipped slightly toward the **negative signs**, giving Jack a more **introverted** than extroverted expression. ❞

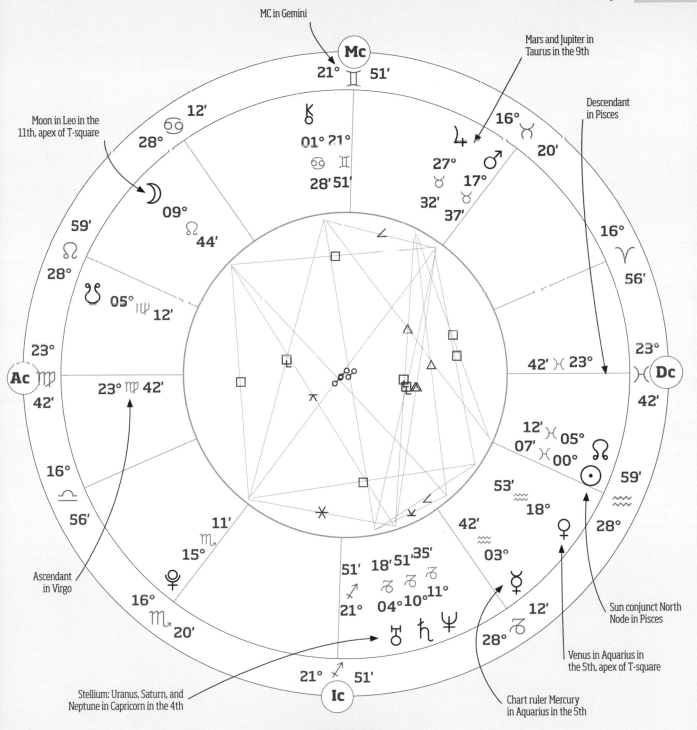

MC in Gemini

Mc
21° ♊ 51'

Mars and Jupiter in
Taurus in the 9th

Descendant
in Pisces

Moon in Leo in the
11th, apex of T-square

⛢
01° 21'

♋ 12'
28°

♋ ♊
28' 51'

16° ♉ 20'

♃
27° ♉ 17°
32'
37'

♂ ↗

16° ♈
56'

09° ♌ 44'

59'
♌
28°

☋
05° ♏ 12'

Ac ♍
23° 42'

23° ♍ 42'

42' ♓ 23°

Dc ♓
23°
42'

16°
♎
56'

12' ♓ 05°
07' ♓ 00°

☊
⊙
59'

53' ♒
18°

♒
28°

Ascendant
in Virgo

11'
♏
15°

42' ♒
03°

♀ 12'

♇
16° ♏
20'

51' 18' 51' 35'
↗ ♑ ♑ ♑
21° 04° 10° 11°

☿
♑ 28°

Sun conjunct North
Node in Pisces

Venus in Aquarius in
the 5th, apex of T-square

21° ↗ 51'

⛢ ♄ ♆

Ic

Chart ruler Mercury
in Aquarius in the 5th

Stellium: Uranus, Saturn, and
Neptune in Capricorn in the 4th

Jack's birth chart
Two fixed T-squares ensure staying power, while
a Leo Moon with Mars/Jupiter in the 9th suggest an
adventurous entrepreneur. The Pisces Sun adds a
spirit of service.

CONTINUED

together a desire for financial power (Pluto in the 2nd) with the determined and adventurous breaking of new ground (Mars in Taurus in the 9th). Jack is tough and resolute. The Moon in Leo in the 11th is brave, extraverted, and needs an audience; Venus in Aquarius in the 5th is sociable and friendly. Both are backed by the unyielding strength of Mars-Pluto, which here pours its energies into making connections and finding opportunities for recognition.

What is emphasized and what is missing

Polarity is tipped slightly towards the negative signs, giving Jack a more introverted than extraverted expression. We can note that his Moon in Leo gives him a performer's instinct, but overall there is a more inward-looking feel to the chart. He is very fixed, with five planets in fixed signs,

giving him resilience and determination but also perhaps a tendency to get stuck at times - of the personal and social planets, only Saturn is in a cardinal sign, so with each new project or phase of life it may take him a while to get out of the starting blocks.

Earth is the most highlighted element, followed by air - Jack may have a slightly "dry" aspect to his character, not given to high drama or displays of emotion. With his Sun as the only planet in water, on the North Node, it may be part of his challenge in life to find ways of developing the more soulful side of himself.

The 4th, 5th, 6th, and 9th houses are highlighted, each containing more than one planet or chart point. Uranus, Saturn, and Neptune in the 4th suggest that home and family is a key area for Jack, albeit subject to a kind of "push-pull", with Uranus suggesting restless

changes of residence and location, but Saturn a need for commitment to one place, and Neptune a longing for the "ideal home".

♂ ♃ **Mars and Jupiter** in the 9th reflect Jack's desire to travel and see the world - he might favour the USA as a "land of opportunity" (Jupiter in the 9th), but no doubt will be drawn generally to the idea of adventures to new places (Mars and Jupiter in 9th).

Aspects with the tightest orbs

Saturn conjunct Neptune is the only major aspect under 1°. Venus square Mars and the Sun trine Chiron are just over 1°. These may well be the most influential aspects in Jack's chart.

STEP 2: **IDENTIFYING THE MAIN THEMES**

Determination

The two T-squares provide much of the chart's inner dynamics and suggest tension but also capacity for hard work. There is an urge for social connection and influence (Moon and Venus), both linked to a capacity for determined survival against all the odds (Mars-Pluto). In addition, both are in fixed signs: Jack may set himself goals which require huge staying power to achieve.

❯ Two fixed **T-squares**

Social connection

The importance of social connections seems strong here. As his only fire planet, the Moon might sometimes be expressed in an exaggerated way, fulfilling a need to feel noticed and special within the group. On the other hand, his Aquarius planets bring a more democratic instinct, but no less needful of human contact.

❯ Chart ruler **Mercury** in **Aquarius** in the 5th, **Mercury** also rules the **MC**
❯ **Venus** in **Aquarius** in the **5th**
❯ **Moon** in **Leo** in the **11th**
❯ **The Moon** rules the **11th**

Work

Working in service to an ideal, behind the scenes or in a supportive role might also be of interest to Jack. With his current work as an estate agent, he seems focused around his 4th house planets, perhaps in particular feeling anchored at present by the safety of Saturn in Capricorn in the 4th – but other areas of his chart may come into prominence later in his life. Chiron in Cancer in the 10th could suggest a professional mentoring role for him, connected to compassion and caring – and the tight trine to his Pisces Sun might put this at the heart of his life.

❱ **Sun** in **Pisces**, Sun rules the **12th**
❱ **Virgo Ascendant**
❱ **Chiron** in **Cancer** in the **10th** trine **Sun** in **Pisces**

Spiritual quest

There is perhaps also a search for faith and meaning, involving tests and challenges. Nothing in this area of Jack's life seems easy – the T-squares are both linked to his 9th house (a place where we seek meaning) and his Nodes pick up the square between the Pisces Sun and 9th house Jupiter, planet of faith and belief. At some point in his life, all this may lead him towards a spiritual or religious crisis or quest.

❱ **Venus** rules the **9th house** and is apex of a **T-Square**
❱ **Mars** and **Jupiter** in the **9th** – Mars is part of both T-squares and Jupiter squares the Nodes
❱ **Sun conjunct** the **North Node in Pisces** (and squares Jupiter)
❱ Low fire – only **the Moon** occupies a fire sign

Home and family

Home and family are highlighted, but with conflicting needs in this area of life. Uranus in the 4th seeks freedom and change, but Saturn (particularly in sensible Capricorn) seeks to feel grounded and safe. His IC is in Sagittarius, ruled by Jupiter in the 9th, so it is no wonder he has the desire to live abroad – but at times this may leave him feeling like a stranger, cut off from his roots (Uranus in 4th) and longing for home (Neptune in 4th).

❱ **Stellium** in the **4th house** – Uranus, Saturn, and Neptune
❱ **Saturn-Neptune** tightest aspect in the chart
❱ **IC** in **Sagittarius** ruled by **Jupiter** in the **9th**

Travel

Jack has identified a desire to go abroad. There are two planets in the 9th house of travel: Jupiter and Mars. Jupiter is itself the long-distance planet and here suggests enthusiasm for far-flung places – it aspects (and co-rules) the Pisces Sun, and also rules the Sagittarius IC making it a perfect symbol for "living abroad". Mars brings an intrepid spirit of discovery and is connected to the Moon (our homing instinct) and to the ruler of the 9th, Venus, reinforcing the travel theme.

❱ **Mars** and **Jupiter** in the **9th house**
❱ **Jupiter rules the IC** and squares/rules the Sun
❱ **Mars squares the Moon** and 9th-house ruler **Venus**

 Uranus, Saturn, and Neptune in the **4th** suggest that **home and family** is a key area for Jack. "

UNDERSTANDING
YOURSELF

UNDERSTANDING YOURSELF
AN OVERVIEW

UNLOCKING YOUR BIRTH CHART

Astrology can shed light on all aspects of life, from the most ordinary of matters to those that hold the most profound significance and shape the course of our lives. It can be used as a helpful guide whenever we need one.

Being yourself

There is no one quite like you. Astrology validates this and suggests what is important to you as an individual. Life is rarely simple and we are continually called upon to adjust and adapt, to fit within the families, groups, and communities we belong to. In the midst of this, your birth chart is a reminder of your inner picture of character and calling, with the power to bring you back home to yourself.

It is also a reminder that personal psychology plays its part in co-creating the situations in which we find ourselves. It is easy to feel trapped by circumstances, believing that nothing will change and we will never achieve our desires. Astrology offers an alternative view, suggesting that self-knowledge can be your most powerful secret weapon in the business of mapping out your path, achieving your goals, living authentically, and finding your own version of happiness and fulfilment.

Symbolic information

Astrology is based on symbols, and so it stands to reason that a birth chart only provides symbolic information. It offers clues and ideas, stories to follow, themes to explore. Symbols might suggest that there is no fixed fate at work in our lives, no set destiny with only one possible outcome. Each symbol in a chart has many different layers and ways of being expressed, and each unfolds its story as life is lived. As we have seen throughout this book, although each symbol must be interpreted in its own terms (Venus things are not Mars things; Sagittarius is not Capricorn), each offers us a wealth of different options. If nothing else, symbols suggest we have choice.

With your own birth chart then, the key might be to work at understanding its patterns on a deeper level, seeing how it reflects your circumstances and the choices you might have made – and what might motivate you in making the choices yet to come.

Exploring life areas in your chart

Each of us has our own very individual needs and style when it comes to anything in life. The following pages offer a road map for exploring each territory, rather than comprehensive information on how you would personally approach each one. For each topic, the most relevant chart factors are listed; you will then need to flex your imagination to apply the ideas to your own chart.

> **Your birth chart** is a reminder of your **inner picture of character and calling**, with the power to bring you back home to yourself.

IDENTITY

HOW TO BE COMFORTABLE WITH WHO YOU ARE

As the picture of your unique character and outlook, we can take the whole chart to indicate "identity". Within this though, some areas of it will provide very specific information about your sense of who you are. The Ascendant, the 1st house, and the Sun form the core of this.

YOUR **HOUSES**

 The Ascendant and the 1st house
This area of the chart denotes your body as the vehicle for your life force and vitality, and so suggests your sense of yourself as a physically separate individual. Being the symbol of the birth moment, it also describes your arrival into the world and the pattern of responses this sets up.

Your Ascendant (or rising) sign is a powerful indicator of how you feel about yourself. For instance, **Gemini rising** brings a feeling of being light and mobile, whereas **Scorpio rising** creates a much more guarded persona.

Planets in the 1st are often the most obvious to others and we use them to present ourselves to the world. If you have **Venus** in the 1st, you might come across as charming, keen to get on with everyone and oil the wheels. By contrast, **Mars** here can come out all guns blazing, a pattern that may reflect emergencies in the birth experience or the early presence of a rival.

If you have planets conjunct your Ascendant, whether in the 1st or 12th, these will strongly colour your identity and how you feel the world out there responds to you.

 **The 5th house
- the inner child**
At the heart of the 5th house is the idea of our seed or life force. We pass this energy on to our children via our DNA and invest it in our creative projects and joyful leisure pursuits. In this house, we create things that express our individuality and creative power. Planets here reflect the essence of this inner gift.

» **1st house** see pp.90-91
5th house see pp.98-99

> " Planets in the 1st are often the **most obvious** to others and we use them to **present ourselves to the world**. "

YOUR **PLANETS**

The Sun stands as a symbol of where we seek to shine, achieve, and take pride. According to the sign and house, to the aspects that the Sun is making, and to the house that the Sun rules (in other words, with Leo on the cusp), we can refine this image.

If your Sun is in the 9th in Capricorn, for instance, you might carve a role for yourself as a teacher, philosopher, or explorer, the solar light growing ever brighter with each journey made or each subject mastered. With a square from Pluto in the 12th, such accomplishments might involve periods of wrestling inner demons—perfect for a psychologist, perhaps, delving into the depths of the unconscious.

The chart ruler is the planet that rules your Ascendant sign, so it gives further information about what it feels like to be you. For instance, if you have **Aries rising**, you might identify yourself as a warrior—**Mars** in your chart will then show what kind of warrior you are and what provokes you to fight.

> >> **The planets** see pp.62-85
> **Chart ruler** see pp.120-121

YOUR **ZODIAC SIGNS**

There are no particular signs that indicate identity more than others—the unique mix of signs occupied by the planets in your chart offers a picture of your temperament. For instance, a person with all their personal and social planets in **Libra** and **Scorpio** will have a very different personality from the person loaded with **Gemini** and **Cancer**. Simply looking at the mix of signs (including the balance of polarity, modes, and elements) offers you a basic picture of who you are.

However, we can flag **Leo**—the house with Leo on the cusp will be ruled by the Sun and will therefore be key to your identity and self-development.

CHANGE

HOW TO NEGOTIATE LIFE'S TURNING POINTS

Change is inevitable, woven into the fabric of life–indeed, many of us actively seek it. We each deal with it in different ways; while some embrace it and prefer never to look back, others can feel it as unwelcome upheaval.

YOUR **ZODIAC SIGNS**

Certain signs respond to change more favorably than others. In particular, the signs of **Taurus**, **Cancer**, and **Scorpio** are conscious of security in one form or another and will tend to hold on rather than let things flow. If you have personal planets here, the devil you know might feel more reassuring than a change of scene. By contrast, **Aries** or **Gemini** welcomes periodic change.

The cardinal signs Aries tends to deal best with change, having all the fiery impetus of being the first sign. Cancer, Libra, and Capricorn possess the cardinal capacity to get on with things, but the cardinal signs prefer to be in control. For a person with personal planets in cardinal signs, change tends to be welcome only if it has been self-initiated.

The fixed signs Lots of fixity in a chart suggests a tendency to stay with what you know, come hell or high water. The instinct of the fixed signs is to stabilize–the winds of change might blow around, but the person remains anchored.

The mutable signs These usually respond positively when change is in the air. If you have personal planets in these signs, you probably hate for things to be static and will spontaneously generate movement in order to reassure yourself that there is always an alternative–even if this is just to move the furniture around from time to time or choose a different place to go on vacation.

> The instinct of the **fixed signs** is to stabilize.

YOUR **PLANETS**

The Moon A significant planet to look at in your chart is the Moon, because it indicates the familiar rhythms and rituals that bring comfort and security. We tend to hoard and collect around the Moon, according to the sign and house. For instance, Moon in **Gemini** might hoard books and magazines (you might want to read them in ten years' time) and Moon in **Cancer** will keep every card, photo, and memento ever received. At the extreme end, compulsive hoarding or returning to the same behaviour patterns can suggest fear of moving on.

Mars can be your ally when it comes to making changes and honouring its particular style will help you to move forward in a way that feels manageable. For instance, if you have Mars in **Capricorn**, this gives you the capacity to forge ahead with determination; with Mars in **Pisces** you might dislike the pressure of making a decision.

Uranus compasses the notion of radical change and wherever it is placed in your chart will tend to be subject to regular overhaul or sudden changes of circumstance. This is where you seek freedom from convention and where you might feel there is always a more exciting possibility awaiting – change may appear to be imposed from outside, but often coincides with an inner need for a fresh start, whether you are conscious of it or not.

> **The Moon** see pp.64-65
> **Mars** see pp.70-71
> **Uranus** see pp.78-79

YOUR **HOUSES**

The Ascendant and the 1st house – new chapters
You can look to your Ascendant and 1st house planets to indicate the energy evoked at the beginning of any new chapter of your life. Wherever the change is occurring, your 1st house and chart ruler are like the hand at the tiller of the boat and will show your style of setting a new course.

With a **Virgo Ascendant** for instance, there might be a degree of anxiety about how things will unfold and a good strategy would be to make sure you have all the details of your new journey organized well ahead of time. By contrast, if you have a **Pisces Ascendant**, each new phase begins with an inner vision, to which you might need to hold fast until dry land appears.

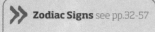 **Zodiac Signs** see pp.32-57

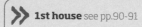 **1st house** see pp.90-91

UNCERTAINTY

HOW TO COPE WITH LIFE'S UNKNOWNS

No matter how decisive you are, we all experience times of doubt, when the way seems anything but clear. Your chart will show the concerns that might give rise to uncertainty and how you can find your way through.

YOUR **PLANETS**

Mars suggests how we keep going through tough times. We might initially cast Gemini, Libra, and Pisces, for instance, as signs that display indecision. What if your Mars is in one of these signs? Perhaps being decisive is not your strong suit. But the sign still offers a strategy for the planets it contains.

With Mars in **Gemini**, you can make a decision, but you might need first to articulate your concerns and fears. By playing devil's advocate for yourself, you can sort through all the options until the right answer emerges.

Mars in **Libra** seeks to act without taking sides. What can appear as equivocation is perhaps more an internal process of giving equal consideration.

Pisces might seem antithetical to the thrusting energy of Mars, and if you have Mars in this sign, it might be difficult for you to feel you can take action. But you are also likely to have strong instincts, and trusting your intuition can be key.

Jupiter is our place of vision and inspiration—our style of keeping the faith. If your Jupiter is in **Aries**, faith is boldly expressed, which probably makes you a confident decision-maker. If your Jupiter is in **Capricorn**, however, you prefer not to let new ventures get out of hand—planning ahead helps you to feel in control. Understanding your Jupiter allows you manage risk in your own way.

The cycles of the planets remind us that there are times to act and times when it might be more useful to wait and see. Crucially, too, astrology suggests it is fruitless to allow ourselves to feel pressured simply to make it look to the outside world that we have "manned up" and seized the day. Sometimes it is more courageous, and more creative, to allow yourself time to retreat and reflect on the issues at hand.

>> **Mars** see pp.70-71
>> **Jupiter** see pp.74-75

"The **cycles of the planets** remind us that there are times to act and times when it might be more useful to wait and see. "

YOUR **ZODIAC SIGNS**

The elements

 Fire offers natural buoyancy and the higher the fire content in your chart, the stronger your faith is likely to be that, no matter what the situation, you believe that somehow it will all be fine.

If you lack fire though, the elements that are strongly represented will flow in to do the job.

Air If you have no fire but several planets in air, you might tackle the unknown by trying to articulate it - talk about it, mind-map it, write lists and plans of what you are going to do.

Earth With lots of planets in earth you might only feel safe with a contingency plan in place - you deal with uncertainty through savings plans and a good insurance policy.

Water With several planets in water, uncertainty might centre around times of emotional crisis - having a good support network of friends and family makes all the difference.

Elements see pp.28-31

YOUR **HOUSES**

 The 9th house - believing in what you can't see

Planets in the 9th house give clues as to how you might feel about encountering the unknown. Whenever we are faced with making future plans, setting off on a long journey, or having to hold a vision of something yet to unfold, our 9th house is conjured. So whatever planets you have here, and the sign on the cusp, will mediate this for you. With **Saturn** for instance, trust in these things might not flow naturally. With **Uranus**, you might actively seek the thrill of the strange and the unfamiliar.

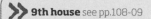 **9th house** see pp.108-09

TROUBLED TIMES

HOW TO COPE WITH LIFE'S DIFFICULTIES

They say that when the going gets tough, the tough get going. But each of us has our own method of finding our way through the storm and we can only call on what we have within us, to help us cope in times of difficulty.

YOUR **HOUSES**

 **The 8th house
– crisis and transformation**

Whilst not all our troubles relate to the 8th house by any means, we can find clues here as to how we react when the pressure is on. More accurately perhaps, it describes a journey into dark places, whether this is the maelstrom of a divorce, financial crisis, or experiences of grief and bereavement.

The 8th house is the dragon's lair and any planets here are forged in the heat of that encounter. Even with no planets here, you can look to the sign on the cusp of this house, and the planetary ruler of that sign, to tell you how you approach life's more extreme experiences and some of the key resources you might call on when things fall apart.

For instance, if you have **Mercury** in the 8th house then it might be an advantage to have a guide in the underworld – a counsellor or therapist, friends with good listening skills or knowledge of the territory, or even just keeping a diary or personal record as a way of sorting through and understanding emotional experiences. Ultimately your birth-right "treasure" is knowledge (Mercury) of deep

things (8th) and this can be both the boon and the reason for entering into troubled waters in the first place.

Or with **Capricorn** on the cusp of the 8th, you no doubt have a stoic approach to hard times, with the ability to lay aside your own feelings if someone else really needs your help. The position of your 8th house ruler **Saturn** in your chart gives clues as to how you can flex this stoicism even further, helping you to stabilize and feel rooted and secure.

 8th house see pp.106-07

YOUR **PLANETS**

The Moon is the barometer of your inner feelings and describes gut reaction, as well as what you need in order to feel nurtured and safe. Anxiety arises when the Moon is under pressure. If you have the Moon in **Scorpio**, for example, your instinct might be to cope with trouble alone, shutting yourself off so that you can draw deeply from your own resources. Or with Moon in **Libra**, you can nurture yourself by trying to create harmony and balance, even if this is just for 1 precious hour each week in a yoga class. The more difficult life gets, the more we need to pay attention to the Moon's promptings, through its particular realms of food, rest, and self-care.

The Sun Keeping our eyes on the prize can be a good way of seeing ourselves through troubled times. From ancient times, in both Eastern and Western traditions, there has been the idea that a human life unfolds, that we begin as a seed containing its own purpose, and that the trials and tribulations we encounter along the way are in fact an integral part of the journey.

Of course, the whole birth chart is the seed moment and the unfolding life, but you might look to the Sun in particular as the central light in your chart, whatever you are in the process of becoming.

The Planets see pp.62-85

> The **Moon** is the barometer of your **inner feelings** and describes gut reaction.

YOUR **ZODIAC SIGNS**

Elements The **fire signs** tend to be confident of finding light at the end of the tunnel. The **earth signs** are focused in the present—staying busy with practical arrangements can bring security. With planets in **air**, your key asset is objectivity; conversely, with planets in **water**, you need to give due importance to deep feelings.

Modes The **cardinal signs** tend to deal with difficulty by taking control and trying to make headway. In the **fixed signs**, there is natural resilience and staying power. If you have strong **mutable signs**, on the other hand, running away might be your preferred option—but if not, you can use your versatility and capacity to adapt.

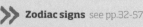

Zodiac signs see pp.32-57

HABIT

HOW TO RECOGNIZE AND CHANGE BAD HABITS

Sometimes even a good habit can eventually become a bad one if it outlives its usefulness. Your chart will show what kind of habits you might fall into and how you might work to break them at times when they compromise your well-being.

YOUR **PLANETS**

☽ **The Moon** As the part of us that governs everyday needs, attachments, and safe havens, the Moon has a lot to say about the habit patterns we build up, often without being aware we are doing it. Being the Moon, much of this is likely to be rooted in childhood. Early atmospheres and dynamics in our family of birth–particularly fears and uncertainties, learned behaviors, anxieties around separation or abandonment, lack of security, or not having our needs met–can become crystallized as negative behavior patterns in later life, particularly those connected to lunar things such as eating habits and emotional intimacy. The Moon's patterns are therefore the hardest to break, because they are likely to be the most deeply embedded. But awareness is a good start.

If you have the Moon in **Taurus**, for instance, a stress response might be to dig your heels in and become immovable or to comfort yourself through food, sex, or physical contact. With the Moon in **Gemini**, you might feel stressed in very emotional situations and cut out if things get too highly charged. Wherever the Moon is in your chart, you can begin to examine the habits you have built up and try to see where they have come from. Unhelpful patterns and addictions can also build up

around the hard aspects in a chart. **Venus** square to **Saturn** suggests that the desire nature has somehow not been given room to grow, which in relationships might emerge as barriers to intimacy or believing that one is unlovable. Or **Neptune** opposite **the Sun** might reflect a sense of loss in connection to the father and therefore a longing for the masculine power that the Sun represents. These kinds of deeper dynamics can become crystallized as entrenched beliefs we have about ourselves, about other people, or about life itself. Self-awareness helps to release us from these.

> " As the part of us that governs everyday needs, attachments, and safe havens, the **Moon** has a lot to say about the **habit patterns** we build up. "

YOUR **HOUSES**

The 6th house - rituals and routines

The 6th house describes the workings of everyday life and planets here are naturally at the centre of habits and rituals. **Mars** here might elicit daily visits to the gym for instance; **Neptune** here might mean you need to build in time for daydreaming or listening to your favourite music.

Such daily rituals are supportive - unless they become obsessive or we are using them to assuage unconscious fear. The extreme version of Mars in the 6th, for instance, is the 18-hour working day or endless gym workouts that hide inner feelings of not being in control - of Neptune in the 6th, being unable to function if you miss your meditation session or if your lifestyle fails to live up to a pre-conceived ideal of spiritual purity. We can accrue unhelpful habits anywhere in our chart - but in the 6th in particular, planets can fall into repetitive rituals.

>> **6th house** see pp.100-01

YOUR **ZODIAC SIGNS**

There are no particular signs that are prone more than others to negative habits - indeed, we might say that each sign has its own array of potential pitfalls. For instance, a bad habit for **Aries** might centre around impatience, for **Taurus** around being sedentary, for **Gemini** around nervous tension, or for **Cancer** around the need for a comfort blanket.

We can perhaps flag **Virgo** though, as the sign most closely associated with the idea of ritual. If you have planets in Virgo, or where Virgo falls on the cusp of a house, this might be a place in your life where you work according to a pre-set formula or method. This is perhaps true of all three earth signs, but Virgo in particular suggests adherence to rules and set procedures, going over and over the same ground in a bid to make it perfect.

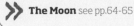

>> **The Moon** see pp.64-65

"**THE WHOLE POINT**
OF ASTROLOGY
IS TO LEARN
SOMETHING
ABOUT
WHAT YOU ARE."

Liz Greene, Astrology for Lovers

HEALTH & WELLBEING

HOW TO KEEP MIND AND BODY IN PERFECT BALANCE

The 6th house is traditionally the house of health. But you can also look beyond this and take an approach to your chart that aims to support and honour each part of it appropriately. Your chart is your health. Everything in your chart contributes to your health and wellbeing.

YOUR **HOUSES**

The 6th house is a good place to begin. Your daily health plan belongs here and so it is wise to create one which reflects your 6th house planets (and/or the sign on the cusp). Sometimes there will be contradictions, such as having both **Jupiter** and **Saturn** in this house, but this simply means that you must pay attention to both and get them to work in tandem in this area of your life.

Even if you have **Chiron** or **Uranus** here, you can devise a way to honour these principles. With Chiron in the 6th, you might be interested in investigating complementary health practices; with Uranus, it might help to exercise in short bursts, and also to

find ways to discharge the high-voltage nervous energy this planet exudes.

The 12th house Traditionally this was regarded as the house of sickness, a place where planets lose vitality and are "weak" in their expression. Other astrologers speak of karma and "past lives" in respect of this house. A psychological approach can shed light on this.

Planets in the 12th are hidden from view – thus our motivations and behaviour patterns around them tend to be unconscious. In addition, the "past lives" can be seen as those of our ancestors; planets here can hint

at complexes or traumas experienced by past generations, which we have somehow inherited.

These hidden feelings often make themselves known to us in psychosomatic form, as physical symptoms. An example of this might be **the Moon** here suggesting an experience of lack of nourishment or care, which might emerge as a longing to be looked after; or **Mercury** here as an experience of not being allowed to speak out, which emerges as illnesses or conditions connected to the voice.

6th house see pp.100-04
12th house see pp.114-15

Each sign has its own **style of expression** and when we do not honour or pay attention to this, our **wellbeing** suffers.

YOUR **PLANETS**

The Moon symbolizes what we need to ensure our basic emotional and physical well-being. The sign and house the Moon occupies in your chart, and the aspects it receives from other planets, all combine to form a picture of what makes you feel happy and at ease. When we cannot "feed" ourselves, literally or metaphorically according to our Moon's needs, anxiety or "dis"-ease can result.

Each planet in a chart contains both positive and negative potentials. Astrology also implies there is a reciprocal relationship between our physical health and our mental, emotional, and psychological health, because each planet incorporates all these levels of expression.

We can use **Mars** to illustrate. As soon as you engage in sports or exercise, you connect to your Mars— so choosing an activity that suits its sign and house can strengthen this planet for you on other levels, too, making you feel mentally and emotionally strong. Conversely, if you feel thwarted in your plans, it can leave you feeling physically tired and listless.

>> **The Moon** see pp.64-65
>> **Mars** see pp.70-71

> " Astrology implies that there is a reciprocal relationship between our **physical** health and our **mental**, **emotional**, and **psychological** health. "

YOUR **ZODIAC SIGNS**

There are no signs that specifically relate to health, but it is important to see what signs are occupied and highlighted in your chart, because each sign has its own style of expression; when we do not honor or pay attention to this, our well-being suffers. For instance, if you have the **Ascendant in Leo**, finding a situation in life where you can shine publicly and be noticed can be one of the keys to well-being. Conversely, with the **Ascendant in Scorpio**, it might feel stressful to you if you are required to be on display, because you prefer privacy. If you have planets in **Taurus**, feeling rushed can bring anxiety; in **Sagittarius**, stress comes from having to fit yourself into a preset plan.

>> **Zodiac Signs** see pp.32-57

LEISURE

HOW TO GET THE BEST OUT OF HOBBIES, SPORTS, AND PASTIMES

The 5th house encompasses the idea of hobbies and leisure time. Mars indicates how we expend our energy and choosing a sport according to your Mars placement ensures you stay interested enough to stick at it.

YOUR **HOUSES**

The 5th house - sports and pastimes
In the 5th, we let our hair down and engage in play. So here you can see what kind of activities will bring joy and a sense of relaxation. The essence of this house is pleasure and you can look to any planets here and the sign on the cusp (and of course its ruler) to get a picture of what engages this for you.

Some planets might seem to suit this house –
the Sun, **Venus**, and **Jupiter** are naturally connected to the idea of enjoying ourselves. Venus in the 5th, for instance, could mean your chosen hobby is dance or dressmaking; Jupiter here might incline you to hobbies that encourage learning and other forms of enrichment.

Other planets might seem not so suited to the 5th house, and yet whatever you have here can be the basis of recreational activities that help to renew and restore the spirit. With **Saturn** here for example, you might garner respect as the referee for the local football team; with the centaur **Chiron** here, perhaps archery would be something to consider.

5th house see pp.98-99

> If you want to take up a **sport**, it is worth assessing your **Mars** and playing to its strengths.

YOUR **PLANETS**

♂ **Mars** If you want to take up a sport, it is worth assessing your Mars and playing to its strengths. If you have Mars in **Virgo** in the 3rd, for instance, you might be better off choosing a solitary activity (Virgo is a self-contained sign) that allows you to explore the local area–walking would suit this. Or if you have Mars in **Aries**, you might prefer something more heated and competitive, such as boxing or mixed martial arts. Mars in **Libra** suggests fencing or tennis (two people on opposing sides politely

outdoing each other according to a strict set of rules); Mars in **Sagittarius** might favor long-distance running.

Mars shows how you like to work up a sweat–or if you like to do this at all. For some, the slow burn keeps them on track far better than a full-on boot-camp workout.

Choosing a hobby or a sport
Aside from the 5th house and Mars, there will always be clues in the rest of your chart as to what you might be interested in doing in your spare time or what kind of athletic activity you might be best suited to. For instance, if you have a prominent **Neptune**, you might be a keen photographer or enjoy

swimming. Or with a powerfully placed **Saturn**, perhaps mountain climbing is your thing. Chess suits the strategically minded–perhaps **Mercury** in Capricorn. Calligraphy might appeal to anyone with a **Mercury-Venus** contact or **Venus** in the 3rd, signifying "beautiful writing." As with most things, many aspects of your chart will be implicated in your choice of pastime, and you might draw on a number of different factors which, combined together in some particular activity, create the perfect day off.

The Planets see pp.62-85

YOUR **ZODIAC SIGNS**

The mix of signs in your chart creates your basic temperament, which in turn inclines you to enjoy certain activities and not others.

The **fire signs** tend to be naturally playful, particularly **Leo**, with **Sagittarius** needing open space and **Aries** the cut and thrust of competition.

The **earth signs** are practical and focused on the physical–**Taurus** might incline to gardening, **Virgo** to crafts, and **Capricorn** to model-making or DIY.

The **air signs** tend to prefer civilized pursuits or ones involving sociable company– **Gemini** enjoys reading or taking a class, **Libra** might favor the gentle movements of yoga or tai chi, and **Aquarius** likes something intellectually stimulating.

The **water signs** imply the use of imagination or emotional involvement: **Cancer** might like nothing better than a magical day by the ocean, **Scorpio** tends toward activities that involve endurance, and **Pisces** (like its ruler Neptune) suggests image-making, perhaps watercolors or photography.

PERSONAL PROJECTS

HOW TO RELEASE YOUR IMAGINATION

Away from the pressures of everyday life, we can come alive when we tap into our creative potential. The Sun and the 5th house reflect the vital life spirit, and Neptune and the 12th the world of imagination.

YOUR **HOUSES**

 **The 5th house
- the creative impulse**

The 5th is traditionally associated with creativity. The most fundamental act of creation is to give birth to a child - children therefore belong to this house, along with all the other creative activities that carry our vital spark out into the world.

Pluto in the 5th might confer the gift of writing a good detective novel; or **Uranus** here might suggest that creative ideas fall like heavenly sparks, trying to find a place to land and take root. Further information is supplied by the sign on the cusp and the planetary ruler of that sign, and of course the aspects that your 5th house planets make to other planets in the chart - all of this will collectively form an image of what creativity means to you.

 **The 12th house -
image & imagination**

The 12th is a place where you can conjure images and connect to non-ordinary worlds. For instance, with **Mercury** here you might be interested in myths and fairy tales, or be attracted to symbolic languages (such as astrology!). Or with **Venus** here, perhaps art or photography appeal to you, or losing yourself in a romantic novel (or writing one). Even **Saturn** enters into the spirit in this house - Saturn here might serve you well if you are a designer, a composer, or the manager of an art gallery, giving form and substance to imaginative conceptions.

5th house see pp.98-99
12th house see pp.114-15

YOUR **PLANETS**

The Sun is the heart center, and its symbol is a reminder of this: a central point of light within a containing circle. Thus your Sun, by sign, house, and aspect, offers an image of whatever you are bringing to life that will stand as a testament to your specialness and unique gifts.

We are all creative in terms of the Sun. If your Sun is in **Gemini**, for instance, then your task might be to develop your linguistic and verbal skills, so that these can shine and attract admiration. If your Sun is in aspect to **Chiron**, then somehow your destiny is to live an aspect of the centaur's story as wounded healer and inventive outsider, creative entirely on your own terms.

Neptune Through Neptune, we enter into the imagination. Neptune distorts reality enough for us to slip through into a more fantastical frame of mind, and any planets or angles that Neptune is in aspect to will be seen through the lens of your imagination and be swept up into a dream or a romance.

>> **The Sun** see pp.62-63
Neptune see pp.80-81

> **Neptune** distorts reality enough for us to slip through into a more **fantastical** frame of mind.

YOUR **ZODIAC SIGNS**

No particular zodiac sign has a monopoly on creativity—with the zodiac being a symbol of the Sun's annual journey, all 12 signs are creative in their own way. Some astrologers describe **Leo** as "creative" and **Libra** or **Pisces** as "artistic," but the unique mix of signs in your chart creates your own unique brand of creativity. People with strong fire and water signs may be inclined to live in their imaginations much of the time, fire focused on vision and water on feelings, but all 12 signs contain their own gifts of creative expression.

For instance, if you have planets in **Cancer** and **Libra**, your creativity may be focused on the domestic sphere (Cancer) where you can use an aesthetic eye (Libra) to develop interior design skills. Or with planets in **Virgo** and **Capricorn**, garden design might appeal, bringing a love of plants together with skills at practical construction. As with everything else in astrology, the key to releasing your imagination is to open up the possibilities of each symbol.

RELATIONSHIPS

HOW WE RELATE TO OTHER PEOPLE

Relationships are at the heart of life. We identify ourselves by them–we are someone's spouse, parent, cousin, friend, boss, colleague, or adversary. Astrology can shed light on how we relate and what issues might emerge in the process.

YOUR **ZODIAC SIGNS**

Compatibility

Popular books on astrology often convey the idea that certain signs will easily get along and other combinations are a recipe for disaster–for instance, that two people with their **Sun** in air signs are compatible, but a couple with different **Moon** signs are bound to run into problems.

The reality is more complex; a relationship can only be understood in the context of the whole birth chart and the life stories of each person involved. The notion of compatibility is an intricate one and, since relationships are arguably the most powerful medium for our growth and self-development, it is worth considering that we are most drawn toward people who help to catalyze this process in us. In other words, the relationship is ultimately to ourselves but conducted through other people, and we are attracted to them because they have something we need

or want, or are trying to process or come to terms with.

This is perhaps particularly so in romantic relationships and long-term partnerships, where complexes and embedded family patterns are often reawakened. But it can apply equally to boss-employee relationships, or colleague to colleague, or with anyone with whom you spend time.

Growth through relationship

Whatever relationships you have experienced, perhaps you might see them all as an important part of your process of understanding and becoming yourself. This makes the notion of compatibility perhaps less important than reflecting on why you might have been drawn to that person in the first place. If it is someone you love, you might ask yourself why you love or admire that person so much; if it is someone you loathe, you might equally ask yourself why, and what your emotional investment might be in maintaining contact with them.

> A **relationship** can only be understood in the context of the whole birth chart and the **life stories** of each person involved.

YOUR **PLANETS**

☽ **The Moon** is perhaps the key planet of relationship in that it suggests how we form emotional bonds – how we nurture and care for others, and what we need from them in return in order to feel safe and comfortable. If your Moon is in a **fire sign** for instance, there is a need for life to be a colourful place of risks and potentials; if your partner or boss conversely has the Moon in an **earth sign**, your enthusiasm might well elicit an annoyingly sensible and risk-averse response that leaves you feeling flat. We are all driven by our basic instincts when it comes to our Moon.

♀ **Venus** suggests a more adult level of affection and bonding – what we want others to appreciate and admire in us. The position of your Venus, by sign and house, as well as the aspects it makes to other planets, indicates what you find attractive and what you need in order to get on well with someone – for a relationship to work, there needs to be mutual appreciation of each other's desire nature. This is harder work of course if your Venus is, say, in **Capricorn** or in aspect to **Saturn** (suggesting a controlled and self-contained relating style) and your partner or friend has Venus in **Sagittarius** or aspecting **Jupiter** (suggesting an extraverted aesthetic and enjoyment of the good life).

» **The Planets** see pp.62-85

YOUR **HOUSES**

Particular houses reflect particular types of relationship. **The 7th** and **8th** reflect the notion of one-to-one encounters and are conjured particularly in longer-term partnerships and marriages. Planets in your 7th house, as well as the sign on the cusp (the Descendant) show what you seek from another person because it is not initially well-developed in yourself and relationship has the power to bring it alive. Planets in your 8th house (and the cuspal sign) suggest the dynamics arising in deeper emotional connections, and the more planets you have here, the more you might be drawn to relationships that have the power to transform you.

The 5th is the house of romance and of children, **the 4th** the house of family. Indeed all the houses reflect some kind of relationship, except perhaps the 1st and the 2nd (which suggest only the relationship to yourself and your personal resources).

» **The Houses** see pp.90-115

RELATIVES

UNDERSTANDING THE DYNAMICS OF FAMILY LIFE

Many chart factors are involved in creating the complex picture of family life – the 4th as house and home, the 10th and Saturn as parental authority, and the Sun and Moon as father and mother, rounded off by siblings in the 3rd and children in the 5th.

YOUR **HOUSES**

The 4th house describes both your home of origin and the one you have created (or will create) for yourself. It is both the bricks and mortar and the atmosphere and dynamic that binds the family unit. This is also the tap root down into your history: your genealogy and family tree. Whatever planets reside here, and planets conjunct to the IC (the cusp of the 4th) will form your foundations.

The MC and 10th house lie opposite the 4th house and between them they denote the idea of parents – mother traditionally in the 10th and father traditionally in the 4th, but we might take the view that whichever parent provided 4th house things (security, lineage, surname) belongs in the 4th, and whichever parent provided 10th house things (socialization, authority, plans for the future) belongs in the 10th, which for most of us is likely to be both parents. Just as the 4th describes the kind of home we create for ourselves, so the 10th will describe what kind of parent you might become, taking control and responsibility.

The 3rd house describes our relationship to siblings and cousins. **Mars** here suggests rivalry, **Uranus** a sense of separation, **Chiron** loss or loneliness. It shows the nature of our sibling dynamics, often reappearing as themes in our adult peer relationships.

The 5th house, and the sign on the cusp, will describe key features of your relationship with your children, including the feelings you have around the whole process of conception, pregnancy, and giving birth. Having **Saturn** in this house doesn't mean your experience of birth or bringing up your children will be a negative one – it might simply suggest that you keenly feel the gravity and responsibility of child rearing. Having no planets here similarly does not mean you will be childless; it merely suggests that other areas of your life are likely to be the more transformative and demanding.

≫ The Houses see pp.90-115

> It is possible to see your relationship to **sisters** reflected in **Venus** in your chart and your relationship to **brothers** reflected in **Mars**.

YOUR **PLANETS**

The Sun and Saturn round out the picture of authority in different ways. Again, this can attach itself to either parent, although the Sun often has a masculine quality, and we find it being descriptive of the relationship we make to our father, as well as the kind of father a man might become.

The Moon is a traditional significator of the mother, although more accurately it describes our need for caretaking and nourishment and the relationship we make to those who provide it–as well as the kind of mother, caretaker, cook, and provider we might become.

It is also possible to see your relationship to sisters reflected in **Venus** in your chart and your relationship to brothers reflected in **Mars** as symbolic images of the young feminine and the young masculine respectively. **Mercury** can suggest your relationship to your siblings.

 **The Planets** see pp.62-85

YOUR **ZODIAC SIGNS**

The mix of signs in your chart can be helpful in understanding the role you play within your family.

For instance, each element behaves quite differently. If you have a predominance of **water** in your chart but your family has an emphasis on **air**, you might feel like you speak a different language to the rest of the household, one that requires you to rationalize your intuitions. Two parents with strong **earth** content in their chart may struggle to understand their **fire** child, who seems like a cuckoo in the nest: boisterous, fearless, and full of life.

Aside from this, certain signs are associated more readily with certain sorts of relationships. For instance, **Gemini** is the sign of the twins, and if you have personal planets in Gemini (particularly your Sun or Moon, or your chart ruler), then your siblings may have played quite a formative role in your life. Alternatively, **Cancer** suggests an affinity with a mothering role, and perhaps by extension a particular closeness to mother herself–and **Capricorn** to father.

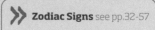 **Zodiac Signs** see pp.32-57

FRIENDSHIP

NURTURING YOUR COMPANIONS

Friendships are a matter of choice, a reflection of our values and ideals. Along with family ties and romantic relationships, friendship is no less important an arena for self-development and for discovering your place in the world. To better understand your approach to friendship, explore the following areas of your chart. A useful place to start is the 11th house.

YOUR **HOUSES**

The 11th house is at the centre of your experience of friendship. Your role in a friendship group echoes whatever planets you have here. Just comparing **Jupiter** and **Saturn** gives us an idea. If you have Jupiter in the 11th, friendship feels liberating and joyful, a source of opportunities for travel or self-improvement. Conversely, if Saturn is here, being in a group might conjure feelings of separateness and self-containment, so that each friendship is a huge investment of time, energy, and commitment.

Tackling problems

Your 11th house also provides clues as to how to approach problems in a friendship, since the 11th can reflect a clash of social values or evoke early memories. If you have **Uranus** here, for example, a clash of views might reflect an unwillingness to compromise your ideals – or **Chiron** might mean being sensitive to rejection or being different.

The sign on the cusp of the 11th also sets the tone for your approach to group activities, and the planetary ruler fine-tunes this. With **Gemini** on the cusp, for example, your approach to friendship will be light and sociable, perhaps with a need for many and diverse contacts.

The 3rd house encompasses school friends, siblings, and other members of your family with whom you have a peer-like relationship. This is a helpful place to look when problems arise in adult friendships as these early experiences can be unconsciously aroused in later life.

For example, if you have **Mars** here, you might have felt the need to compete with siblings and schoolfriends, a dynamic that could persist as an instinct to see off rivals or dominate the conversation. On the other hand, if you have **Pluto** here, an early experience of betrayal involving a sibling, or trauma connected to schooling, can impact levels of trust within your companionships.

 11th house see pp.112-13
3rd house see pp.94-95

YOUR **PLANETS**

 The Sun shows you what you seek to develop in yourself. This can be reflected in your choice of friends, as you often feel most comfortable with people who reflect the characteristics of your Sun. For example, if you have the Sun in **Cancer**, you might seek emotional closeness, since the journey of the Cancer Sun is to find one's tribe and then take care of it. By contrast, if you have the Sun in **Capricorn**, you may choose friends who show self-reliance and authority because you admire these skills and are developing them within yourself.

 Venus is a cohesive force, suggesting your style of making bonds and finding common ground. Even in the closest friendship, the Venusian dance of mutual respect is at work. If this fails, so might the friendship. If you have Venus in **Aquarius**, for example, the eclectic nature of your friendship group might be based on a belief of giving equal value to all; by contrast, if your friend has Venus in **Leo**, they might not fully appreciate your tendency to treat everyone the same and begin to doubt your loyalty.

The Sun see pp.62–63
Venus see pp.68–69

> Even in the closest friendship, the Venusian dance of **mutual respect** is at work.

YOUR **ZODIAC SIGNS**

Polarity
- **Positive** signs tend to need more social contact than the negative ones.
- **Negative** signs are often happier in their own company or prefer smaller groups.

The elements
- **Fire** signs tend to seek fun and adventure with friends.
- **Air** signs prefer intellectual and social connection.
- **Water** signs seek an emotional type of bond.
- **Earth** signs often conduct relationships at a slower pace than other signs.

Polarity & elements see pp.28–31
Zodiac signs see pp.32–57

ROMANCE & SEX

HOW TO FIND JOY IN INTIMACY

Your chart will reveal different levels of the experience of love, from brief romantic encounters to the deeper connections that can develop out of sexual intimacy. From erotic love to devoted affection, astrology reflects all these.

YOUR **HOUSES**

 The 5th house is where ancient astrologers located the procreative act – after all, this is the house of children, and the one leads to the other.

But this is also a house suggesting the idea of our creative seed, on all sorts of levels, so the sex we have in the 5th reinforces our personal reproductive power. This is perhaps the essence of romance and the mating game – that it is ultimately an expression of our essence, fertility, potency, our "pulling power".

What this revolves around for you will be shown by any planets here, the aspects they make to other planets in the chart, and of course, as always, the sign on the cusp and its planetary ruler. If you have **Mars** here for example, your assessment of your strength, vitality, and effectiveness will be directly linked to your sexuality; with **Mercury** perhaps the game and intrigue of romance, or the sound of a lover's voice, is the spark that fans the flame. Libra on the cusp suggests you like to play fair with lovers – **Venus** rules

Libra, and if your Venus is in the 12th house for instance, it adds a sense of longing and fantasy to your romantic life.

The 8th house is the house of deep intimate involvement, and also describes aspects of sexual experience, albeit very different to the joyful experience the 5th is designed to be. In the 8th we let down our guard in order to share ourselves completely with another person. The Victorians referred to the orgasm as "la petite mort", the little death, which fits perfectly with the meaning of the 8th house as a house of transformation through renunciation of personal power and separateness. So having **Saturn** here might suggest some wariness and barriers to intimacy – whereas **Neptune** might generate feelings of being open and porous in the sexual act, and thirsty for complete union and merging with a lover.

>> **The Houses**
see pp.90-115

Venus and Mars contribute directly to our picture of **sex and romance** in the chart.

YOUR **PLANETS**

Venus and Mars contribute directly to our picture of sex and romance in the chart.

♀ **Venus** reflects the classic feminine deities of erotic love, such as Aphrodite, Inanna, and Ishtar–images of the romantic impulse.

♂ **Mars** reflects the classic masculine warrior deities, such as Ares and Nergal–fiery and potent.

In the chart, Venus and Mars balance and complement each other and combine to show the seductive, sensuous, affectionate (Venus) and heated, passionate, ardent (Mars) aspects of sexual attraction. We each show these in our different ways according to the placements by sign and house, the aspects that Venus and Mars make to other planets, and the houses they rule in our chart.

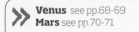

Venus see pp.68-69
Mars see pp.70-71

YOUR **ZODIAC SIGNS**

Some astrologers cast **Scorpio** as the sexpot of the zodiac, citing its reputation for passion and its rulership by fiery Mars. We might note Scorpio's affinity with the deep, the dark, and the dangerous. But conversely, Scorpio is also a very private sign and often very self-contained.

Virgo is often portrayed as fussy–the dozen red roses don't mean anything if the sheets aren't clean–but it is after all an earth sign, needing physical connection, unlike **Pisces**, where the focus is on romantic fantasy.

The **earth signs** in general are focused on the physical side of sex–how it feels in the body. The **fire signs** make adventurous lovers, the **air signs** fall in love with a person they can talk to, and the **water signs** need to be on the same emotional wavelength for love to blossom.

MARRIAGE

LONG-TERM PARTNERSHIPS: CLOSENESS OVER TIME

Marriage and long-term partnership belong to the 7th as the house of contractual relationship and to the 8th as the relationship lays down ever-deeper bonds. Saturn in your chart too can indicate commitment and longevity.

YOUR **HOUSES**

The 7th house - the hook of love

Whatever is in your 7th house (even if this is just the sign on the Descendant and of course by extension its planetary ruler) provides a powerful "hook" for your relationships and it is unlikely that any long-term partnership will take hold that does not pivot on this. This is the place in your chart where something lies in shadow and is waiting to be ignited within you, and one of the primary ways you will do this is through your relationships.

So if your relationship has run into difficulties, or if your efforts at partnership always seem to end in disaster, it is worth examining your 7th house for clues as to why. From this point of view, astrology suggests that there is no such thing as a "failed relationship" – there is only relationship, as a vessel for the work of becoming yourself.

The 8th house - till death us do part

After the contractual side of things in the 7th, the 8th takes us into deeper processes of intimacy and sharing. It is here that we take a dive into the unknown, entwine our financial fortunes with someone else and risk laying ourselves open to loss, divorce, grief, or betrayal. After a time, any relationship must move into this territory and weather the emotional storm – or be dashed on the rocks. An even more profound alchemy occurs here than in the 7th house – at least, one which is perhaps enacted at a more internal and emotional level, rather than an outer one. Any planets you have here, and the planetary ruler of the sign on the cusp, will be players in this process, a part of you which is likely to be completely transformed by relationship.

> " The **8th** house takes us into deeper processes of **intimacy and sharing**. "

7th house see pp.104-05
8th house see pp.106-07

YOUR **PLANETS**

♄ **Saturn** initializes a process of development within each of us that demands our dedication. If Saturn falls in one of your relationship houses, or it aspects the Moon or Venus in your chart, you might seek a long-term commitment.

☽ **The Moon** will always be conjured in a marriage or romantic partnership–the Moon is our basic ground, the needs that must be met in order for us to thrive.

♀ **Venus** is the beautiful garden of attraction, respect, and sensual love that makes a marriage more than just an exercise in mutual caretaking.

>> **The Planets** see pp.62-85

YOUR **ZODIAC SIGNS**

We can get an overview of the signs by exploring how the **three modes–cardinal**, **fixed**, **and mutable** signs–might operate in relationship. Apply this to your own chart by counting the number of planets in each mode. You can also look at the signs on the cusp of your relationship houses, the 7th and the 8th.

The cardinal signs (Aries, Cancer, Libra, and Capricorn) like to keep things moving–a relationship may need to feel as though it is going somewhere. Even for safety-conscious Cancer, a partnership may begin to feel stale if there is no clear trajectory or sense of development.

The fixed signs (Taurus, Leo, Scorpio, and Aquarius) fare best when there is stability and time to put down roots. Although Scorpio conjures the idea of deep transformation, this tends to happen over a long period of time. For these signs, it is important to stay the course.

The mutable signs (Sagittarius, Gemini, Virgo, and Pisces) can be wary of commitment. If you have these signs dominant, this does not mean you are incapable of a long-term relationship, merely that the relationship needs to have built-in flexibility or variety to engage your focus year after year–otherwise, you can feel trapped or bored. Freedom is a key ingredient.

>> **The Modes** see pp.28-31

"A PERSON'S CHART IS THE **DOOR OPENING** US INTO THEIR **MYTHICAL SYSTEM**."

Richard Idemon, Through the Looking Glass:
A Search for the Self in the Mirror of Relationships

PROFESSIONAL RELATIONSHIPS

WORKING WITH OTHER PEOPLE

Professional relationships draw on certain areas of your chart. The 6th house describes your relationship to work colleagues, whereas the 10th describes your relationship to the boss, as well as how you yourself might function in a position of management.

YOUR **HOUSES**

 The 6th house
– getting on with your colleagues

The 6th house specifically covers the idea of working relationships. It describes not only how you relate to those you work alongside, it also describes how it might feel to be an employee. So the 6th house covers different dimensions of working life: being a cog in the company machine, employing other people, and getting on with your co-workers.

 The 10th house
– hierarchies and chains of command

The 10th is associated with the idea of rulership and management. Crucially for working relationships, the 10th is where your feelings about the boss, and equally your feelings about taking command, will kick in. Whatever planets you have here will colour very closely the kind of relationship you are likely to create with those who manage you at work, as well as how you may feel about giving professional instruction to others.

Being a parental house, the link is made to early relationships with authority figures which can re-emerge in later life as an issue with the boss or a crisis in your own capacity to lead the troops.

Whatever was constellated in your relationships to your parents, schoolteachers, and other community leaders has the power to shape all other expressions of this house in the years to come. As children, we watch how our parents do things and absorb this into our view of how things ought to be done – so it is useful to think about how your parents might have felt about being in control and being responsible, how they felt about being out in the world and making their professional mark, since all of this can be reflected in your 10th-house planets and signs.

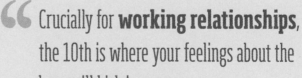
> Crucially for **working relationships**, the 10th is where your feelings about the boss will kick in.

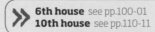

6th house see pp.100-01
10th house see pp.110-11

YOUR **PLANETS**

There are no planets specifically associated with professional relationships – but we can explore here a few examples of different planets in the "work houses", 6th and 10th:

♅ Uranus If you have Uranus in the 10th, perhaps you prefer a freelance lifestyle, or a job with freedom, where you neither have to issue orders nor bend yourself to them.

♄ Saturn With Saturn in the 10th on the other hand, you might seek to fit into the office hierarchy and fulfil expectations.

☿ Mercury in the 6th makes dialogue and lines of communication a potential skill for you in the workplace, a way to smooth things over with your colleagues or get those who work for you alongside – or you might naturally assume a role as the office grapevine.

You can extend your understanding of this by looking, as ever, at the aspects which any 6th-house planets are making to other planets in your chart. For instance, an opposition from **Pluto** in the 12th to the **Mercury** in the 6th adds a darker turn to communication, perhaps suggesting sensitivity to intrigue or keeping secrets in the workplace which might threaten to undermine good relations.

YOUR **ZODIAC SIGNS**

As with all things, each sign will have its own style when it comes to conducting professional relationships. No one sign is better suited to this than the others and we must all play to our strengths. Recognizing motivations can go a long way to creating a happy workplace.

To illustrate this, if you have the **Sun in Leo**, wherever this is situated in your chart, you probably want to take a central and controlling position. It is hard for you to be in a subordinate role. Thus, professional relationships can become strained if you feel ordered around, or your view is questioned by your colleagues.

As another example, if you have a **cardinal T-square** in your chart, particularly if it includes planets in **Aries** and **Capricorn**, this suggests you possess an inner dynamo of energy - you are goal focused and tend to get things done quickly.

Getting on with others in the workplace can be challenging, but even a simple knowledge of someone's **Sun, Moon, or Ascendant sign** can help you to understand their actions and create a smoother working relationship.

》 The Planets see pp.62-85

》 Zodiac Signs see pp.32-57

CAREER

ACHIEVING YOUR AMBITIONS

The MC and the 10th is the place to look for a view of your career and ambitions. But we can also look to the Sun as the creative heart of your chart and to Saturn as an image of striving for worldly success.

YOUR **PLANETS**

The Sun should be able to shine its light at the heart of any career. If we are not using our solar qualities and gifts in the work we do, it is unlikely to be satisfying, and we may end up straying from it–or having a crisis at midlife or at a time of a major planetary transit to the Sun.

Uniting the Sun's creative impulse toward individuality with the worldly ambitions of the **MC and the 10th house** can sometimes be a challenge, particularly if the Sun is not connected in any way to your 10th or is connected by a hard aspect to a planet there (indicating stress at trying to reconcile the two).

Saturn in your chart shows a place where you seek to achieve something concrete–the fruit of hard labor. Often then, this can be implicated in your professional choices, since Saturn can bring a sense of tremendous satisfaction and is a place where we seek recognition and respect. We typically "professionalize" things where Saturn is–we demand high standards and strive to be a success.

The Nodal Axis Although not connected directly to your professional aspirations, the Nodes reflect a process of moving between past and future, taking natural skills and then pushing to develop new ones that stretch you out of your comfort zone.

The Nodes indicate a process of self-development, so you might look to your **North Node** to describe something that you are in the process of making or creating. Whatever it is might not show obviously in what you do for a living, yet you might be prompted by it in your yearnings for achievement.

>> **The Planets** see pp.62-85
The Nodal Axis see p.124

YOUR **HOUSES**

 The MC and the 10th house
The MC is where planets are said to "culminate" in their daily journey across the sky. On a metaphoric level, we can say that this is where life culminates too, where we reach for recognition, success, and accomplishment.

By extension the **10th house** (which the MC forms the "cusp" or beginning of) is also implicated to a high degree. Planets in this house will form the basis of your career path, either literally (**Uranus** in the 10th as the electrician, **Neptune** in the 10th as the chiropodist, **the Moon** in the 10th as the care assistant, and so on) or psychologically (Uranus as the person who rejects orthodoxy and goes their own way; Neptune as the person who drifts for a time and then finds their destiny through a spiritual awakening; the Moon as professional "mother" who seeks to nurture and foster).

In this area of life, we might initially follow in our parents' footsteps, carrying on the family business or doing the job we think is expected of us. Sooner or later though, we are likely to connect with our own destiny and carve out a space for ourselves.

>> **10th house**
see pp.110-11

YOUR **ZODIAC SIGNS**

Each sign suggests a particular orientation and field of experience. So your choice of career will reflect the motivations, skills, and drives of the signs that are most prominent in your chart. Your Sun and MC signs will lead this, as we have seen, but other planetary placements will be significant too, as will your Ascendant sign.

For instance, if you have **the Sun in Gemini**, you might choose a profession that revolves around communication, allowing you to develop talents at writing or languages. This is your creative purpose. If you also have the **Ascendant in Pisces**, there might be an imaginative slant to your writing, a touch of poetry or magic in the way you express things.

Or with **the Sun in Virgo**, your life purpose might be to develop technical proficiency in your chosen craft. If you also have planets in **Libra**, the creation process benefits from your artistry and love of beauty and good design.

>> **Zodiac Signs** see pp.32-57

> " **Saturn** in your chart shows a place where you seek to **achieve** something concrete, the fruit of hard labour. "

MONEY

HOW TO HANDLE FINANCIAL MATTERS

The axis of the 2nd and 8th houses supplies much of our information concerning money and finance, showing the interplay between personal and shared material resources. Venus adds to our definition of worth and value.

YOUR **HOUSES**

The 2nd house - what's mine is mine

If you want a window onto your own personal finances, look to your 2nd house. As ever, the 2nd consists of an interweave of factors – any planets here and the planets they are making aspects to, plus the sign on the cusp and its planetary ruler/s. What you will find here describes both your attitude to money and your material circumstances, the latter arguably arising from the former.

The 8th house - what's ours might be a problem

The 8th describes everything to do with money and goods that are shared with a partner – anything from major items such as a mortgage or a shared bank account to everyday things such as the weekly shared shopping. They say that money is one of the flash points in any relationship and we can perhaps see the connection here to the deeper meanings of the 8th, as a place where a relationship can easily slip into a power battle. No doubt many an argument might be averted by understanding better the kind of feelings that are evoked for us when it comes to joint decisions over money.

Implicit with the 8th is the idea of indebtedness, so whatever planets and signs you have here will show how comfortable you feel around this. For example, Aries on the cusp of the 8th might mean you charge headlong into financial arrangements. On the other hand, a water sign on this cusp might suggest an emotional approach and being best guided by your instincts.

>> **2nd house** see pp.92-93
8th house see pp.106-07

> We are inclined to accord **value** to whatever **Venus** touches in our chart.

YOUR **PLANETS**

♀ **Venus** We are inclined to accord value to whatever Venus touches in our chart, and it will therefore describe what we are prepared to spend money on, because we count it as valuable and desirable. So you can look to your Venus for an image of what you are inclined to throw your resources into.

For instance, if you have Venus in aspect to **Jupiter** in your chart, perhaps you enjoy traveling and are happy to spend money on this; or if you have Venus in aspect to **Saturn**, perhaps you like things that are well made, like tailored clothes, and are prepared to pay a little more for something classic. Venus in **Leo** suggests a desire for good quality–Venus in the 11th suggests you value your social life and are happy to spend a little more to have a good time.

>> **Venus** see pp.68-69

YOUR **ZODIAC SIGNS**

♉ **Taurus** The sign of Taurus is also implicated in financial matters. Where Taurus is in your chart, you will want to consolidate–energetically, it suggests the idea of physical or material goods through being the fixed earth sign. While this does not equate directly with money, as a sign many astrologers associate it with finance and banking, and this might be an area of professional interest or talent for you if you have personal planets in this sign.

The other two earth signs can suggest a similar talent or facility with money and material things, if you have personal planets here–**Virgo** for its careful thrift and **Capricorn** for a sensible and level-headed approach to pretty much everything.

>> **Zodiac Signs** see pp.32-57

MOTIVATION

HOW TO GEAR UP FOR ACTION AND ACHIEVEMENT

Action and initiative suggest the planet Mars. Whatever house your Mars occupies will be a major focus for your energy and a place where you can come alive. Dynamic Aries, the cardinal fire sign, is also worth exploring.

YOUR **PLANETS**

 Mars If you want to locate the "get up and go" in your chart, look to your Mars. We all have a different martial style and you can play to the strengths of your Mars to create the right climate for achievement.

Some are suited to dynamic action (Mars in **Aries** or **Capricorn** for instance), others suit the slow burn (Mars in **Taurus** or **Scorpio**); some may often appear not to be acting at all (Mars in mutable **Gemini** or **Pisces** perhaps) but given the right set of circumstances their will is engaged and achievement is possible. If you have Mars in the so-called "double-bodied" signs of **Gemini**, **Virgo**, **Sagittarius**, or **Pisces**, it might be natural to you to prevaricate, hedge your bets, or change your mind, but when engaged in activities that suit the sign (communicating for Gemini, crafting for Virgo, travelling for Sagittarius, and devoting yourself for

Pisces) you can summon up significant strength and motivation. Even Mars in Venus-ruled Libra can focus energy – this is a good placement for dance or yoga.

Hard aspects
It is worth taking a look at the mix of aspect types in your chart. Planets that are linked by **square**, **semi-square**, or **sesquiquadrate** tend to form complexes of dynamic energy where you work hard to move and shake.

As a rule of thumb, the more you have of these, the busier your life is likely to be and the more driven you might be to show dynamic action – particularly if the planets are in cardinal or mutable signs, all of which contain an inbuilt desire for movement.

> **"** If you want to locate the **'get up and go'** in your chart, look to your **Mars**. **"**

The Planets see pp.62-85
Aspects see pp.130-31

YOUR **ZODIAC SIGNS**

Aries The Mars-ruled fire sign of Aries is also significant, if only to indicate a house in your chart that galvanizes you to action. If you have no planets in Aries and it just lies on the cusp of one of your houses, that will be an area of your life where "carpe diem" will be your motto – Mars will be the planetary ruler of this house and the two things will be linked.

For instance, if you have Aries on the cusp of the 11th house, making new friends or creating a new social network are things that you can easily do from a standing start. Indeed, your life path may mean you having to do this more than once. Then if ruler Mars is placed in the 9th, perhaps the motivation for being socially proactive is to travel with exciting go-ahead friends and bravely explore more of the world.

>> **Aries** see pp.32-33

YOUR **HOUSES**

The Ascendant and the MC These two points in your chart each play a role when it comes to gearing up for action.

Your Ascendant sign and any planets here (and in the 1st) will shape how you begin each new project and it is important that you honour this. With **Taurus** rising, each new beginning cannot be rushed; with **Capricorn** rising, you might be eager to begin but only if you feel in charge; with **Libra**, perhaps you seek to make sure that everyone is happy before proceeding.

Your MC is a point where you actively reach for achievement and success – so the sign on the MC and planets here (and in the 10th) will indicate whether you see a glass ceiling or an unlimited sky. If you have **Cancer** here you might count success in emotional terms rather than material ones; or if **Leo**, then you need your accomplishments to shine and be noticed.

>> **The MC** see pp.122-23

BELIEFS

HOW TO ANSWER THE BIG QUESTIONS

Religion and spirituality in a birth chart centre around the 9th and 12th houses, and around Jupiter and Neptune, along with the signs ruled by these planets. These will form the basis of your particular belief system.

YOUR **HOUSES**

Religion and spirituality are often defined differently and it is not unheard of for people to identify themselves as "spiritual" but not "religious". So we need to take a broad view of what might contribute to the overall picture of a person's belief system.

Like most things, it is also true that the whole chart somehow plays its part in shaping our view of the divine; the god we worship arguably reflects our own outlook on life.

The 9th house - the "house of god"
It is here that you will find the foundation of whatever creed or moral philosophy you espouse. **Saturn** here might suggest you prefer a fully worked-out system that supplies concrete answers, and a deity who exudes authority and holds you to the rule of law. **The Moon** here might suggest a feminine aspect to deity or a preference for

a spiritual system centred around family and community. Aspects to any planets you have here will extend this by denoting what conflicts or crises of faith you might experience in grappling with the metaphysical (in the hard aspects) or what feels supportive and nourishing to your beliefs (in the soft aspects).

The 12th house - spirituality
Although not traditionally associated with religion or belief, many modern astrologers look to the 12th house, and to **Neptune** and **Pisces**, as signifiers of spirituality. This perhaps has its roots in the decline of organized religion in the West and the increasing interest in global spiritual outlooks, which has resulted in very individual definitions of spirituality, often drawn from a kaleidoscope of traditions.

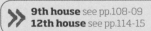
9th house see pp.108-09
12th house see pp.114-15

YOUR **PLANETS**

Jupiter represents the capacity within us to make a leap of faith, and its placement can describe aspects of your chosen religion or system of thought. Or if you have personal planets in **Sagittarius**, one of the two signs that Jupiter rules, perhaps you have a philosophical frame of mind—and/or the house with this sign on the cusp might be an area of your life in which you are particularly inclined to quest and search for answers.

Any planets you have in your 12th house will express themselves as much in your imagination as they do in the world of form and matter, and these planets, along with your **Neptune** placement and planets/house cusps in Pisces, can suggest the ways in which you connect to unseen worlds.

The Planets see pp.62-85

YOUR **ZODIAC SIGNS**

The elements

Fire Of the four elements, fire is the most naturally attuned to the idea of belief, and the more planets you have in fire signs, the more you might be comfortable with believing in something you cannot see. This does not necessarily mean you are religious—but if you are, then it suggests you might be less driven to question the reality or provability of your chosen creed.

Air On the other hand, air tends to be the cynic, needing a logical argument and trying to apply rationality to matters of faith.

Earth is the pragmatist, perhaps more given to living life in the here and now—or perhaps God is to be found in nature rather than floating on a cloud.

Water is usually content with the unanswered questions that abound in religion; for a watery person, it does not need to be neatly worked out, as long as it makes sense inside.

" We need to take a **broad view** of what might contribute to the overall picture of a person's **belief system**. "

ASTROLOGY IN
LIFE EVENTS

LIFE EVENTS
AN OVERVIEW

FORECASTING WITH ASTROLOGY

Important to an understanding of life events is an appreciation that no chart is ever still – the planets continue to orbit around, producing "transits" over your planets, angles, and houses that reflect the energy of any given moment.

Planetary transits

Transits are astrology's key forecasting tool. They reflect the current situation, but also the past and what the future might hold. The word means "'crossing": a planet moving across something in your chart. You can follow the planets as they move on from their birth positions. They cross angles, enter and leave houses, and form aspects to the planets and other chart factors, creating a constantly moving dynamic picture.

At any given time, your transits will highlight certain areas of your chart. Each reflects how you feel at that time, the deeper meaning of the events that arise, and what response might be appropriate and fruitful. A planet can transit in conjunction – or in square, opposition, trine, or any other type of aspect, each of which brings its own particular quality of experience.

Checking your own transits

You can check current planetary positions in an "ephemeris". For instance, if your Sun is at 27° Aries, check to see what transiting planets are within close range (1°-2° orb) of this. You can either invest in a paper ephemeris or use one of the many free online versions (try www.astro.com).

The planets from Mercury outwards all go retrograde at some point in their cycle. This means that by transit they can pass three, or even five, times over a point in your birth chart.

Pluto, Neptune, and Uranus

transits take at least one year from first to last "hit". They bring the most profound events and changes. **Jupiter, Saturn, and Chiron** transits can also have deep impact but are shorter – up to a year for Chiron if it

retrogrades, less for Jupiter or Saturn. A one-hit Jupiter transit lasts a week or so, but nine months (and three hits) if it goes retrograde.

Mars, Venus, and Mercury take two or three days for one hit but with the possibility of three hits if they go retrograde.

The Sun and Moon never go retrograde. A transit of the Sun lasts a day or so – the Moon a few hours.

Planetary cycles

As well as transits to your planets or angles, each planet has a cycle in relation to its own place in your chart. For instance, if Saturn comes opposite your natal Saturn, you can see this in context of Saturn's full cycle of 30 years; astrology sees it all as one integrated experience. Astrologers refer to the "mid-life transits"; Pluto

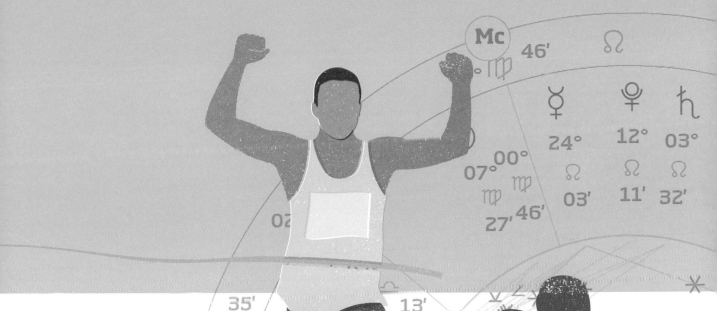

square Pluto (late 30s or early 40s), Uranus opposite Uranus and Neptune square Neptune (41-42), and the Chiron return (50). We are never quite the same after mid-life!

Fate and free will

Astrology suggests we have choices – no matter how "fated" or beyond our control a situation may seem, it suggests we can alter our reality through a change of perspective, using imagination to re-vision our approach.

We can apply the same attitude to forecasting as to the natal chart. Symbols do not tell us precisely what to do; instead they open our creative awareness and invite participation as co-creators of our own destiny.

> **Astrology** suggests we have **choices** – no matter how **'fated'** or beyond our control a situation may seem.

MEETING NEW PEOPLE

FIRST ENCOUNTERS AND MAKING NEW CONTACTS

Some encounters have the potential to bring profound change–even a passing acquaintance can be significant for what it evokes in us. Your chart shows how you approach new meetings, and transits to it point to what such meetings might mean in the flow of your life.

YOUR **HOUSES**

 The Ascendant and the 1st house show how we initially come across–our opening gambit or initial style of engagement. For instance, chatty **Gemini rising** invites exchange and wants to know all about you–on the other hand, **Scorpio rising** will be enigmatic, forcing you to make the first move.

This part of your chart describes dress and presentation, key elements of anyone's persona. Like the person with Saturn on the Ascendant whose wardrobe is heavy on blacks and grays, what you wear has the power to convey to others what you want them to see and know about you.

YOUR **PLANETS**

Mercury in your chart will be key in making and maintaining contacts. Mercury is to the Sun what an ambassador is to the head of state– the official envoy, conveying messages and checking the lay of the land. If you have a prominent Mercury (say, conjunct the Sun or on the Ascendant), the need to communicate will be strong; tucked away in the 8th or the 12th house, on the other hand, might suggest a more circumspect style of conversation. In aspect with Pluto or with Saturn, Mercury might be downright shy, preferring to observe rather than speak out.

 **The Ascendant** see pp.120-121
1st house see pp.90-91

 Mercury see pp.66-67

YOUR **ZODIAC SIGNS**

The elements

While the **air** signs thrive on social contact, anyone with planets in **water** might favor solitude or the company of a few familiar faces. The **fire** signs tend to approach new situations with confidence and skill, while the **earth** signs tend to take things at a more measured pace.

Your Sun sign in particular will show how you project yourself on first meeting—while your Moon sign is a barometer of how you feel inwardly, you tend to project your Sun outwardly, using these qualities to help you shine in social situations.

 Elements see pp.28-31

Case study

When Tatiana returned to work after having children, it was a challenge to find her niche again.

Tatiana has an 11th-house Leo Moon and Venus. These make her a fun-loving person who wants to be popular and enjoys socializing. There is showmanship and glamour in this Leo pair—and with Libra rising, she has great charm, too. Her Venus is the apex of a T-square with Jupiter-Uranus opposite Chiron, so she likes to be different and individual, not just one of the crowd.

But she also has a Saturn-Pluto conjunction in her 1st house, so she can feel reticent and shy at first meetings, trying hard to fit in. She began her new job as Saturn transited this duo, bringing doubts about being taken seriously by her colleagues. Luckily, the Sun was also making a brief transit through her 1st house, bringing her the initial spark of confidence to connect with them.

The Sun   **Venus**   **Uranus**

KEY **TRANSITS**

New people often act as catalysts for the next stage of our development. It can therefore be useful to check the transits to your chart at times when you met someone significant, whether this is social, professional or romantic, fleeting or long-term.

The type of experience will be shown by the transiting planet—a **Uranus transit**, for instance, brings an unexpected encounter. The planet being transited indicates the significance of the relationship—a transit to **Venus** evokes your desire nature, and to **the Sun** your sense of identity.

PLANNING CELEBRATIONS

GETTING INTO THE FESTIVE SPIRIT

A celebration is perhaps an acknowledgment of the vital human spirit, a brief flare of sunshine and exuberance. Our year is punctuated by special events and holidays that renew our energy, bring the family or community together, or celebrate an individual's life and achievements.

YOUR **HOUSES**

The 5th house is the house of celebrations–your planets in this house, and the sign on the cusp (and its planetary ruler), will show what you bring to the party and the ways in which you go about planning for leisure events.

You might of course have **Saturn** here, or **Pluto** or **Chiron**–not typically associated with indulgence or spontaneity. But we might imagine Saturn as the organized party-planner, Pluto as preferring a trip to a nightclub for a birthday surprise, and Chiron having the ingenuity to come up with unconventional ideas for an outing.

⟫ **5th house** see pp.98-99

Case study

Miriam is planning a lavish surprise party for her parents' wedding anniversary. Her brother would prefer a small family get-together.

Miriam's chart is dominated by a Stellium in Taurus in the 11th. Although down-to-earth, the 11th house emphasis inclines her toward group involvement, so she wants to invite a wide selection of friends and acquaintances. With Neptune in the 5th, she enjoys celebrations unhampered by budgets or practical considerations–and Leo on the cusp of her 2nd suggests wanting the best that money can buy.

Venus rules her 5th house and sits on her Cancer Ascendant–it is perhaps no wonder she sees this event as a chance to show love for her family. On the day of the party itself, transiting Venus was conjunct her MC, an apt symbol of Miriam as party host and mistress of ceremonies, and the celebration a gift to her parents.

YOUR **PLANETS**

 The Sun and Jupiter both have a celebratory feel to them—or at least, whatever signs and houses they occupy in your chart will say something about what, or who, brings out a sense of goodwill, generosity, and playfulness in you.

With the Sun in the **7th**, for instance, you can make other people feel special and golden—or in the **6th**, work colleagues can bring out your sunny side.

Jupiter in **Sagittarius** or **Leo** might naturally lean toward joviality and good cheer—Jupiter in **Capricorn** or **Virgo** might be more circumspect but are more likely to keep the party budget under control.

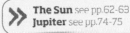
>> **The Sun** see pp.62-63
Jupiter see pp.74-75

YOUR **ZODIAC SIGNS**

Some signs are naturally more celebratory than others, and inevitably it tends to be people with the **fire** and **air** signs well-represented in their charts who enjoy a good party. **Water** and **earth** signs tend to be more introverted as a rule, and if your chart has a predominance of personal planets in these signs, you might be more inclined toward low-key events.

Each sign will have its own style of celebrating—if you are a **Leo**, you enjoy being at the center, bringing sunny warmth to the proceedings; by contrast, **Cancer** suggests a preference for family gatherings or enjoying time with trusted friends.

>> **Leo** see pp.40-41
Cancer see pp.38-39

KEY **TRANSITS**

Transits of **Jupiter** can bring optimism and party spirit, putting you in the mood for festivities or indicating a time when you would rather play than work.

You can also chart the transiting **Sun** through the houses in your chart—it takes 1 year to go around. The weeks when it travels through your 5th will feel very different to its passage through the 12th, the former a time to be creative and festive, and the latter a time for escape or solitude. The Sun returns to its own place at your birthday—a day of celebration, naturally.

 The Sun

 Jupiter

TAKING A RISK

STEPPING BRAVELY INTO THE UNKNOWN

Whether you're relocating, starting a new business, or taking a sabbatical, astrology reveals how you might respond and the inner resources you can bring to bear. Even if you did not choose the changes you face, the following areas of your chart, and transits through it, will point to a part of you that is ready to make a transition.

YOUR **ZODIAC SIGNS**

The elements

🔥 **Fire** is the daring element, focused on the vision without worrying about the details. For you, life is always an adventure.

🏔 The **earth** signs are risk-averse, managing it through planning ahead.

☁ With planets in **air**, you can take a risk if your interest is piqued or there is a companion alongside.

🌊 The **water** signs can be unsettled by change; you put up a protective barrier behind which to feel your way.

Your rising sign sets the pattern for new beginnings, whether taking the plunge into a new job or signing up for your first mortgage. Each is different—at opposite ends of the spectrum, **Aries** charges out head first, while **Gemini** hesitates to commit.

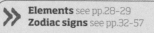

» **Elements** see pp.28–29
Zodiac signs see pp.32–57

YOUR **HOUSES**

🏠 **The 5th house** is traditionally connected to gambling–both literal and metaphorical. Use your 5th-house planets to create a strategy for handling risk. For example, with **Jupiter** here, you might feel happy to plunge straight in, recognizing an opportunity for growth; by contrast, with **the Moon** in your 5th house, you might prefer to navigate the situation more intuitively, reserving the right to withdraw if the tide becomes unfavorable.

✈ **Risk evokes the 9th house** as our sense of what awaits in the distance, suggesting the feelings that might arise in us at the start of a journey. For example, **Saturn** in the 9th, the planet of limits and rules, might suggest reticence or a fear of flying.

» **5th house** see pp.98–99
9th house see pp.108–109

Case study

Emma's passion is sailing. When Jupiter transited her 9th house, she had the opportunity to sail around the world.

Emma has several planets and the Ascendant in fire, bringing enthusiastic spontaneity. Leo rising gives her faith in her capacity for success in new ventures, and with chart ruler Sun in Aries

in the 9th, she can carve a role for herself as intrepid adventurer. Jupiter in Aries means she also deals with obstacles head on. With the Sun, Jupiter, and North Node all conjunct in Aries in the 9th—and when the transit of Jupiter brought such an exciting opportunity—Emma felt

convinced that it was her destiny to head fearlessly into the unknown.

Mars in Taurus meant she could uphold her decision with steadfast courage and stamina, and Uranus and Neptune in her 5th house enabled her to fully express her creative ingenuity and vision in the new role, all guided by the cautious practicality of Saturn, also in her 5th.

YOUR **PLANETS**

♂ **Mars** suggests a capacity for seizing opportunities or making decisions. In taking a gamble, you should honor your own style. For example, Mars in **Libra** needs to weigh the odds, while Mars in **Pisces** can respond and bend to the prevailing wind. Mars in **Aries** is single-minded, quick, and decisive, while Mars in **Cancer** takes a more subtle and indirect route.

♃ **Jupiter** expresses your drive to expand on the opportunities you seize. With Jupiter in **Gemini**, for example, the benefit of acquiring new skills for yourself makes the risk worthwhile. Jupiter in **Libra**, on the other hand, sees growth as a two-way exchange and an exercise in sharing.

» **Mars** see pp.70–71
» **Jupiter** see pp. 74–75

KEY **TRANSITS**

The transits of Jupiter and Uranus often bring unexpected opportunities.

Uranus brings change, fueled by the excitement of a new idea or vision. The single-mindedness this planet generates often allows you to pull off the impossible.

Jupiter serves to broaden and enlarge your outlook, offering new possibilities in whatever part of your chart it is moving. Jupiter also instills confidence and an unshakable faith in the outcome.

Jupiter

Uranus

"ARE WE COURAGEOUSLY AND JOYFULLY RIDING **THE WHEEL OF FORTUNE** IN OUR OWN LIVES, ENGAGING ACTIVELY WITH THE **DANCE OF TIME**, OR ARE WE **AFRAID OF IT**?"

Clare Martin, Mapping the Psyche:
Volume 3: Kairos–the Astrology of Time

KEY MOMENTS IN RELATIONSHIPS

STARTING A RELATIONSHIP AND MAKING A COMMITMENT

Relationships offer some of the most joyful moments of our lives, but also some of the most painful and challenging. Each chart is unique and suggests a particular style of making attachments.

YOUR **HOUSES**

The 7th and 8th houses
These are the relationship houses, reflecting how you feel about emotional commitment. The 7th suggests a contract and a part of you encountered through the partners you choose. The 8th takes you into emotional entanglement on a soul level.

If you have **Saturn** here, the issue of long-term alliance is likely to arise at some point. With **Jupiter** or **Uranus**, the issue of freedom might be top priority.

If you have no planets here, it does not mean you will never have a relationship–merely that this is not your life's main focus.

7th house see pp.104-105
8th house see pp.106-107

YOUR **PLANETS**

The Moon indicates your emotional style and colors how you interact emotionally with others.

If you have the Moon in **Scorpio**, for instance, deep emotional bonds come more naturally than with the Moon in **Gemini**–or perhaps more accurately, a person with a Gemini Moon forms bonds through seemingly light things such as conversation and sharing ideas.

Venus is the other planet of relationships, indicating affection and issues of value. Venus in **Sagittarius** wants a partner with a sense of adventure, whereas Venus in **Capricorn** values commitment.

The Moon see pp.64-65
Venus see pp.68-69

YOUR **ZODIAC SIGNS**

The modes
Certain signs seem more suited to commitment than others, although looks can be deceptive.

The **mutable signs** often seem commitment-shy, although it is also true that people born under these signs need room to breathe and to feel free–commitment works if it incorporates these things.

The **fixed signs** are the most inclined to seek the stability and permanence of long-term partnership, sticking with it through all weathers–even when the fire has gone out.

The **cardinal signs** often fall in love quickly, but these people are also inclined to move on swiftly, too, once the relationship is over.

Modes see pp.28-31

Case study

Darren married young. The relationship was stormy, and they separated when Darren found out his partner was having an affair.

Darren has a Sun-Mars conjunction in Cancer in his 7th house, conjunct a Cancer Descendant. Relationship is focal for him, based on mutual protection and bringing a sense of purpose.

The Moon in Aries is square this Mars in Cancer, suggesting a defensive and combative side. With the Moon also opposite Pluto, it would be easy for him to feel undermined or betrayed; loyalty will be key for him.

He married at his Saturn return, a highly significant time: Saturn is his chart ruler and is conjunct his Midheaven. He discovered the affair when Uranus transited over his Aries Moon, activating the Moon-Pluto opposition and bringing emotional secrets into the open. He came to see that he had become dependent on his partner to the exclusion of the more self-willed and vibrant Aries Moon and Venus in Gemini.

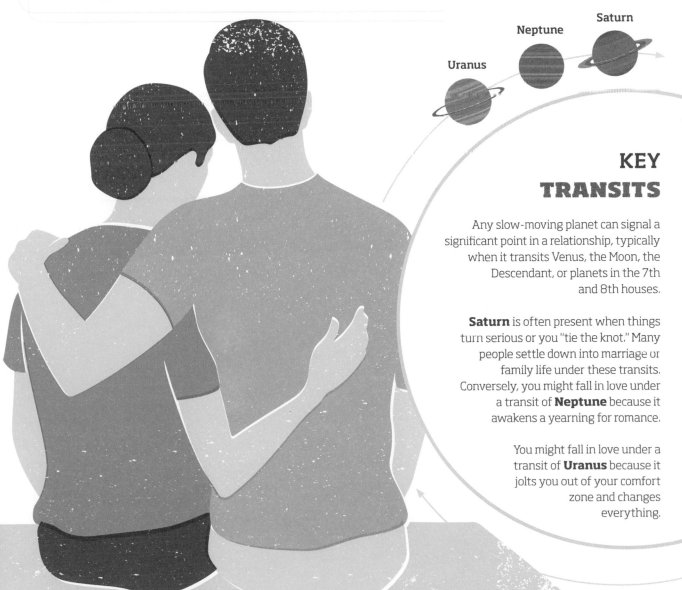

KEY TRANSITS

Any slow-moving planet can signal a significant point in a relationship, typically when it transits Venus, the Moon, the Descendant, or planets in the 7th and 8th houses.

Saturn is often present when things turn serious or you "tie the knot." Many people settle down into marriage or family life under these transits. Conversely, you might fall in love under a transit of **Neptune** because it awakens a yearning for romance.

You might fall in love under a transit of **Uranus** because it jolts you out of your comfort zone and changes everything.

STARTING A FAMILY

HAVING CHILDREN AND BEING A PARENT

They say there is never a right time to have children, but astrology shows that children come along when a key aspect of a chart is highlighted–classically, the 5th house of children. Indeed, your child's chart represents your transits at that time, reflecting what the experience means for you.

YOUR **HOUSES**

The 5th house The experience of pregnancy and birth is reflected here, and the powerful, creative act of bringing a child into the world.

If you have **Jupiter** here, perhaps you want a large family, and children feel like gifts from the gods. **Saturn** slows things down, perhaps bringing children later in life or placing the focus on solo parenting or developing parental self-reliance. **Chiron** here might manifest as adoption or fostering.

The 4th house is the house of home, the crucible or container of the family. It is our foundation, reaching down into the past–it offers a sense of family legacy and dynasty.

The 10th house suggests your role of parent as responsible guardian; any planets you have here, and the sign on the cusp, will color this for you.

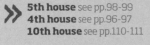

5th house see pp.98-99
4th house see pp.96-97
10th house see pp.110-111

YOUR **PLANETS**

The Moon is a key player when it comes to having children and looking after a family. Your own style of caretaking will be shown by your Moon placement by sign, house, and aspect, and you can think about what your strengths and challenges might be in this respect.

For instance, if you have the Moon in **Leo**, you can easily identify with the playful world of children and be master of the bedtime story or coming up with fun things to do on a rainy afternoon.

By contrast, if you have the Moon in **Virgo**, your focus may be toward physical well-being and establishing regular routines.

The Moon see pp.64-65

YOUR **ZODIAC SIGNS**

A quick poll among your friends will serve to prove that no particular sign is more inclined to have children than another. **Cancer** is associated with children, family, and the instinct for protective nurturing, and if you have personal planets in Cancer, a family might be a significant focus of your life. But each sign brings its own skills and challenges to child-rearing—the signs occupied by your **Sun**, **Saturn**, and **MC** (images of parental authority), and your **Moon** and **IC** (caretaking style and the family nest), will all contribute to your needs and experiences in this sphere of life.

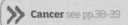

Cancer see pp.38-39

Case study

Andrea never wanted children. Her partner has two from a previous marriage, and Andrea finds herself in the role of stepmother.

Andrea has four planets in the 1st, including the Sun, placing focus on personal self-development. The 10th is also key, containing Mars and chart ruler Saturn—she puts her time and energy into a demanding and high-powered job.

Chiron in Gemini in the 5th suggests ambivalence around having children, perhaps feeling she is not skilled enough. Given Chiron's mythological story of surrogate upbringing, Chiron in the 4th, 5th, or 10th, or in aspect to the Sun or Moon, can sometimes manifest as fostering, adoption, or stepparenting.

For Andrea, Chiron opposite Saturn has brought fear of not being accepted by her stepchildren and the enormity of the task. She met her partner as transiting Chiron squared her natal Saturn-Chiron opposition; a few years later, her Saturn return saw her settling more comfortably into the role.

The Sun   Saturn   The Moon

KEY **TRANSITS**

Transits to any of these places in your chart can coincide with the arrival of a child. Transits to the 4th house, for instance, can signal shifts in the family structure and the addition of another member (or indeed a death in the family, which then alters the hierarchy of the generations).

For a man, transits to **the Sun** or **Saturn** might coincide with becoming a father, just as for a woman a transit to **the Moon** (or to the planetary ruler of the 5th house) can coincide with getting pregnant.

PARENTING DECISIONS

SUPPORTING YOUR CHILD'S GROWTH AND HAPPINESS

Parenting must surely be one of the hardest jobs, requiring constant attention and decision-making that supports your child and allows them to grow, develop, and fulfill their potential. Knowing your own chart, and that of your child, can be a great help.

YOUR **HOUSES**

The 10th house is where we stand on our own and develop, over the course of time, a sense of our inner authority and capacity to guide and lead. It is also one of the parental houses, traditionally denoting mother, but more accurately perhaps denoting the parent who socializes the child and introduces them to the world.

Whatever planets you have here, the aspects they make to other planets, and the sign on the cusp, will all say something about how you feel in this role, which in turn can shape the decisions you make as a parent.

YOUR **PLANETS**

The Moon is pivotal in parenting decisions, being fundamental to caretaking style. In **Aries** or **Sagittarius**, for instance, you might give your children more latitude than the average parent, since you nurture through encouraging independence; on the other hand, if you have the Moon in **Cancer**, you are likely to put safety and security first, prioritizing interdependence and the family nest.

Jupiter and Saturn make an interesting contrast, like "good cop, bad cop," and reflecting the interplay in you between joy and duty. They are classic indicators of this balancing act—Jupiter your expression of freedom and adventure, and Saturn your view of what the rules should be.

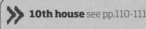
10th house see pp.110-111

The Moon see pp.64-65
Jupiter see pp.74-75
Saturn see pp.76-77

Case study

Patrick is the father of two boys. The eldest is not yet 16 but wants permission to go traveling with a friend.

Patrick's chart is dominated by Cancer, the sign containing his Ascendant, Mercury, Saturn, Sun, and chart ruler the Moon, all in the 1st and 2nd houses. Cancer is protective and conservative, and oriented strongly toward family–here, the protection is as much toward himself as anyone else, something for Patrick to consider when assessing whether his son is able to look after himself. Patrick would probably not have dreamed of leaving the safety of his own family at 15.

At the time, Patrick had Pluto transiting opposite his Saturn. We might see this as a challenge to the protectionist policy of Saturn in Cancer, generating fear over all the things that might go wrong but also a chance to reassess deep-seated fears from his own childhood.

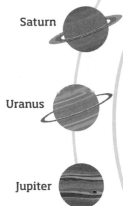

Saturn

Uranus

Jupiter

KEY **TRANSITS**

In making a decision, the chart can reveal the underlying issues for both parent and child. For instance, if you have a **Saturn transit** and your child is under the influence of **Uranus**, you might be busy pointing out the pitfalls while they want to seize a new opportunity, perplexed you do not share their excitement. A compromise may be needed.

The planets' cycles show what stage each family member has reached. For instance, at the first **Jupiter return** at 11-12, many children change schools for the first time and take a leap in their learning. The **Saturn half-return** at 14-15 suggests the hurdle of high school as a stage on the journey to adulthood.

YOUR **ZODIAC SIGNS**

Elements
Each parent-child relationship is different. Knowing that you are, for instance, a fiery person, active and outgoing, but your child has most of their planets in water can be enough to appreciate that their sensitivity and introspection takes them on a different path.

Modes
If you have planets in **cardinal signs**, making a decision tends to be uncomplicated. Cardinality suggests clarity about the road ahead.

For the **fixed signs**, the instinct is to ruminate and take time to decide–perhaps frustrating for the child who is cardinal in nature.

The **mutable signs** prefer not to make decisions at all, so important matters can evoke anxiety and self-doubt–you need to allow yourself time to explore all the options.

»» Elements, Modes see pp.28-31

COMPETING

PROMOTING YOUR OWN TALENTS

There are those who consider themselves to be naturally competitive and those who seem reticent at the idea of putting themselves forward. However, we all compete in our own way. What drives you to competition might be very different to the next person, but no less motivating.

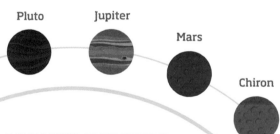

Pluto Jupiter Mars Chiron

KEY **TRANSITS**

A transit to your 7th can herald a new relationship, but equally the presence of an opponent. Sometimes these can be one and the same person. For example, with **Pluto** transiting here, a competitive situation might arise that feels like a fight to the death, involving feelings of jealousy or betrayal. Or with **Jupiter**, perhaps the rivalry centers on who is richer or more influential.

A transit to Mars suggests the latest chapter in your relationship to this planet. Again, the nature of the transiting planet defines this–**Chiron**, for instance, might show you that compassion and forgiveness can be just as powerful as winning.

YOUR **HOUSES**

The 7th house is known in traditional astrology as the house of "open enemies," and if you have any rivals on the horizon, they might have character traits that conjure the planets and signs in your 7th. Planets here can become the focus of contests or a desire to prove supremacy over someone, since these drives are typically developed in the cut and thrust of a relationship.

For instance, if you have **Mercury in Aries** in the 7th, you might test and develop your communication skills through engaging in heated debate and argument.

7th house see pp.104-105

Case study

Rachel is a writer. She had never considered herself to be competitive until she entered a competition to write a radio play.

Rachel's Mars is in Capricorn in the 5th. In Capricorn, Mars is focused and productive, and in the 5th house, Rachel puts this energy into her creative work. Having her creativity recognized keeps the pulse and the power going.

Mars rules her 9th house—she wants to break new ground in terms of

higher thinking (Aries on cusp of 9th), bringing these pioneering ideas into her creativity (ruler Mars in 5th).

Neptune rules her 7th and is in the 2nd, square to Mars. She has never been wealthy, often feeling her work was not financially valued. Pluto in Capricorn was transiting this Mars-Neptune square at the time of the writing competition. The spur of professional paid work proved enough to win the contest.

YOUR **PLANETS**

♂ **Mars** is a key place to look in assessing your competitive spirit. Mars in a **fire sign** suggests you compete openly, using dramatic flair to beat the competition. With Mars in an **earth sign**, you might be keen to prove your efficiency and practical drive. Mars in **air** suggests intellectual competition, or with Mars in **water**, you might seize the day through subtlety and subterfuge.

The house it occupies indicates where you seek to come out on top. With Mars in the **2nd**, for instance, you are prepared to fight for your share of the money; if in the **10th**, you might be keen to climb the career ladder.

YOUR **ZODIAC SIGNS**

Aries and Scorpio are worth considering, as the two signs ruled by Mars. If you have more than one planet in these signs (you can include your Ascendant in the count), it suggests Mars is an important planet for you— and although the position of your Mars will shape your style of competing, the fact that it is a strong influence at all suggests you gravitate toward situations where you can test and develop your fighting spirit.

If you have no planets here, you can look to the houses with Aries and Scorpio on the cusp; these will be life areas that galvanize you to action and conflict.

» Mars see pp.70-71

» Aries see pp.32-33
Scorpio see pp.48-49

"**EVERY TRANSIT** HAS A PURPOSE AND CARRIES A **PERSONAL MESSAGE** IF WE ARE PREPARED TO **ASK THE RIGHT QUESTIONS** AND **ENGAGE WITH WHAT IS GOING ON.**"

Clare Martin, Mapping the Psyche:
Volume 3: Kairos–the Astrology of Time

HANDLING DISAGREEMENTS

MAKING PEACE AND GETTING ALONG WITH OTHERS

We all run into disagreements from time to time. Some might be petty disputes or face-saving exercises; others might be pivotal moments in a relationship, the cause for separation. Either way, astrology helps us to see what underlies each dispute.

YOUR **HOUSES**

Some disagreements revolve around the **7th** and **8th** houses because their contents tend to be unconscious and emotive, and because partnership invokes these sides of us.

Disputes with neighbors often revolve around the **3rd**. If you are having a dispute with a friend, you might look to your **11th** for clues as to what underlies it, whereas a spat with a work colleague might be a **6th** or a **10th** issue.

You can examine the nature of the disagreement itself and try to find it in your chart. When you hold a strong opinion about something, it can be found as a theme in your own planetary placements and configurations.

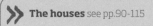
The houses see pp.90-115

YOUR **PLANETS**

Venus and Mars In the time of the ancient Greeks and Romans, myths and stories of Aphrodite and Ares, or Venus and Mars, reflected an ancient philosophy of Love and War as powerful cosmic forces of love/attraction and conflict/separation.

The same thing is true of the relationship between Venus and Mars in a chart. You fight according to your Mars—maybe a disciplined military maneuver (**Mars in Capricorn**) or emotional combat (**Mars in Cancer**). You make peace according to your Venus—perhaps via a verbal apology (**Venus in Gemini**) or through the classic peace offering: food (**Venus in Taurus**).

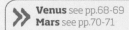
Venus see pp.68-69
Mars see pp.70-71

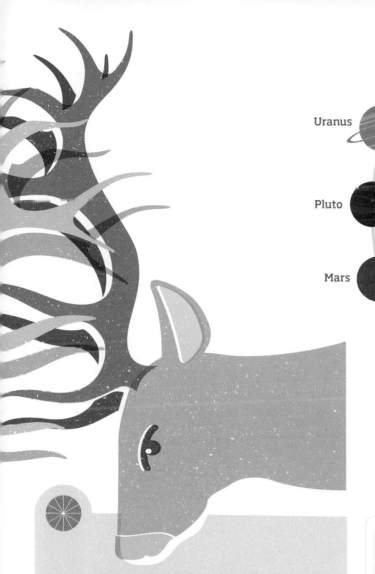

KEY **TRANSITS**

Disagreements imply the testier planets. In a long-running dispute, a transit of **Uranus** or **Pluto** might form the backdrop, particularly in square or opposition to one of your natal planets, igniting tension or provocation.

A brief flare-up suggests a shorter-lived transit of **Mars**. When it transits through your 7th or 8th, or in square or opposition to a personal planet, there is the potential for disagreements. Just being aware of this can be enough to avert an ill-timed or inappropriate retaliation – or indeed, allow the eruption to occur and clear the air.

Uranus

Pluto

Mars

YOUR **ZODIAC SIGNS**

Some signs are more argumentative than others, without necessarily meaning to create conflict. **Aries** is the Mars-ruled sign that tends to be blunt and direct; **Scorpio** is also ruled by Mars but favors covert action and wars of attrition. Comparing the signs occupied by a particular planet in the charts of rivals can show radical differences of viewpoint. For instance, someone with **Jupiter in Sagittarius** tends to be idealistic and convinced of their own truth. Someone with **Mercury in Gemini** debates with humor, whereas **Mercury in Leo** likes to sound authoritative.

» **Zodiac signs** see pp.32-57

Case study

Christine and Robin are colleagues. They disagree about the best way to manage a joint project, and it is holding up progress.

Christine's chart is fiery compared to Robin's. She has Sagittarius rising ruled by Jupiter in Aries in the 3rd; her enthusiasm can run over into either verbal or intellectual dominance.

Rebellious Uranus sits on her Ascendant, and its opposition to Mars in Gemini can ignite verbal flares. Her fixed Taurus Sun and Scorpio Moon make her reluctant to compromise – unlike Robin's mutable Pisces Moon and Virgo Sun.

Robin has an emphasis on Virgo and Libra – she likes to be helpful and work as part of a team. We can immediately see a conflict of styles with Christine's more forceful chart patterns.

They can make a good team if they appreciate each other's strengths, however: Christine's capacity for new ideas and for strong management alongside Robin's Virgoan attention to detail and Libran people skills.

FIGHTS AND TENSION

FINDING YOUR WAY OUT OF AN IMPASSE

Most of us shy away from conflict. Once a dispute has erupted into a full-blown fight, it can be difficult to handle, and we might say something we later regret. In the heat of the moment, there are ways in which astrology can help discharge the tension.

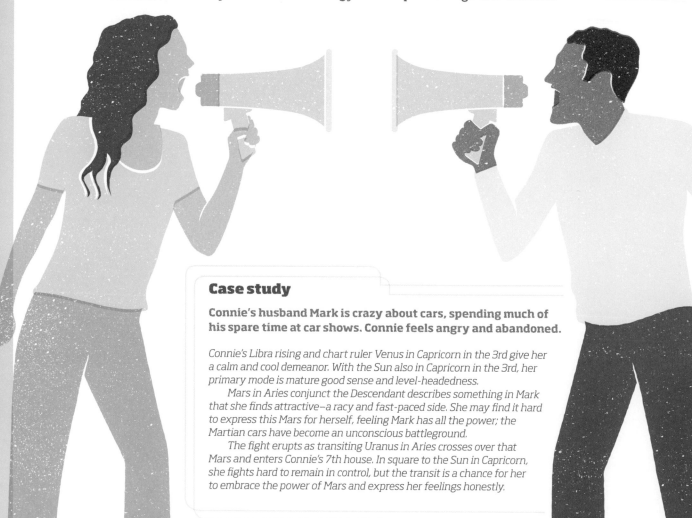

Case study

Connie's husband Mark is crazy about cars, spending much of his spare time at car shows. Connie feels angry and abandoned.

Connie's Libra rising and chart ruler Venus in Capricorn in the 3rd give her a calm and cool demeanor. With the Sun also in Capricorn in the 3rd, her primary mode is mature good sense and level-headedness.

Mars in Aries conjunct the Descendant describes something in Mark that she finds attractive—a racy and fast-paced side. She may find it hard to express this Mars for herself, feeling Mark has all the power; the Martian cars have become an unconscious battleground.

The fight erupts as transiting Uranus in Aries crosses over that Mars and enters Connie's 7th house. In square to the Sun in Capricorn, she fights hard to remain in control, but the transit is a chance for her to embrace the power of Mars and express her feelings honestly.

YOUR **HOUSES**

No particular house is implicated more than others—
we tend to engage in conflict when we are challenged
or undervalued, when our security is threatened, or
when our style clashes with someone else's. Thus, any
area of your chart can be involved.

 The 7th house We might look to the 7th house,
though, as a place where we can be unaware of
our feelings or behaviors, since here these are so often
projected onto others and encountered in relationships.
With **Chiron** here, for instance, you might feel you don't
fulfill a partner's expectations, or with **Pluto**, that the
other person has more power, bringing tension into
the frame.

7th house see pp.104-105

YOUR **ZODIAC SIGNS**

The elements

The fire signs are most given to conflagration; with
personal planets in fire, being caught up in your own
beliefs can sometimes blind you to other's viewpoints.

The earth signs show a calm and unruffled
response; with planets in these signs, you are
probably not easily riled.

The air signs are the most peaceable of the 12,
concerned with civilized interrelationship. You tend
to conduct fights and conflicts using logic and reason.

The water signs work on hidden emotional
undercurrents—with personal planets in water,
you might not articulate your feelings, but your mood
can dominate the atmosphere.

Elements see pp.28-31

YOUR **PLANETS**

Mars is often a tricky planet, and many of us do
not have a good relationship with it. No wonder
that it was traditionally known as "the lesser malefic," a
symbol of humankind's natural warlike and destructive
tendencies. Owning your own Mars is a major step on
the road to handling conflict successfully.

Aspects to Mars influence how you express this
planet. Saturn squaring it suggests great effort to
rein in its fiery tendencies, making the person
measured and slow to anger. Uranus squaring
it, on the other hand, suggests urgency
and impatience.

Mars see pp.70-71

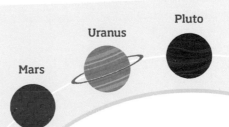

Mars

Uranus

Pluto

KEY **TRANSITS**

Transits to **Mars** galvanize our warrior spirit
and often see us fighting back. With transits
of **Mars**, these have influence in the context of a
longer-lasting social or outer planet transit, where this
quick-moving planet might act to set light to a situation
that is already smoldering under the surface.

As with disagreements, transits of **Uranus** or **Pluto** suggest
times of tension and strain, often ignited by the profound
changes these planets bring about. Particularly when they
transit opposite to a planet in your chart, you can be aware of
resistance or opposition from others.

SEPARATION– SHOULD I STAY OR GO?

DEALING WITH CRISIS IN A RELATIONSHIP

Relationships provide us with some of the most testing moments of our lives. Sometimes going our separate ways seems inevitable; astrology helps us to choose whether or not this might be the best course of action.

YOUR **HOUSES**

If you have planets in the **7th house**, these can explain what attracted you to your partner–and what might also pull you apart, if the relationship no longer feeds this. All too often, we end up hating the other person for everything we used to love them for, and at least some of this will pivot on the sometimes enigmatic 7th, where we are prone to project onto others.

The 8th house We might say that marriage is made in the 7th house, but so often broken in the 8th. Money is a classic flashpoint, as is infidelity, both of which can conjure 8th-house feelings of betrayal.

>> **7th house** see pp.104-105
8th house see pp.106-107

YOUR **PLANETS**

The Moon is often at the heart of a relationship–while Venus might be the more obvious planet in terms of attraction, sooner or later the Moon becomes significant in holding a relationship together.

This planet indicates your basic needs, and if these are not honored in a relationship, it can make you feel uncomfortable and unsupported. You do not need to have the Moon in the same sign or element or mode as your partner– indeed, many relationships thrive on differences in lunar style–but understanding a partner's inner needs makes all the difference.

 The Moon see pp.64-65

KEY **TRANSITS**

People often break up under transits to the Descendant or its ruler, to planets in the 7th or 8th houses, or to Venus or the Moon; transits from **Uranus**, **Neptune**, or **Pluto** are often at work during a relationship's critical times.

Uranus transits coincide with sudden events and realizations–this planet can bring separation or make us act without caution. **Neptune** transits can feel like moving through fog, and one strategy is not to make a decision until it clears. **Pluto** can feel inexorable, taking away our control–perhaps the only way is to submit and trust our eventual emergence from darkness into a new chapter.

Uranus

Pluto

Neptune

YOUR **ZODIAC SIGNS**

Your Descendant sign

The sign on your Descendant is potently invoked in relationships, so it is worth exploring this because it reflects experiences that can make or break a partnership. For instance, with a **Taurus Descendant**, you might look for material security from your partner and feel let down if this is compromised. Similarly, a **Scorpio Descendant** implies an exchange based on deep passion–unconscious testing of your partner's loyalty can see the relationship falter by bringing about the betrayal that Scorpio most dreads.

 The Descendant see pp.120-121

Case study

Melanie has been married to Paul for 15 years, and they have two children. She is no longer in love with him and feels restless.

The key houses in Melanie's chart are the 4th and 5th. The 4th contains her chart ruler Moon in Virgo, and a tight Venus-Pluto conjunction in Libra. This places great emphasis on family life and on relationship as its foundation. Perhaps she perceived her own parents as tightly bonded–a "power couple" (Venus-Pluto in Libra in 4th).

Five planets in the 5th, including the Sun, makes this house hugely important, too. It is the house of children, but also of romance and of creativity. For Melanie, Mars-Uranus here indicates a need for romantic excitement–very different from the stable, mature partner of her Capricorn Descendant. Transiting Pluto was on her Descendant at the time, soon to square the Mars-Uranus. The relationship might prevail if she can release this energy within herself through feeding her creative independence.

SAYING SORRY

RESTORING PEACE AND HARMONY

As the song goes, sorry seems to be the hardest word. Apologizing means admitting we were wrong and is seen by some as a weakness. How can we bring back some Venusian harmony to a situation while retaining our dignity and strength?

Venus

Mercury

KEY **TRANSITS**

During a time of difficulty in a relationship or friendship, the act of saying sorry implies a willingness to see things from the other person's point of view. The spirit of conciliation then suggests a moment when **Venus** is given precedence over Mars, or perhaps **Mercury** as mediator and ambassador can convey the right words to smooth things over.

Such transits are ephemeral, but within the context of a longer-term transit of, say, Uranus or Pluto, which has given rise to an entrenched dispute, it might turn the tide and encourage the work of peace-making.

YOUR **HOUSES**

The 3rd house is implicated in any kind of communication, and your planets here will say a lot about your verbal style. Depending on the sign, **Venus** here tends to be diplomatic, **Mars** forthright and unwilling to compromise. **Jupiter** can be effusive, **Saturn** more taciturn. Your planets in the 3rd certainly suggest how you deliver the message.

The 7th house is also useful to explore if you find yourself at an impasse with someone; it suggests some of the unconscious undercurrents that inform your relationships with others. The feistier planets here, such as **Mars** or **Uranus**, tend to be less willing to give ground than, say, **Venus** or **Neptune**.

3rd house see pp.94-95
7th house see pp.104-105

Case study

During a protracted fight with his best friend over a debt, Nick said some things that jeopardized the friendship and that he regretted.

Nick has Leo rising with chart ruler Sun conjunct Mercury and Uranus in Leo in the 1st. With so much in Leo, backing down is not really Nick's style—a Leo does not like to lose face, and getting past that may be a challenge.

With four planets in the 2nd house, it is perhaps not surprising that this fight involved money. Being in Virgo, this might both help and hinder. Although Virgo

contributes a more self-effacing side, his Mars-Pluto conjunction does not feel particularly forgiving.

His 11th house is ruled by Venus. Despite the uneasy situation, it is likely that he values the friendship, and focusing on this may be the way forward. When Venus transited through his 7th house, opposing his Leo planets, he used this brief opportunity to offer an apology.

YOUR **PLANETS**

Venus helps us on the road to an apology—being the prime planet of social nicety, Venus in your chart suggests how you offer the olive branch. Venus in **Aries** is perhaps less amenable than Venus in one of the air signs or in **Pisces**. But with Venus in Aries, the apology, when it comes, is likely to be swift, clean, and fair—in Pisces, it might come loaded with a dose of self-pity.

Mercury can be viewed alongside your 3rd house in showing your communication style—and whatever aspects your Mercury makes to other planets will further shape this.

YOUR **ZODIAC SIGNS**

Scorpio and Cancer tend to hold on to grudges or hurts for longer than other signs. Scorpio in particular, as the fixed water sign, generates deep feelings that are not easily released; a scorpion does not like to concede defeat.

But those with ever-helpful **Libra and Virgo** are hardwired to say sorry, even when it is not their fault. The mutable signs in general tend to shy away from conflict. "Sorry" can then sometimes be an escape clause, breaking the tension of an argument so the mutable person can wiggle out and be free once again.

 **Venus** see pp.68-69
Mercury see pp.66-67

 Zodiac signs see pp.32-57

CHANGING CAREERS

UNFOLDING YOUR PROFESSIONAL PATH

Judging what career moves to make and when to make them usually takes thought and planning. Timing is important, and the planetary cycles in your chart will show you what kind of move or change might be right for the time.

YOUR **HOUSES**

The MC and 10th house Planets in the 10th, plus the sign on the MC and its ruler, show what you are trying to achieve career-wise, what might prompt a change of direction, and how you navigate such changes–**Saturn** here, for instance, is focused on gaining mastery and disinclined to take a risk; **Uranus** needs excitement and catalyzes change.

The 6th house If your job seems better described by your 6th than your 10th, perhaps it puts food on the table rather than lighting your fire. Of course, if you have planets here, a 6th-house field may be your vocation–administrative, craft-driven, or connected to health.

10th house see pp.110-111
6th house see pp.100-101

YOUR **PLANETS**

The Sun As we have seen before, the Sun is at the heart of what you do for a living, because it is the heart of what drives you as a person and describes the essence of your life's path.

So if the qualities and talents described by your Sun are not showcased and developed through your work, it is unlikely to feel fulfilling in the long run and could well be the reason behind major career changes.

While even the most glamorous jobs contain routine aspects, it is important for you to develop and display your solar gifts as part of your vocation.

The Sun see pp.62-63

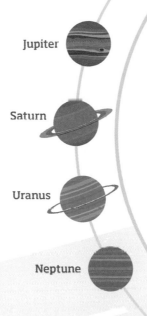

Jupiter

Saturn

Uranus

Neptune

KEY **TRANSITS**

Transits to your **6th** and **10th**, to your **MC ruler**, and to your **Sun** are the main things to watch for. Pay attention also to the configurations that describe your work. For instance, if you have planets in the 3rd and are a preschool teacher, a transit to those planets will impact your professional life.

Major shifts can happen under any transiting planet. **Jupiter** transits suggest promotions or further training, whereas **Saturn** suggests increased responsibility or specialization. **Uranus** can bring a sudden change of tack–or, with **Neptune**, doubts about which direction to take.

Case study

Judith is in her late 30s and was recently made redundant. She now has to plan for her future and think about what to do next.

It is not uncommon for people to make career changes during the midlife transits. These include Pluto squaring its birth position. At the time of her redundancy, Pluto was approaching this square as it transited through Capricorn. In Judith's chart, Pluto is conjunct the Ascendant and squares the MC-IC axis, so the Pluto square Pluto is part of this bigger picture.

To be "redundant" conjures images of no longer feeling useful. But the action of Pluto is to strip away anything that no longer serves us–it might feel disempowering for a time, but we hopefully re-emerge stronger and more purposeful. A strategy for Judith is to allow herself to contemplate a radical change of direction personally (1st house Pluto), domestically (IC), and professionally (MC), and indeed that, for her, all three are linked.

YOUR **ZODIAC SIGNS**

Explore the balance of the modes in your chart for an overview of how you respond to a career change.

Cardinal You like a career that offers you a chance to move quickly up the ladder–a dynamic environment and one that gives you a measure of executive control.

Fixed You prefer to develop your skills in a slower and more measured way. You might be inclined to stick with one employer or one type of work for some time.

Mutable Variety is the spice of life–a predominance of this mode suggests a winding career path with many changes, allowing you to refresh your interest from time to time.

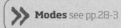 **Modes** see pp.28-3

"ASTROLOGY CAN SHOW HOW PERIODS OF **PERSONAL CRISIS** ARE, IN FACT, **TESTING TIMES**, WHICH HELP US TO **DISCOVER OURSELVES**."

Lindsay River and Sally Gillespie,
The Knot of Time

RELOCATING

NAVIGATING A CHANGE OF RESIDENCE

Relocating tends to be one of life's more stressful events. This is perhaps not surprising, since from an astrological point of view, the areas of the chart that indicate home are also places of deep emotional connection.

YOUR **HOUSES**

The IC and the 4th house describe home, both as a physical place and as an inner sense of roots, safety, and foundation.

If you have Jupiter in the 4th, it might feel natural to you to travel around, or you might even choose to live abroad–or with Uranus here, you may experience many changes of address. With the Sun or Moon in the 4th, you might be so strongly connected to home and homeland that uprooting yourself will not be easy–your Sun here suggests your life revolves around home in some way, and the Moon that your emotional well-being is closely tied to it.

>> **The IC** see pp.122-123
4th house see pp.96-97

YOUR **PLANETS**

The Moon is our interior sense of safety–not just our own behavior patterns that bring this about, but also the kinds of people, experiences, places, and atmospheres that help us to thrive. Just the sign your Moon occupies will give major clues as to how you might feel about relocating; the Moon in **Aries**, for instance, implies willingness to leap into the unknown, whereas the Moon in **Cancer** might find it hard to cut ties. A strategy with Moon in **Pisces** might be to choose a peaceful environment and take your time to settle into the energy of your new place.

>> **The Moon** see pp.64-65

YOUR **ZODIAC SIGNS**

Your IC sign

The IC begins the 4th house, and the sign here will reflect your experience of early home life and the kind of home you want to create for yourself.

You can look to the sign it occupies to help you navigate a change of residence. If you have **Taurus** on the IC, for instance, moving might feel like a huge upheaval, and one way to cope is to prepare yourself for the change as far in advance as possible. On the other hand, **Aries** here might see you acting like a bullet from a gun—ready to move on domestically and not look back.

>> **The IC** see pp.122-123

Case study

Millie was sharing a house with two friends. She had saved enough to afford a place of her own and decided to buy her first property.

Millie's 4th house contains a Moon-Saturn conjunction in Virgo. This has an interesting link to both of her money houses, through the Moon's rulership of her 2nd and Saturn's co-rulership of her 8th—thus the purchase represents (and needs to be) a sound financial investment. In short, Millie's emotional well-being (Moon) is connected to her ability to pay her mortgage. Fortunately, Moon-Saturn in Virgo would tend to be exceedingly prudent with money.

The purchase happened very quickly, as transiting Uranus transited over her 11th house Mercury, ruler of the Virgo IC, and made a quincunx to the Moon-Saturn. This was unnerving for Millie (with Cancer rising, three planets in Virgo and the Sun in Taurus, she prefers caution) but was mitigated by careful attention to the small print in the mortgage paperwork.

The Moon

Uranus

KEY **TRANSITS**

Changes of home often occur under a transit of a social or outer planet to the IC, the IC ruler, or planets in the 4th. The effect is to reshape our foundations, the inner reorientation being mirrored in the outer experience of the move itself.

Transits to the **Moon** reflect the emotional impact. A square from transiting **Uranus to a Cancer Moon**, for instance, implies a time of emotional disorientation, which generates feelings of insecurity. If this coincides with relocating, it suggests the hermit crab, urgently trying to re-establish a sense of safety.

TAKING TIME OFF

VACATIONS, SABBATICALS, AND BREAKS

We all need a decent break from time to time. Whether this is a week by the ocean, a sabbatical from work, or time away to travel the world, these periods not only recharge us, but can also empower us for the next stage of life.

YOUR **HOUSES**

The 5th house Although anything significant in your chart can determine what kind of vacation you enjoy, leisure time focuses around the 5th house, a place that contributes to our life force and vital spirit. It might not do much to persuade the boss, but the 5th house of vacations is one-twelfth of the wheel of life experience, and regular breaks are fundamental to our well-being.

Make the best of your time off by choosing something that suits this picture–with **Mercury** here, for instance, you might choose hiking, or **Jupiter** might call you to a more cultural type of experience.

⟫ **5th house** see pp.98-99

YOUR **PLANETS**

The Sun is the central flame of our vitality. Acting according to your Sun sign and engaging in activities denoted by the house it occupies are important ways to increase your energy and vigor.

For instance, with the Sun in the **1st**, you might need time alone in order to recoup your energies–the presence of others can drain you. Or with the Sun in the **6th**, maybe you like to spend your spare time working in the garden or catching up on projects. The Sun in **Sagittarius** might mean you like to explore; if in **Aquarius**, maybe you like to vacation with a group of friends.

⟫ **The Sun** see pp.62-63

YOUR **ZODIAC SIGNS**

Some signs are naturally more work-oriented, while some are more suggestive of needing a slower pace. **Capricorn** (or its ruler, the cosmic task-master Saturn) is often highlighted in the charts of anyone with a strong work ethic–by contrast, **Leo**, **Libra**, or **Pisces** might engender a bit more need for time off to play, relax, or dream.

Each zodiac sign has its ideal sabbatical or vacation. The **fire** signs might favor adventurous breaks, the **air** signs a chance to meet new faces, the **earth** signs maybe an eco tour, and the **water** signs a sojourn by the ocean or in quiet, restful places.

⟫ **Zodiac signs** see pp.32-57
Elements see pp.28-31

KEY **TRANSITS**

Jupiter takes about 1 year to go through an average-sized house, while **Saturn** takes 2 to 3 years. With Jupiter transiting through your 9th, for instance, you might think of taking a break to travel. Or Saturn through the 12th might create a desire for time alone on retreat.

On a smaller scale, it takes 1 year for **the Sun** to transit around your chart. Going on vacation when the Sun transits your 5th emphasizes it as "me time," or you might visit relatives when it goes through your 4th. Even just a long weekend when the Moon is in these same houses will honor the tides of your chart.

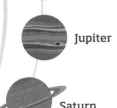
Jupiter

Saturn

The Sun

Case study

Ray had worked since he left school at 18. At 41, he decided to take a year off to travel.

With the Sun in Sagittarius in the 9th, conjunct his chart-ruler Neptune, the siren call of faraway places is strong; a foreign vacation might assuage the longing for a while, but the Sun here suggests he needed something more significant.

At the time, Neptune was transiting square to his Sun-Neptune. The trip could therefore serve to open up his artistic side. After all, this conjunction, alongside Pisces rising, suggests a dreamer, poet, or romantic traveler. The sabbatical may thus represent an important threshold into the next chapter of his life.

FINANCES

HOW TO COPE WITH FINANCIAL DIFFICULTIES

Trying to cope on a restricted income, or managing a debt, is a significant challenge. Astrology cannot instantly bring you more money. But when life brings a period of financial difficulty, your chart gives clues as to how you might work your way through it.

Saturn   Neptune

KEY **TRANSITS**

Look to transits through your 2nd and 8th and work with the transit energy rather than against it. Explore your natal picture first as the starting point.

A transit of **Saturn** through your 2nd, for instance, suggests a need to tighten your belt, visit a financial advisor, or finally get out that spreadsheet and calculator. At the end of it, the idea is to feel more in control.

Transits to the 8th often draw us into financial tangles. **Neptune** transiting here might see you sleepwalking into an unwise investment or lending money to someone who disappears without paying it back.

YOUR **HOUSES**

 The 2nd house reflects your underlying relationship to money, and patterns around money are often deeply ingrained. For instance, with the **Moon** here or **Cancer** on the cusp, your emotional well-being rises and falls with your bank balance, both of which may be subject to fluctuation. You can be a rags-to-riches success, but with **Saturn** in the 2nd, you might always feel poor, the millionaire who still buys the discount items at the grocery store.

 The 8th house is concerned with debt and our relationship to institutions that provide loans, mortgages, and overdrafts. **Capricorn** on the cusp of the 8th suggests paying your dues and insisting on a legitimate contract, while **Sagittarius** gives no more than a glance at the figures before signing on the dotted line.

>> **2nd house** see pp.92-93
8th house see pp.106-107

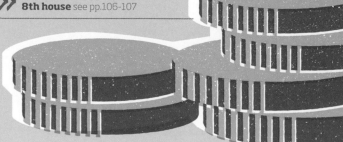

Case study

With the death of Colette's husband, several debts came to light. No longer able to retire, she was forced to sell her house.

Colette has a Grand Cross, with Moon-Mars in Taurus in the 2nd opposite Jupiter in Scorpio in the 8th, and Uranus in Leo in the 5th opposite Chiron in Aquarius in the 11th.
This combines a need for financial stability (Moon-Mars in Taurus in 2nd) with a capacity for canny investment (Jupiter in Scorpio in 8th) but an element of unpredictability, too, via Uranus and Chiron. Jupiter plus Sun-Venus in Sagittarius in the 8th suggests an expectation that money will flow in; she had handed the power to her husband and failed to monitor their joint finances.
At the time, Pluto, co-ruler of her 8th, was transiting her MC. She felt there was no option but to face the crisis, bring the secrets into the open, and take control.

YOUR **PLANETS**

♀ **Venus** Although this planet is not traditionally a significator for money, it is a place in your chart where you want to acquire things that give you pleasure. It is also bound up with self-value, and we often see this in monetary terms. For instance, if you have Venus in **Gemini**, perhaps you want to be valued for your writing skills, and it is important to you that this appreciation takes a monetary form. Or if your Venus is in your **1st house**, you yearn for the money to dress in expensive clothes because this enhances your identity and confidence.

Venus see pp.68-69

YOUR **ZODIAC SIGNS**

Elements

🏔 **Earth** is most attuned to the material world, and anyone with personal planets in earth signs usually has the knack to make, save, and invest money.

🔥 If you have several planets in **fire**, on the other hand, perhaps you work more on trust. While earth patiently saves, fire speculates or lives on credit.

Signs

Taurus and **Leo** are traditionally associated with money, finance, and banking. People with personal planets in these signs often find they have something of the Midas touch. **Pisces** is the least worldly of the signs, tending to care less about it than most.

Elements see pp.28-31
Zodiac signs see pp.32-57

HEALTH ISSUES

SUPPORTING YOUR WELL-BEING

When you acknowledge the needs and rhythms of your chart, it can support your health and well-being. The 6th and 12th houses are traditionally the houses of health and illness, although ultimately your whole chart is involved.

YOUR **HOUSES**

The 6th house suggests the approach you can take to support efficient physical (and therefore emotional) functioning. Health issues may not arise under transits to the 6th, but if they do, it is useful to strengthen your natal planets there and try to understand the deeper significances of the transit.

The 12th house is traditionally the house of sickness. That's not to say that you are likely to get ill if you have planets here–more that they can represent unresolved emotional material. For instance, if you have **the Moon** here, you might not express how you feel–a transit to that Moon might release those feelings, coinciding with a period of emotional and physical stress.

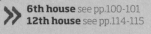
6th house see pp.100-101
12th house see pp.114-115

YOUR **PLANETS**

Each planet can be thought of as a process–**Mercury** moves things from A to B, **Jupiter** expands, **Saturn** contracts, and so on. Like the signs and houses, these processes are both physical and psychological, and understanding the stresses you are under psychologically can help you to understand physical symptoms in a wider context, and vice versa; the one often echoes the other.

In this sense, your whole chart is the key to health, and a health issue can arise under a transit to any planet– perhaps the soul speaks through symptoms, expressing some of the deeper issues connected to each planet.

The planets see pp.62-85

Case study

Joshua was about to take his college final exams when he had a panic attack, which threatened to derail his finals.

Joshua's chart is highly mutable–he has the Ascendant and three planets in Gemini, including Mercury-Venus in a mutable T-square with Jupiter and Mars. His Moon is in Aries tightly quincunx Mars in Virgo. This suggests a good deal of active, edgy, nervous energy, which can benefit from being discharged through regular exercise–he has a very mobile Gemini mind and finds it hard to turn off.

At the time, Saturn in Sagittarius was transiting the T-square. Talking things through with a counselor worked well– Gemini often gets trapped in internal dialogue with no resolution, and transiting Saturn in the 7th is a good symbol for consulting an external advisor.

Neptune

YOUR **ZODIAC SIGNS**

The signs and the body

Every sign rules a region of the body, from **Aries** at the head to **Pisces** at the feet. **Taurus** rules the throat, **Gemini** the arms and hands, **Cancer** the lungs, **Leo** the heart and spine, **Virgo** the intestines, **Libra** the kidneys, **Scorpio** the sex organs and eliminatory systems, **Sagittarius** the thighs, **Capricorn** the knees, and **Aquarius** the ankles.

Everything in a chart has both physical and emotional dimensions. Astrology is thus holistic, linking soul to body. **Mars in Virgo**, for instance, suggests heat generated in the intestines, and a transit to this might show outwardly as a condition that mirrors the symbolism, like irritable bowel. At times when health is compromised, it can be useful to think on a psychosomatic level.

⟫ **Zodiac signs** see pp.32-57

KEY **TRANSITS**

To support yourself at any given time, it is helpful to track your transits and respond in kind.

For instance, if you are experiencing **Neptune** transits, it is perhaps not the time to work long hours or take on additional responsibility. More likely, it is a time to dream, float, imagine, and disengage a little from the everyday world. To the extent that you are unable to do this or do not pay attention to this need, it would not be surprising to find that tension builds and, typically with Neptune, a sense of exhaustion.

FACING RETIREMENT

MAKING THE MOST OF YOUR SENIOR YEARS

For many of us, retirement is not at all about retiring—indeed, many people are more active in their later years than at any other time in their lives. Traditionally, astrologers placed retirement in the 4th house—nowadays, staying at home is often the last thing on our minds.

YOUR **HOUSES**

The IC and 4th house are traditionally associated with retirement. This makes sense if we consider that this house is literally about withdrawing from the world, being opposite the MC and 10th house of profession.

Retirement can sometimes bring feelings of loss of professional status or worldly purpose. However, at a certain stage of life, many people begin to reorient away from the pressure to "be someone" and carve a path. We may not be "withdrawing," but home perhaps becomes more of an anchor point in our later years, as worldly achievement becomes less important.

 **The IC** see pp.122-123
4th house see pp.96-97

YOUR **PLANETS**

The Sun is your central sense of identity and purpose. In our retirement years, we hopefully have the chance to explore new levels of our solar development. No doubt we all have long lists of things we would like to do, continually shelved due to lack of time.

In retirement, we might have the chance to turn our Sun into something different and finally do things that unashamedly celebrate and reinforce our sense of self— and perhaps find that what we achieve in these final decades is at least as important as what we achieved in our working years, if not more so.

 The Sun see pp.62-63

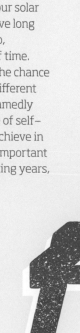

Case study

Louise is in her 50s. She would like to retire to spend more time with her grandchildren and indulge her creative projects.

With Taurus rising, Louise's chart ruler is Venus, in the 4th conjunct the North Node and IC in Cancer. Her Sun is also in the 4th. The Node and Venus point toward the IC as a key place; the major task of her life has been to create a safe family nest, with Louise at the center of it.

Her Leo Sun rules her 5th—and the 5th contains Mercury in Leo and the Moon in Virgo. Children have been pivotal in her life, and personal creativity (5th) is clearly crucial, too.

Transiting Uranus in Aries squared her MC-IC and her Nodal Axis when she first felt the need to make a change. Uranus transits often arouse a need for increased freedom, and this was a chance for her to take a radical step.

YOUR **ZODIAC SIGNS**

If we take the idea that retirement gives us time to attend to unfulfilled solar goals, you can look to your **Sun sign** to explore what you might achieve in your twilight decades.

If you have the **Sun in Aquarius**, for instance, perhaps it becomes a time to open up your social life—or with the **Sun in Pisces**, you take up scuba diving. Of course, as with most things, we bring all of our chart to bear. So you can also look to the rest of your personal planets in their respective signs and envision for yourself all of their as-yet-unlived potentials.

 Zodiac signs see pp.32-57

Saturn

KEY
TRANSITS

The second **Saturn return** at age 58-59 is the classic transit equating to retirement. Of course, retiring at 58 is often not feasible, and many prefer to continue working anyway. But the Saturn return remains a significant watershed, a rite of passage into seniority and a new chapter of life.

At this point, it is not uncommon to rearrange our lives to fit in the things we never managed to do during the second Saturn cycle, when we were busy bringing up children and paying off the mortgage. Saturn reminds us that time is a precious commodity.

BEREAVEMENT

ENCOUNTERING LOSS AND GRIEF

Death is part of the circle of life–and with its focus on cycles, astrology helps us to encompass death and bereavement as part of life's current. The 8th house speaks directly to this experience, as do transits of Saturn, Neptune, and Pluto.

YOUR **HOUSES**

The 8th house is the house of bereavement. This does not mean that if you have planets here you are destined to suffer loss–but you may feel an affinity with this side of life.

For instance, people with 8th-house placements often have the capacity to be alongside someone experiencing bereavement. Some might work professionally as grief counselors or funeral directors–others are just good with people who are going through tough times, unafraid of the complex emotions aroused. This might be particularly true of the **Sun**, **Moon**, or **Mercury**. **Mars** here suggests bravery at times of crisis, and **Saturn** indicates stoicism. Your planets here give clues as to how you might react.

>> **8th house** see pp.106-107

YOUR **PLANETS**

♆ ♇ **Neptune and Pluto** can correspond to experiences of loss. Neptune in the chart is where we create a relationship based on the spiritual rather than the physical–it reminds us that the material world is transitory, and what remains beyond death are intangible things such as love, memory, and soulful connection.

Pluto by contrast is where we can undergo an "underworld journey," a stripping away until only the core of us is left, from which we then rebuild and recreate that part of our lives. Pluto is also one of the two significators that suggest "death" in some format–**Saturn** being the other one. Pluto suggests an experience of death as transformation, while Saturn indicates an experience of death as the final boundary of life.

>> **Neptune** see pp.80-81
Pluto see pp.82-83

KEY **TRANSITS**

It might be typical to find transits of **Saturn**, **Neptune**, or **Pluto** active at times of grief and loss–they can certainly describe the testing circumstances these experiences usually bring. That's not to say that, if you have a transit of Saturn over your Moon, your mother will die–or that your father will die when Pluto transits over a planet in your 4th. Astrology cannot say when someone will die; the chart is a map of symbols showing how things feel for us inside and how we might respond.

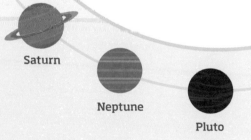

Saturn

Neptune

Pluto

YOUR **ZODIAC SIGNS**

The elements

Earth tends to be stoic and realistic–with planets in earth, you might throw yourself into the practical arrangements, seeing the rituals of funerals and will-readings as ways to honor the dead.

Fire, a symbol of immortality, rages against "the dying of the light," perhaps needing to acknowledge a spirit that outlives the mortal body.

People with a good deal of **air** in their charts might react by cutting off from the complex emotions generated by grief; seeking out opportunities to talk can be valuable.

For a **watery** person, emotions flow more easily, so perhaps there is a converse need to find ways of containing or channeling them.

» **Elements** see pp.28-31

Case study

Clive's wife died in 2007, which brought his world crashing down. Since then, he has rebuilt his life and retrained as a bereavement counselor.

When his wife died, Pluto was transiting over Clive's Sagittarius Moon. This 7th-house Moon describes a strong emotional bond in the marriage and, as his only personal planet in fire, it might have seemed to him that the fires had somehow gone out. Rekindling this would have been understandably hard, and he might have needed to draw on the energy of others (7th) to keep his spirits high. Pluto entered his 8th house in 2012, passing over Mercury, then Chiron and on toward the Sun, all in the 8th. This long procession of Pluto transits had a profound reshaping effect, allowing him to use very purposefully his own personal experiences of grief and loss in his counseling work with others.

"BECOME WHAT YOU ARE!"

Dennis Elwell, Cosmic Loom:
The New Science of Astrology

RESOURCES

FURTHER READING
There is a vast array of published astrological material. Here is just a small selection of books on contemporary psychological astrology.

Chart Interpretation

Horoscope Symbols Rob Hand (Schiffer Publishing, 1997)

The Houses–Temples of the Sky Deborah Houlding (Wessex Astrologer, 2006)

Through the Looking Glass: A Search for the Self in the Mirror of Relationships Richard Idemon (Wessex Astrologer, 2010)

Mapping the Psyche Volume 1: The Planets and the Zodiac Signs and **Volume 2: The Planetary Aspects and the Houses of the Horoscope** Clare Martin (Wessex Astrologer, 2016)

Incarnation: The Four Angles and the Moon's Nodes Melanie Reinhart (Starwalker Press, 2014)

Chiron and the Healing Journey Melanie Reinhart (Starwalker Press, 2011)

The Twelve Houses Howard Sasportas (Flare Publications, 2007)

Aspects in Astrology Sue Tompkins (Rider, 2001)

The Contemporary Astrologer's Handbook Sue Tompkins (Flare Publications, 2009)

Publications by Liz Greene are too numerous to list, but are all excellent, including those written in conjunction with Howard Sasportas as part of the "Seminars in Psychological Astrology" series.

Transits and Planetary Cycles

Planets in Transit: Life Cycles for Living Rob Hand (Schiffer Publishing, 1997)

Mapping the Psyche, Volume III: Kairos, the Astrology of Time Clare Martin (Wessex Astrologer, 2015)

The Gods of Change Howard Sasportas (Wessex Astrologer, 2007)

Raphael's Yearly Ephemeris provides information on the positions of the planets each day. Or you can invest in an ephemeris covering the 20th or 21st centuries–try **The American Ephemeris** by Neil F. Michelsen and Rique Pottenger.

The History and Philosophy of Astrology

The History of Western Astrology, Volumes I and II Nick Campion (Continuum, 2009)

Cosmic Loom: The New Science of Astrology Dennis Elwell (Wessex Astrologer, 2008)

The Astrology of Fate
Liz Greene (Thorsons, 1997)

Journey Through Astrology: Charting the Astrological Voyage of Discovery The Faculty of Astrological Studies (Faculty of Astrological Studies Press, 2015)

Outlets for books in the US include:

Inner Traditions:
www.innertraditions.com

Goddess Isis Books & Gifts:
www.store.isisbooks.com/
Astrology_Books_s/230.htm

TRAINING
The Faculty of Astrological Studies is regarded as one of the best astrological schools anywhere in the world.

Founded in London in 1948, it offers a range of opportunities for study, from webinars and short courses to a full astrological training, available online and as classes in London. It also holds a Summer School in Oxford, UK.
www.astrology.org.uk

WEBSITES

Astrodienst:
www.astro.com
Articles and information on many different subjects and branches of astrology. Also offers a free chart calculation service, a list of free astrological software, and a free online ephemeris.

Skyscript:
www.skyscript.co.uk
Articles and information on many different subjects and branches of astrology.

AstroDatabank:
www.astrodatabank.com

A comprehensive online collection of birth charts, including actors, musicians, writers, politicians, and other public figures, both contemporary and historical.

Astrolabe:
www.alabe.com
A seller of astrological software, which offers a free birth chart calculator.

PROFESSIONAL BODIES

AFA
(American Federation of Astrologers):
www.astrologers.com
NCGR (National Council on Geocosmic Research):
www.geocosmic.org
ISAR (International Society for Astrological Research):
www.isarastrology.org

Consulting a professional astrologer
You can find expert astrologers at www. astrologers.com/afa-certified-astrologers/united_states, all of whom are certified by the AFA.

GLOSSARY

Air signs Gemini, Libra, and Aquarius.

Angles The four angles are the Ascendant, Descendant, MC (Midheaven), and IC. They represent the four directions of the compass: the east-west horizon (Ascendant-Descendant) and the north-south meridian (IC-MC).

Aspect The angular relationship between two planets or factors in a chart. Astrology uses a set of aspects based on division of the circle by certain key numbers. Other minor aspects not included in this book, and used less frequently by astrologers, are the quintile (division of the circle by five), the septile (division by seven), and the novile (division by nine).

Aspect pattern A distinct pattern of planets connected together by aspect and thereby creating a particular dynamic based on the energies of the planets and aspects involved. The aspect patterns included in this book represent a standard selection of recognized and frequently-occurring forms, but other patterns exist.

Cardinal signs Aries, Cancer, Libra, and Capricorn.

Cusp The boundary between two houses. For instance, the cusp of the 1st house is the Ascendant and the cusp of the 7th is the Descendant.

Cycle A full circuit of a planet around the chart or in relation to another planet (such as the lunation cycle).

Dissociate An aspect or aspect pattern is said to be dissociate when one of the planets does not occupy the sign we might naturally anticipate and is therefore "out of sign". For instance, when a planet in Aries is conjunct a planet in Taurus this would be termed a "dissociate conjunction".

Earth signs Taurus, Virgo, and Capricorn.

Elements The four elements are fire, earth, air, and water. Each zodiac sign is connected to one of the elements. Also referred to as the triplicities.

Ephemeris A listing of planetary positions each day at noon or at midnight. The ephemeris also usually records information about lunar phases and eclipses.

Fire signs Aries, Leo, and Sagittarius.

Fixed signs Taurus, Leo, Scorpio, and Aquarius.

Geocentric Earth-centred. Astrology is a geocentric system, placing the chart's owner in the centre looking out at the zodiac and planets around them.

Hemisphere One half of the chart, divided at either the Ascendant-Descendant axis or the MC-IC axis.

Horizon The horizontal line linking the Ascendant (in the east) and Descendant (in the west) across the chart.

Horoscope The birth chart. Originally, "horoscope" referred just to the Ascendant but is now used to refer to the whole chart.

House A one-twelfth division of the chart. A house represents a territory, both physical and psychological.

House system The method used to divide a chart into the 12 houses. There are many different house systems, the most popular being Placidus (which is used in this book) and Equal House (which divides the chart into 12 equal portions beginning at the Ascendant).

Lights The Sun and the Moon. Also known as the Luminaries.

Longitude Distance measured along the zodiac. On a birth chart, planetary positions are given in zodiacal longitude, i.e. their position from 0-30° in the zodiac sign they occupy.

Luminaries The Sun and the Moon. Also known as the Lights.

Meridian The "observer's meridian" is a circle running through the north and south points of the horizon and directly overhead and underneath the observer. In a chart, the zodiac intersects the observer's meridian at the MC and IC, the chart's north-south axis.

Modes The three modes are cardinal, fixed, and mutable. Each zodiac sign is connected to one of the modes.

Mutable signs Gemini, Virgo, Sagittarius, and Pisces.

Natal Pertaining to birth. The natal chart is the birth chart.

Negative signs The negative zodiac signs are the earth and water signs.

Nodes or Nodal Axis The crossing points of the paths of the Sun and Moon as seen from Earth.

Orb The space (in zodiac degrees) either side of an exact aspect between two planets, in which the aspect is still held to be effective.

Placidus A house system, i.e. a method for dividing a birth chart into the 12 houses. The Placidus system is based on dividing the wheel in terms of time as the Earth turns on its axis, rather than division according to space. In the Placidus system, the MC and the IC form the cusps of the 10th and 4th houses respectively.

Polarity The two polarities are positive and negative. Each zodiac sign is connected to one of the polarities.

Positive signs The positive zodiac signs are the fire and air signs.

Quadruplicities Division of the zodiac into three groups of four signs each, according to the three modes.

Qualities An alternative name for the three modes.

Retrograde An optical illusion whereby planets (although not the Sun or Moon) can appear to move "backwards" in the sky, contrary to their usual "direct" motion. This occurs when the Earth overtakes a slower-moving planet or is overtaken by a faster-moving one. Retrograde motion is necessary in working with transits. Many astrologers believe that when a planet is retrograde in a birth chart, it indicates a more introspective or philosophical expression of that planet. The idea of backwards movement also suggests that the person is less sure of themselves in this area of life, maybe feeling they need continually to digest and review, or that they go against the conventional way of doing things.

Rulership Each planet "rules" either one or two zodiac signs. The ruler of an angle or house is the planet ruling the sign occupied by the angle or house cusp; this ruler has influence over the affairs of that angle or cusp.

Significator A chart factor taken to "signify" a particular desire, drive, object, emotion, or type of experience. For instance, Mercury is a significator for communication, the Descendant is a signficator for relationships.

Singleton A planet which alone occupies a particular polarity, mode, or element. It forms the main funnel for the qualities of that polarity, mode, or element.

Table of houses A reference book used by astrologers when calculating a birth chart by hand. It lists the zodiacal position of the Ascendant, MC and intervening house cusps for different times of day at different latitudes.

Transit The movement of a planet around the chart. Each planet moves through houses and crosses over angles, planets and other chart points, giving rise to dynamic life events.

Triplicities Division of the zodiac into four groups of three signs each, according to the four elements.

Water signs Cancer, Scorpio and Pisces.

Zodiac The "circle of animals" based on the 12 main constellations which lie along the ecliptic (the apparent path of the Sun during the year).

INDEX

ABOUT THE AUTHOR

Carole Taylor, BA (Cantab), MA, FFAstrolS, is a full-time astrologer who combines teaching, writing, and client work. She is Director of Studies at the Faculty of Astrological Studies, where she was awarded a fellowship. Carole is co-author and co-editor of *Journey* *Through Astrology*. She is also a past editor of the journal of the Astrological Association of Great Britain and holds an MA in Myth, Cosmology, and the Sacred from Canterbury Christ Church University. She lives in West Sussex, England.

ACKNOWLEDGMENTS

Author's Acknowledgments
The author would like to thank Sue Tompkins, who over many years has been an inspirational tutor, colleague, friend, and trusted astrological guide.

Publisher's Acknowledgments
DK would like to thank Katie Hardwicke for proofreading, Marie Lorimer for the index, and Megan Lea and Alice Horne for editorial assistance.

Charts created using Solar Fire v. 9, published by Astrolabe, Inc., www.alabe.com

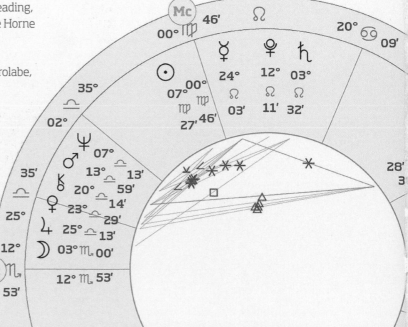